JANUARY 2013, THIRD EDITION

Sources, indexes and agreements can be found on pages 262-27¹

A SKYBORN WORKS
PRODUCTION
WWW.SKYBORNWORKS.COM

NOTE

Attempts have been made to reach all copyright holders. Should anything be omitted or be wrong I'm grateful for information on this for future editions. If you wish for your company or yourself to be removed from the book, please be sure to contact me.

BIG THANKS TO

My supportive and lovely fiancée, friends and family. To all the creative people behind these stories. To those of you I had the great honor of meeting and interview. To teachers and guest lecturers.

CREOGRAPHY

In what category would you put a book which sole purpose is to retell stories of creative acts of individual people and companies? Since I couldn't find an answer to that question I'm coining the new term *creography*.

ABOUT THE WRITER

Simon Zingerman is a newly graduated graphic design student from Stockholm, Sweden. *We All Need Heroes* is the quite astonishing result of his thesis for his last year studying Media Design at *Luleå University of Technology*. As school finished Simon started up his own business *Skyborn Works*, with strong intention to finish and self-publish the book as his very first professional project. Although he spent many months writing this book Simon chooses not to label himself as an author. In his own words: "I'm simply a young and hungry entrepreneur retelling stories in a fun and exciting way, hoping that the result of my hard work in putting it all together will convert the skeptical into believers, make heroes out of cowards and turn dull entrepreneurs and directors into trendsetters".

Simon is a graphic designer at heart and writing and designing this book has been a great learning process for him. Follow the unstoppable creative force at: **www.skybornworks.com.**

We All Need Heroes

Stories of the Brave & Foolish

SIMON ZINGERMAN

COPYRIGHTS

Text: All text is written and copyrighted by Simon Zingerman.
Proofreading/correction: Johanna Hagstedt, Stefan Nordström, Ivana Kovacevic, Karin Vincelette and Erik Vincelette.
Design: Simon Zingerman.
Typography: Corki (Free type by Typedepot™), League Gothic (Free type by Micah Rich & Caroline Hadilaksono), Miso (License, Mårten Nettelbladt), Carton (Free type by Nick McCosker), Practique (License, Blindfrog Industries), Lobster (Free type by Pablo Impallari), Molesk (Free type by Pedro Lobo), Pacifico (Free type by Vernon Adams), Cubano (Free type by Chandler Van De Water), Ostrich Sans Rounded (Free type by Tyler Finck), Chunk Five (Free type by Meredith Mandel) and Adobe Garamond Pro.

The owners of the freeware types grants permission to use them freely for 'all your personal and commercial work'.

ACKNOWLEDGEMENTS

Attempts have been made to reach all copyright holders. Should anything be omitted or be wrong I'm grateful for information on this for future editions. In advance I apologise for any unintentional mishaps and I'm pleased to correct any errors in the acknowledgements. If you wish for your company or yourself to be removed from the book, please be sure to contact me.

SOURCES & INDEXES

The sources for the stories are displayed at the bottom of the left page of each story spread. The index of all the used names, products and companies, the creative library and the copyrights/agreements for the illustrations can be found on pages 262-271.

PUBLISHING

This paperback version of *We All Need Heroes* is published by *Skyborn Works* through *Amazon CreateSpace*. First edition was released in December 2012. The third edition (this one) was released in January 2013.

ISBN-13: 978-91-637-1720-8
ISBN-10: 91-637-1720-4

CONTACT

Skyborn Works
Lyckselevagen 38, LGH 1102. 162 67 Vallingby. SWEDEN.
T: +46 73 649 83 11
contact@skybornworks.com

www.skybornworks.com
www.weallneedheroes.com

TO LEO

INDEX

INDEX

Adventure

Art

Architecture

Biography

Cooking

Computers

Creography

Creō: the English word creativity comes from the Latin term creō "to create, make".

-graphy (grə fē): a process or method of writing, recording, or representing (in a specified way): calligraphy, photography.

Economics

Erotica

Fantasy

Graphic Novels

History

Horror

Nature

Romance

Science Fiction

Sports

WE ALL NEED HEROES

This book contains a collection of stories from all around the world. I've been gathering them by travelling, reading books/magazines, listening to teachers presenters/lecturers, making interviews, watching documentaries, eavesdropping on the train/bus and much more. This is a collection of three years of inspiration, made possible by my curiosity. From the beginning, I never had any intentions of writing this book, nor did I ever chase after these stories. They came to me, and I just kept writing them down. Now here we are with a book packed with 120 stories!

The stories are narrated, and as we all know, each time a story is told, a few changes are made to it. Thus, I cannot promise that all the stories are true, and that all the information is correct. It's important for you to know that these facts are not to be fully trusted, something that all stories have in common. This is pure entertainment with the goal of encouraging, inspiring and entertaining with hope of lighting a spark in your mind. A "feel-good" book with fairy tale movie endings. The focus is not set on who or which company, but on the act of bravery and/or foolishness itself.

No matter if you are an entrepreneur, part of a working team, a student or someone thinking of starting a business – I hope this book will be of inspiration to you. The stories might be told about a completely different line of business than the one you're in, but the main idea behind them and the essence of finding new ways to tackle problems – are universal.

The idea for you as a reader is to pretty much never know what to expect. What determines what kind of experience you get from your reading depends only on yourself, where you are in life and what your needs consist of right now. This allows the book to always be up-to-date. You can pick it up at any time, and hopefully, a story you didn't care for earlier may now lead to action on your part. To draw an analogy: A music band you never thought you'd be listening to five years ago, is perhaps today one of your favourites.

The projects and people portrayed in the book have encouraged me to follow my crazy dreams and do what I want careerwise. This book will have done its job if it affects you in a way that makes you improve one or two things about yourself or your life on Monday morning.

We all need heroes – these are some of mine.

SIMON ZINGERMAN
SKYBORN WORKS

Note: My intention with this book is to charge people with energy, not to advance falsehoods. I want to clarify that my goal is not to defame individuals or companies in any way. Enjoy your reading!

The search for stories continues at www.weallneedheroes.com

THE DIGITAL STORY

LATEST NEWS

To read the latest story, use this QR-code

I wanted to create a book that never gets outdated. In a way most of the stories found here are timeless. But I know I'll always come across inspiring stories that are new to me (old as fresh), and I want to share these as well. So I thought I'd implement something digital within my analog product, simply by using a *QR-code*. This code lets you keep track of the latest story uploaded on the site. I'll be able to control the re-direction for the future. So, if you're the comfortable type – be sure to open the book and scan the code from time to time to keep updated.

INSTRUCTIONS

Download a *QR-reader* application for your smartphone/tablet.
They're free, check out: *QR Reader*, *QR Droid*, *QR Scanner*.

Scan code

Read story!

ABSURD YET TRUE

STUCK IN LIMBO

REFUGEE AIRPORT FRANCE
THE TERMINAL 17 YEARS

Mehran Karimi Nasseri, also known as *Sir, Alfred Mehran*, is an Iranian refugee who lived in the departure lounge of Terminal 1 in Paris *Charles de Gaulle Airport* between the years 1988 and 2006.

Due to protesting against the Shah in 1977, Nasseri was imprisoned, tortured, and later expelled from his country. He then applied for asylum in many European countries without luck. When he decided to go to the United Kingdom, he claimed that he had been mugged and that his shoulder bag was stolen while waiting at the train platform to go to *Charles de Gaulle Airport* and take a flight to *Heathrow Airport*. Nasseri managed to board the plane but when he arrived at Heathrow without the necessary documentation, Heathrow officials sent him back to *Charles de Gaulle*. Nasseri was unable to prove his identity and his refugee status to the French officials and so he was moved to the *Zone d'attente* (waiting zone), a holding area for travelers without papers. He was initially arrested by the French, but then released as his entry into the airport was legal. Although Nasseri had no country of origin to be returned to, and so began his residency at Terminal 1. With his cart and bags, he almost looked like a traveler, so people either didn't notice him or ignored him as if he were a homeless person. Normally Nasseri wouldn't speak with anyone. He kept his luggage by his side and spent his time reading, writing in his diary, or studying economics. He received food and newspapers from employees of the airport. He also received mail to the address "Sir Alfred, Terminal 1, Charles de Gaulle". Newspaper and television reporters from around the world visited him for interviews. In England and Germany a book about Nasseri was released. In 1999 he was granted refugee status by the French authorities and would have been able to leave the airport for the first time but he refused to sign the necessary papers, claiming that his real name was *Sir Alfred* and therefore wasn't allowed to leave. Theoretically this meant Nasseri could have left the terminal at any time.

Nasseri was reportedly the inspiration behind the 2004 movie *The Terminal*. Unlike Tom Hanks' character in the movie, from around 1994,

Sources: "Terminal Man", Alfred Merhan, 2004. "Mehran Karimi Nasseri – In Transit", h2g2, BBC, May 28, 2008.

Nasseri didn't live in the duty-free transit area but simply in the departure hall, in the circular boutiques and restaurants passage on the lowest floor. *DreamWorks*, the company behind *The Terminal*, paid Nasseri for the use of his story. However, he couldn't access checks reportedly sent to his lawyer because he didn't have a bank account.

Nasseri's stay at the airport ended in July 2006 when he was hospitalized. Towards the end of January 2007, he left the hospital and was looked after by the airport's branch of the *French Red Cross*. He was lodged in a hotel close to the airport for a few weeks and on March 6 of 2007, he transferred to an *Emmaus* charity reception centre in Paris. As of 2008, he continues to live in a Paris shelter. Nasseri's strange and unbelievable destiny became a legend during his 17 years at the airport.

POSSIBLE MORAL

I like to use stories like this one as a tool to spark new ideas of mine. Stories of absurd events in life get my creative juices flowing and have so far given birth to some of my best ideas. Nasseri's fate makes me reflect upon life and ask: "What would I do if I got stranded at an airport?".
I believe that there must be something good to be gained by putting yourself in a fake scenario and using your creativity to, in this case, make the best of a horrendous situation. I think it's also a great thing to try and find inspiration in unexpected places. Furthermore I believe that this story can serve as an eye-opener about how you can feel alienated and lonely despite being surrounded by throngs of humans.

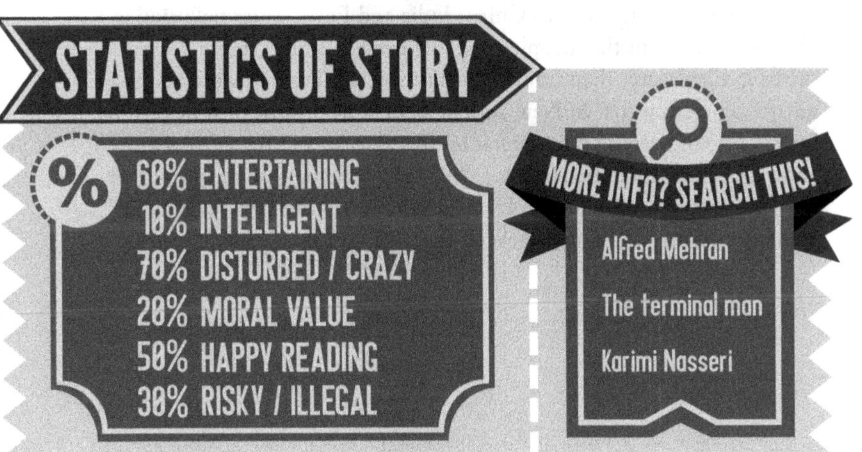

ABSURD YET TRUE

SWIMMING FOR NATURE

BIG RIVER MAN RIVERS AMAZON
ENDURANCE POLLUTION

Long-distance swimmer Martin Strel has become the world's most unlikely philanthropist – he's out to save the world's dirtiest rivers. Martin comes from Slovenia and he taught himself to swim in a nearby stream when he was six years old and became a professional long distance swimmer in 1978. Nowadays, he's not so fit and is considered the world's heaviest elite endurance swimmer. With this in mind, it comes as a big surprise that it's in Martin's latest years he's achieved his most impressive swimming goals. He has swum the Mississippi, the Danube and the Yangtze rivers. Why? To bring attention to how polluted they are. In February 2007, Martin began an insane attempt to be the first person ever to swim the entire length of the world's most dangerous river, the mighty Amazon. He faced piranhas, bull sharks and pirates when he swam the 3,272-mile stretch in 66 days. This amazing achievement was filmed and the movie-documentary, which became a big success, was released in 2009 with the title *Big River Man.*

Our world has a lot of water, but only 1-3 percent of it suffices as drinking water. This is one of the greatest problems of today: Drinking water is sparse and Martin points out that we have to take better care of it because no one should have to buy drinking water from the grocery store. He's trying to change this. In China, India and Egypt water pollution is serious to the point that people are dying from it. In fact, more people die from dirty water than from war. Martin sees himself as a teacher or an adviser on clean water. In New York he held motivational speeches on the importance of keeping the Manhattan Island clean and to get the Hudson and Harlem Rivers in better shape. Martin's next step is to make another film that focuses on pollution. He says there is still much to do when it comes to cleaning up drinking water and that's what he's intending to do.

Sources: "Big River Man" documentary, 2009. "The Amazon Swim Project" official site, "Martin Strel" official site.
Quote: From Martin Strel's speech after the Amazon Swim, 2007. "English Channel Triathlon Dover-Heidelberg", Sri Chinmoy.

POSSIBLE MORAL

Martin Strel's driving force should be an inspiration to us all. Using your talent, hobby or profession in a way that makes you contribute with something good to this world is truly the way to go. After his Amazon swim, Martin held a speech about simplicity: "My Name is Martin. You can see I'm not Lance Armstrong. I'm a little fat and a little old. I like to drink a little. I'm a simple man. There are many people like me. I hope they see this swim and realize they can do impossible things, even save the world. I hope people remember this rainforest is our friend and stop destroying it. Now I'm very tired I just swam Amazon... Please excuse me".

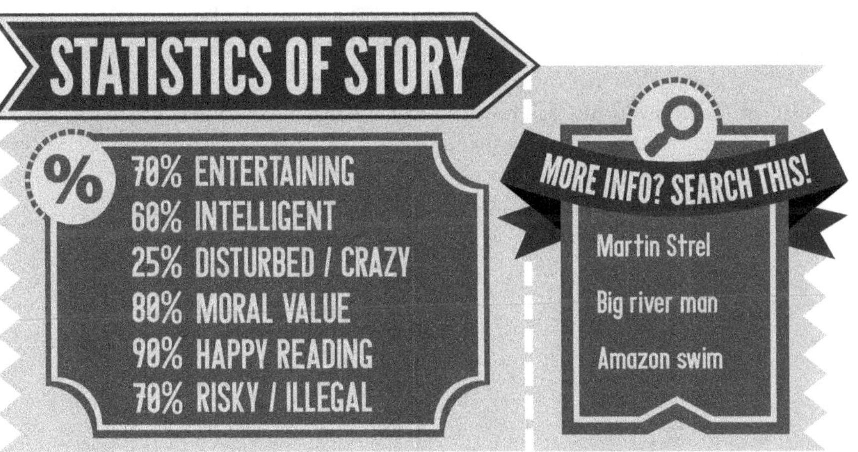

ABSURD YET TRUE

THE KNOWLEDGE

TAXI CABS LONDON SPECIAL TEST CHALLENGING FAILURE

The Knowledge is the world's most demanding training course for taxi drivers. All licensed London taxi drivers need to pass a special test before they can drive one of the capital's famous black taxis. The test was initiated in 1865 and has changed little since. It's claimed that the training involved ensures that London taxi drivers are experts on London, and have an intimate knowledge of the city. The taxi driver is required to be able to decide routes immediately in response to a passenger's request or traffic conditions, rather than stopping to look at a map, relying on satellite navigation or asking a controller by radio. *The Knowledge* is based on learning 320 routes (or runs). This helps them learn the 25,000 streets and 20,000 landmarks and places of interest in the six mile radius of Charing Cross (the "centre of London").

Applicants will usually need at least twelve "appearances" (attempts at the final test), after preparation averaging 34 months, to pass the examination. It takes between two and four years to pass the All-London Knowledge. Two-thirds of all applicants who apply will fail, some will sustain serious injuries and many more will become divorced while studying *The Knowledge*. People have compared this education with a Ph.D thesis. These taxi drivers really are the "Doctors of the Road" in that sense.

What is unique is that these drivers are independent contractors that own their own taxis, and have more or less no association with the government. The drivers can choose to work more or less depending on their own circumstances. Once you are licensed you can work anywhere in the Greater London area. It's said that working 50 hours per week all year will give these taxi drivers around 50,000 GBP (almost $80,000) in salary.

Sources: "Did You Know That...?", Marko Perko, 2001. "The Knowledge", Public Carriage Office, Transport for London.

POSSIBLE MORAL

Benefits of becoming a black-taxi driver? Your independence, better pay than most London workers and the right to be called one of the best at what you do.

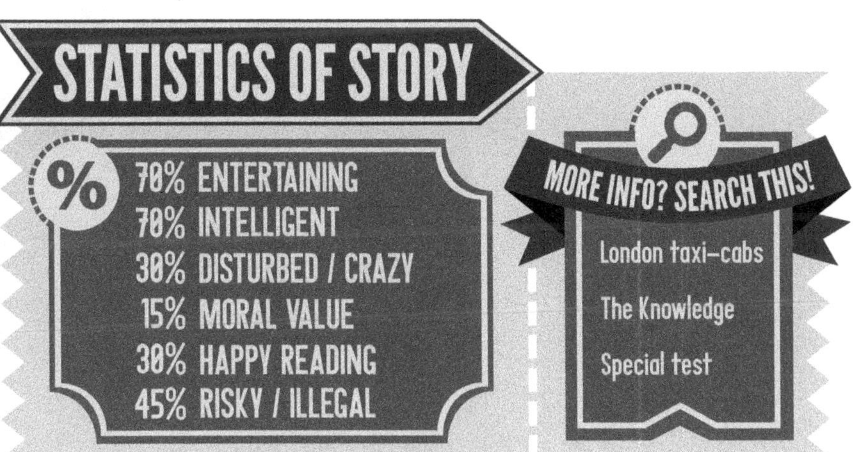

ABSURD YET TRUE

THE TRADE OF A LIFETIME

RED PAPERCLIP TRADING DREAMER
ADVENTURE A HOUSE

In 2005, Canadian blogger Kyle MacDonald had bills to pay and a patient girlfriend who was paying the rent while he was searching for work. He also had a red paperclip and a big dream. Kyle wanted to be able to provide for himself and his girlfriend. He dreamed of owning his own house. One day he got this crazy idea. Kyle decided to put an advertisement on the popular classified advertising website *Craigslist*, with the intention of trading that red paperclip of his for something better. It didn't take long before he got contacted by a girl from Vancouver who offered him a fish pen in exchange for his paperclip. He then traded the fish pen for a doorknob and the doorknob for a camping stove. Kyle seemed to be on a steady course to bigger and better things. He started a website where he shared his trading stories with the world. At the end of this project, he had traded his way from this single red paperclip to a house (!) in a series of online trades, all in over the course of a year.

Kyle was inspired by the childhood game *Bigger and Better* and his website received a considerable amount of attention for tracking the transactions. In 2007, Kyle released the book *One Red Paperclip: How a Small Piece of Stationery Turned into a Great Big Adventure*.

Sources: "One Red Paperclip" book, Kyle Macdonald, 2007. "Man turns paper clip into house", BBC News, July 11, 2006.

POSSIBLE MORAL

Believe it or not, to get that house for the price of a paperclip, Kyle MacDonald only had to make 14 trades. There is a valuable lesson to be learned here: Folks who are patient and adept at recognizing value can actually get more through bartering than by selling the same item for cash. Simply put, both bartering and patience are skills worth mastering. In less than a year, Kyle took a one-cent paperclip and turned it into a house worth tens of thousands of dollars. Good luck getting returns like that from the stock market.

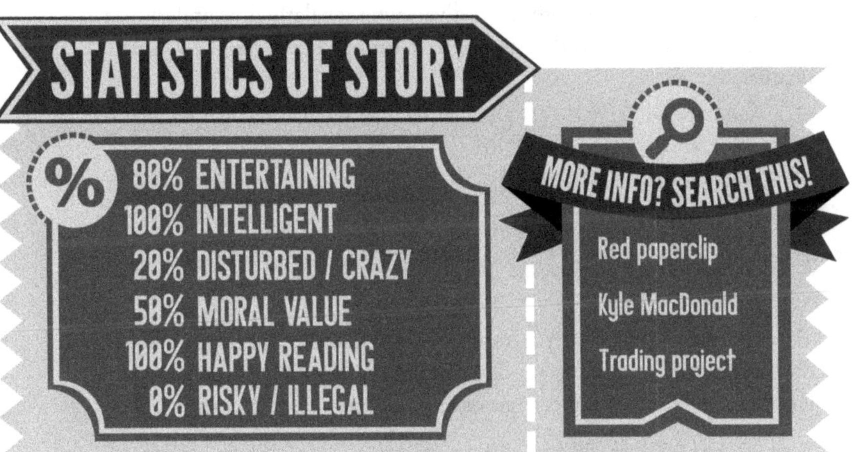

ABSURD YET TRUE

URBAN GOLD MINING

PROSPECTOR DIAMONDS TREASURES
SIDEWALKS DIAMOND DISTRICT

Raffi Stephanian makes a living scraping the sidewalk for gold and diamonds. He eases up mud from the cracks in the sidewalk using a butter knife, and then takes it to a nearby polishing studio where he pans the dirt using a bowl and a sieve, just like a 19th-century prospector. Using only a styrofoam cup, a butter knife and tweezers, 43-year-old Raffi scours the streets of New York's *Diamond District* searching for gold, diamonds and other precious jewels. People walking on 47th street hardly realize the riches that are hidden right beneath them. Raffi is most likely the only one who has ever thought there was something valuable hidden on the sidewalk. His daily treasure hunt started several years ago, when he was working as a stone setter and found gold scraps on the floor of a diamond exchange. He realized if he could find gold inside, it must be outside too – so he started scouring the sidewalks. Material falls off clothes, from the bottom of shoes, it drops off jewelry and it falls in the dirt and sticks to the chewing gum on the street. The precious materials which he collects are sold to merchants at *The Diamond District.* Raffi says he brings in over $500 a week.

It's not only in New York one can find urban gold prospectors. In Brighton, England, there are scuba divers who regularly dive underneath the pier to pick up coins that people have dropped between the wooden boards.

POSSIBLE MORAL

The urban landscape clearly has some hidden treasures for those willing to find them, but you have to get down and dirty to get your hands on them. For these prospectors this isn't an issue, just a great way to pay the bills.

Sources: "Got his 'mined' in the gutter", New York Post, June 20, 2011. "Diving South Coast England" at Divesitedirectory.

STATISTICS OF STORY

70% ENTERTAINING
70% INTELLIGENT
30% DISTURBED / CRAZY
20% MORAL VALUE
85% HAPPY READING
0% RISKY / ILLEGAL

Raffi Stephanian

Gold digger

New York/Brighton

ABSURD YET TRUE

WINNER AND LOSER

GIVING NAMES CRIMINAL FAILURE
SUCCESSFUL POLICE OFFICER

This is the absurd story of Robert Lane, a father who in 1958 decided to name his first born son Winner, thinking it would give the kid a boost in life. Three years later he had another son, and, in the spur of the moment, decided to call him Loser. It doesn't appear that Robert was unhappy about the new baby: He just seemed to get an absurd kick out of the name. First a Winner, then a Loser. But if Winner Lane could hardly be expected to fail, how could Loser Lane possibly succeed?

These two brothers are notable primarily for their unusual first names, but also for their fate being quite the reverse of what their names would suggest. The only noteworthy achievement of Winner Lane is his criminal record – nearly three dozen arrests for burglary, domestic violence, trespassing, resisting arrest and other crimes. Loser Lane on the other hand, born in 1961, graduated from *Lafayette College* in Pennsylvania, and joined the *New York Police Department.* He eventually advanced to become sergeant. Although he never hid his name, people were uncomfortable using it. His friends threw a French pronunciation on it, calling him "Losier". To his colleagues he's known as Lou. These days Loser and Winner barely speak with each other.

Interesting questions to ask yourself: Can a persons name affect their destiny? Whether you're naming your first born baby or your newly started business, be sure to think twice out the outcome before deciding.

Sources: "Family's winner becomes...", Sydney Morning Herald, Aug 1, 2002. "Freakonomics" by Levitt and Dubner, 2009.

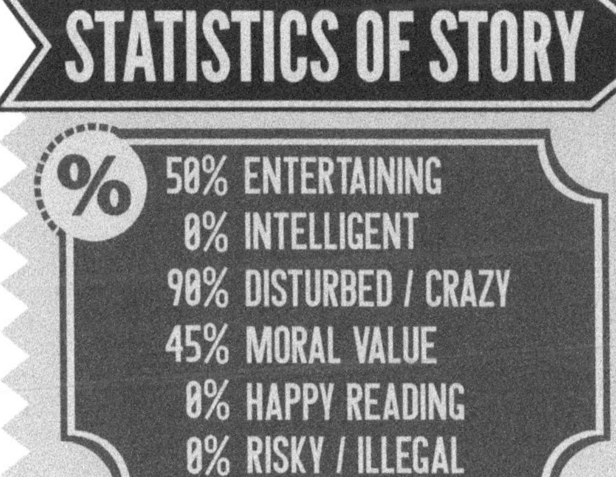
STATISTICS OF STORY
%
50% ENTERTAINING
0% INTELLIGENT
90% DISTURBED / CRAZY
45% MORAL VALUE
0% HAPPY READING
0% RISKY / ILLEGAL

MORE INFO? SEARCH THIS!
Winner and loser
Robert Lane
Giving names

AWESOME MARKETING

BEST JOB IN THE WORLD

CARETAKER ISLAND TOURISM
AUSTRALIA PUBLICITY

In 2009, the Australian government tourist office in Queensland wanted to improve their tourism. They needed to launch a new campaign to promote the Islands of the Great Barrier Reef to *Global Experience Seekers* across eight key international markets. The advertising agency *Cummins Nitro* presented their solution: *The Best Job In The World.* The idea was to search for someone to look after a desert coral island in the Great Barrier Reef, for half a year. The tourist office liked the idea and started working on promoting the Great Barrier Reef as a global tourism destination with a website encouraging people worldwide to apply for *The Best Job In The World*: To become a caretaker and "house-sitter" of the island. The caretaker would live in a three-bedroom villa with an unbeatable views of a crystal clear lagoon, surrounded by palm trees and white sandy beaches with a temperature of around 29°C (84°F).

The new hire was supposed to live in this fantastic house on this paradise island for six months and get paid $110,000 to do so. The only catch? Writing a weekly blog. That's right, weekly, not even daily. The job requirements were quite simple: The ability to speak English and swim. Job benefits except the large salary and free lodging in a multi-million dollar villa, was transportation with free return flights, transfers, and transport around the island included.

All this was advertised as a typical job advertisement in newspapers and online around the world, creating a huge interest among the media that reported on this "dream job". Those who wanted to apply for the job were asked to upload a one minute long application video. In total, 35,000 applications were submitted from 201 different countries. The advertisement made a massive impact in other words (no wonder!). The submission website crashed from excessive visits and application video uploading two days following the launch of the campaign.

The tourism bureau announced the winner: Ben Southall, a 34-year-old British man who claims he once kissed a giraffe.

Sources: "Wanted: Paradise island 'caretaker'", BBC, 12 Jan, 2009. "Best Job In The World", Utalkmarketing.com, 12 Apr, 2010.

POSSIBLE MORAL

A massive and bold campaign that really paid off. I think *Tourism Queensland* did something highly unexpected and gutsy. In my experience, most government owned agency's hardly ever step out of their comfort zones. The comfort zone can be seductive. Many of us desire comfort. It's human nature. However, the right level of risk-taking yields vitality and a higher level of achievement. We don't know the rewards we will enjoy by our willingness to take thoughtful risks, but we do know that the really big rewards will not occur unless we are willing to take those risks. *The Best Job In The World* was a big bet that in the end gave back a lot. By the campaign's end, it had generated more than $200 million in global publicity value for *Tourism Queensland.* The Australian government is setting a good example for governments of other countries – dare to try something new!

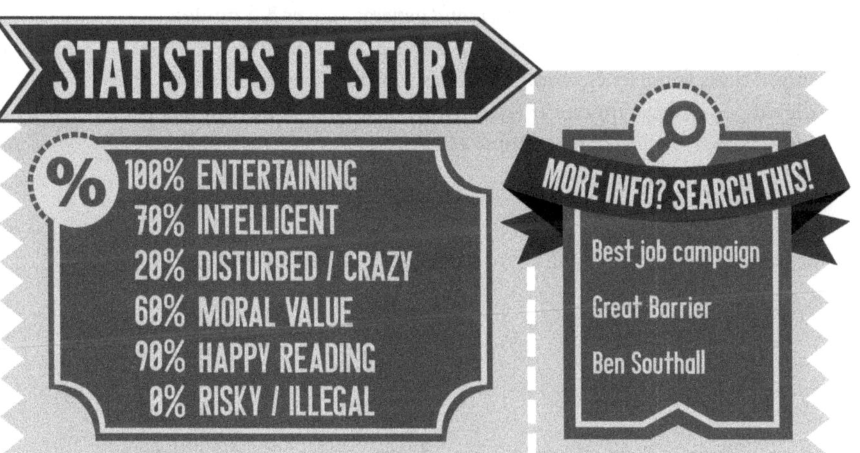

AWESOME MARKETING

DAVID ON DEMAND

LIVE-STREAM WEBCAM TWITTER
FOLLOW UP AD FESTIVAL

In 2010, David Perez from Chicago begged his bosses at the advertising agency *Leo Burnett Worldwide* to send him to the *Cannes Advertising Festival.* They agreed to send him, on one condition – he had to do anything that anyone told him to through *Twitter.* What will he do next? That was simply up to whoever sent him a *tweet.* So, David strapped on a pair of webcam-enabled glasses and gave up his free will for seven days. The buzz became huge. Everyone wanted to be a part of it. David ended up doing everything from flying a helicopter, drinking beer from his shoe, getting a *Fail whale*-tattoo (read more on page 205) and a lightning bolt haircut. He received over 20,000 requests.

DavidOnDemand showcased the *Cannes Advertising Festival* in a way no one had ever done before. With over 144 hours of live streaming content, *Leo Burnett Worldwide* brought the seminars, parties and the galas outside of Cannes – and straight to the viewers. It gave the festival a broader audience than ever before. By the end of the week, almost half (45.3 percent) of all mentions of the festival, were about David. *Facebook* founder Mark Zuckerberg, who also attended at the festival only received 7.1 percent mentions.

In just a few days, *DavidOnDemand* generated over 3.5 million *tweets*, from over 132 countries, and over 100 million estimated media impressions from articles and interviews. Instead of using a printed or digital poster engaging the festivals theme "real time marketing", David himself became the prime example of it.

Sources: "David On Demand", Leo Burnett Worldwide, YouTube video, 21 Nov, 2010."About the Project", davidondemand.com.

POSSIBLE MORAL

Today more than ever before consumers are demanding immediate and interactive relationships with the brands and products that impact their lives. With the *DavidOnDemand* experiment *Leo Burnett Worldwide* and *Arc Worldwide* stepped away from the traditional advertising methods and tried something new. By knowing their target audience well, staying updated with trends, using the latest technology and doing something no one else was doing – they created a truly successful marketing story.

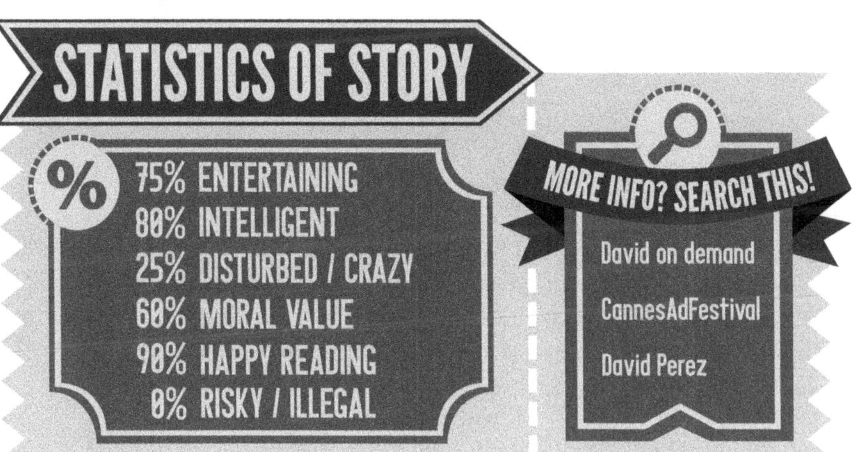

AWESOME MARKETING

HAPPINESS MACHINE

EXPERIMENT RIGGED SURPRISED
REACTIONS ENGAGEMENT

Together with the marketing agency *Definition 6*, *Coca-Cola* took their *Happiness Factory* concept from 2010 out of the television and into the common room of *St John's University* in Queens, New York. With the purpose of spreading joy, a specially rigged *Coca-Cola* vending machine was set up overnight with five hidden cameras ready to catch the reactions of the students. The next day they were surprised to find that the machine was prepared to break the users pays rule, handing out (literally in some cases) pizzas, flowers, cupcakes, extra coke bottles, balloon animals and a six-foot sub sandwich. *The Happiness Machine* was *Coca-Cola*'s first attempt to get in on the whole "viral internet marketing" trend. With no big budget for the project, *Definition 6* took a regular working *Coca-Cola* vending machine and re-built it.

Coca-Cola's goal was to create a real experience, with real reactions. According to themselves, other than the janitor loading the machine, nothing was scripted. The girl mouthing "Oh My God," students helping each other lift the huge sub, and hugging the machine are what gave the video life. You can film people being given free stuff all day long and it can still fall flat on the audience. The way people reacted was the success behind this project.

POSSIBLE MORAL

Coca-Cola gave and shared a sense of happiness which created an emotional connection with their brand. Students involved in this video were caught up in their everyday lives, and this little moment touched them. *Coca-Cola* used free stuff to surprise people but what they gave away at the end of the day was happiness and a smile. The key was engagement, and free stuff was the catalyst.

Sources: "Coke Scores With First Viral Video", Marketing Daily, 19 Jan, 2010. "Coca-Cola Happiness Machine", YouTube.

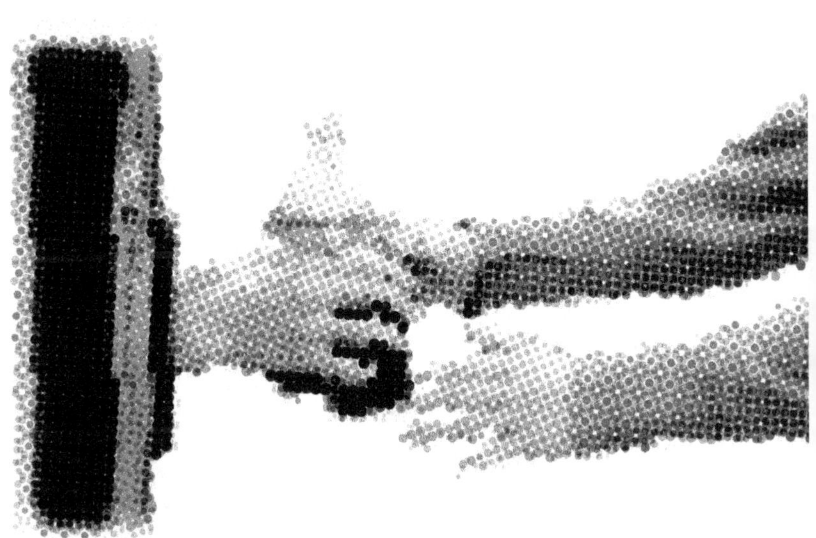

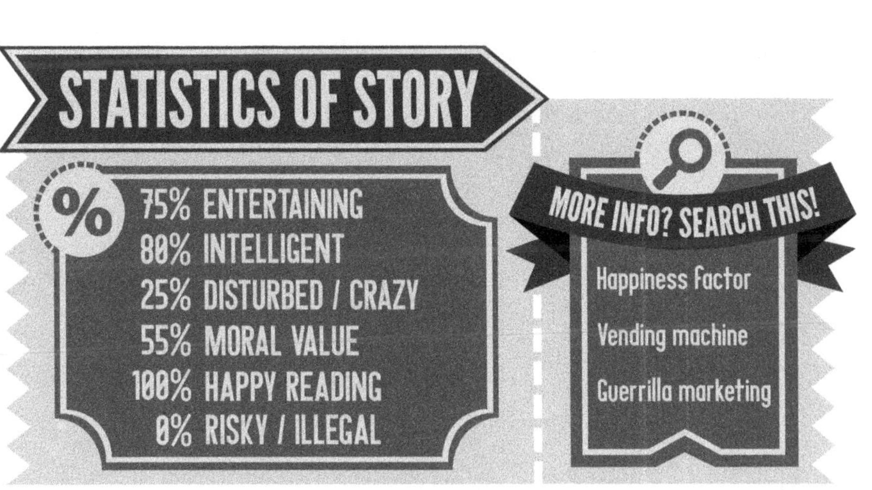
STATISTICS OF STORY
75% ENTERTAINING
80% INTELLIGENT
25% DISTURBED / CRAZY
55% MORAL VALUE
100% HAPPY READING
0% RISKY / ILLEGAL
MORE INFO? SEARCH THIS!
Happiness factor
Vending machine
Guerrilla marketing

OASIS' NEW RECORD

UNRELEASED LIVE GIG MUSICIANS
INSPIRABLE STREET PERFORMERS

In 2008, New York City street performers gathered at a loft in Brooklyn to rehearse unreleased songs from Oasis' upcoming record – *Dig Out Your Soul*. The main idea behind the project was, would it not be cool if street musicians played the songs first and not last for a change?

Many of the invited performers were part of the *Metropolitan Transportation Authority*'s (*MTA*) *Music Under New York* program, dedicated to presenting quality music to the public throughout New York City's transit system. The street musicians were taught the music and lyrics of four songs, led by Oasis themselves, and then ordered to spread out around the streets and subways. They all performed the songs while playing different instruments, taking the music of Oasis to new levels. The selected street musicians came from all parts of the city, and had a broad variety of different ethnic, musical and creative backgrounds.

They performed the previously unheard new songs at different locations throughout the city including *MTA* approved subway station platforms at Grand Central, Times Square, Penn Station and Astor Place, subtly premiering the album before it came out. The musicians all had signs with them saying: "You are the first to hear this new Oasis song". *New York City Tourism*'s website offered a page where you could use *Google Maps* and *Google Earth* to find live performances. Fans were encouraged to upload their own videos of the performances to a dedicated *YouTube* channel.

Sources: "Dig Out Your Soul In The Streets", YouTube, Jan 15, 2009. "Oasis train buskers to sing...", IndieLondon.

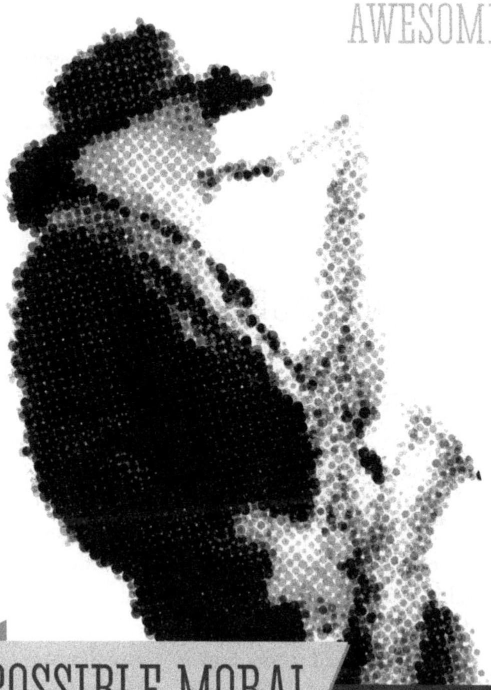

POSSIBLE MORAL

Together with music video and film directors *The Malloys* and advertising agency *Bartle Bogle Hegarty,* Oasis did something very inspirable. They also tried something completely different, marketing their music in a whole new way. It was also a good way for the street musicians to gain publicity – if they performed well, people would notice them as well which would help them boost their own careers.

STATISTICS OF STORY

%

70% ENTERTAINING
70% INTELLIGENT
0% DISTURBED / CRAZY
90% MORAL VALUE
80% HAPPY READING
0% RISKY / ILLEGAL

MORE INFO? SEARCH THIS!

Dig out your soul

Street musicians

Live in New York

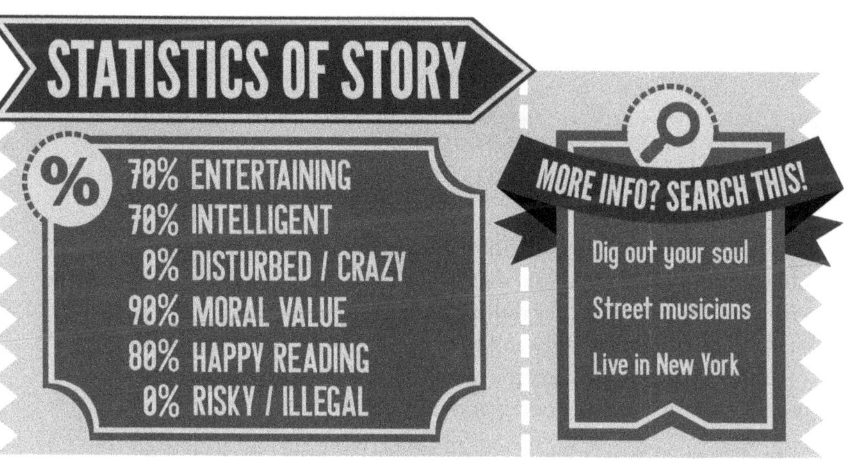

AWESOME MARKETING

SUBWAY BAND CREATIVITY

ATOMIC TOM IPHONES STOLEN
CONNECTION INSTRUMENTS

In October 2010, little-known New York City band, Atomic Tom, had their instruments stolen, but bad luck wasn't going to stop these musicians from doing what they love. Riding over the Manhattan Bridge on the subway, the band gave a performance of their song *Take Me Out*, by using four *iPhones* to simulate the drums, guitar, bass and vocals (microphone) they had recently lost. The performance was recorded and the video uploaded on *YouTube*, reaching millions of people world-wide.

While performing on the train they were physically close, had eye contact with each other, smiled, and used technology in a way that was connective with others. Atomic Tom used the power of social media to help get their name out there, and whether the story of the stolen instruments was true or not, their story and video became a huge viral hit and the act brought focus to their music.

POSSIBLE MORAL

So often can you see people with their faces buried in their gadgets, oblivious to the world around them. It's great to see a story where technology is being used for real-time, in connection, with people. With the help of a capturing story and by using an original and unexpected venue for their performance, the members of Atomic Tom successfully promoted their band to a new worldwide audience.

Sources: "A Subway, 4 iPhones and a Little Serendipity", Bits blog NyTimes, 15 Oct, 2010. "Take Me Out", YouTube.

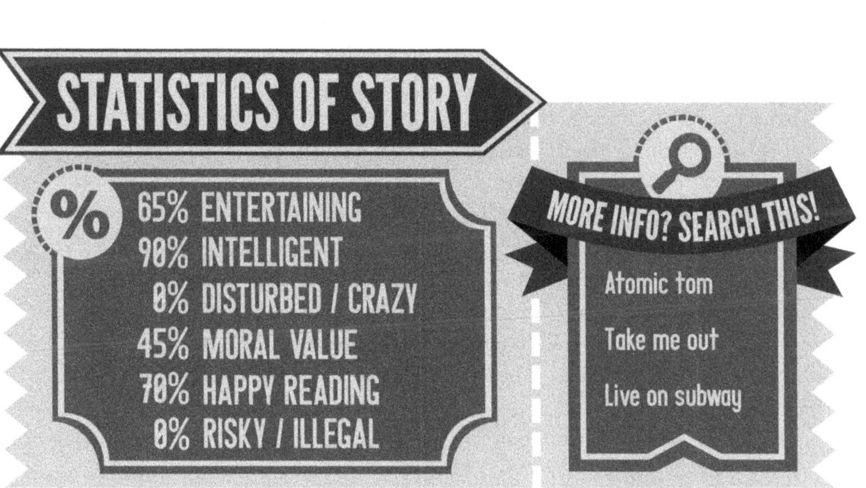
STATISTICS OF STORY
%
65% ENTERTAINING
90% INTELLIGENT
0% DISTURBED / CRAZY
45% MORAL VALUE
70% HAPPY READING
0% RISKY / ILLEGAL
MORE INFO? SEARCH THIS!
Atomic tom
Take me out
Live on subway

AWESOME MARKETING

THE ANGRY BIRDS STORY

BANKRUPTCY ROVIO SUCCESS
BRANDING SMARTPHONE GAME

This is the short story about how a great product, marketing and a strong and fearless attitude saved a small company from bankruptcy, and turned them into a huge empire. It's the story of *Angry Birds*, which made the transition from a smartphone game into a huge brand.

Early in 2009, programmers at *Rovio Entertainment* got together to brainstorm some new smartphone applications ideas. The game studio located in Espoo, Finland, had already produced 51 games in its six-year history. None of them had become a real success. For a time, the specter of bankruptcy shadowed the door. *Rovio* needed a hit, and boy did they get one: *Angry Birds* – an infectiously cute game in which the player uses a slingshot to help flightless fowl exact revenge against some green pigs who've stolen their eggs. The game has been praised for its successful combination of addictive gameplay, comical style, and low price. Its popularity led to versions of *Angry Birds* being created for personal computers and gaming consoles, a market for merchandise featuring its characters and even long-term plans for a feature film or television series. With over 700 million downloads across all platforms, the game has been called "one of the most mainstream games out right now" (original quote from digitaltrends.com, November 2010).

Blessed with a success of this magnitude, most application developers expand by creating new games. But *Rovio*'s flown horizontally instead and is busy hatching merchandise (plush toys, t-shirts, phone cases, etc.) which is making *Angry Birds* as much an analog brand as a digital one. *Mattel* released an tabletop game, making cardboard the latest incarnation of a digital idea. *Rovio* have quickly worked their way to success. First in the gaming industry and currently in all sorts of industries, ranging from Hollywood to the local toy stores. *Mickey Mouse* generates annually about $9 billion in revenues (including props) for *Disney*, and the *Hello Kitty* illustration from the 70's have become a theme park in Japan. So what can become of *Angry Birds* in the future? It seems everything is possible.

One of the secrets behind the success is the strong belief from *Rovio*

Sources: "Angry Birds: the story behind iPhone's gaming phenomenon", The Telegraph, 7 Feb 2011."Rovio.com – About us".

employees that they were simply going to succeed and at the same time have a workplace that allowed them to have fun. How else can one even think of sending the small colorful birds into space? (see page 140). Other than gaining financial success they have also helped to export Finland's expertise in pedagogy to the rest of the world, something the Finnish government has been unable to carry out successfully to date.

There is no easy way to reach the top: *Rovio* had produced more than 50 games before hitting the jackpot. There is an accumulation of knowledge and a large number of mistakes to be learned from before you find that one idea that will take you far.

POSSIBLE MORAL

Angry Birds is one of the first brands to launch from the digital to the physical world and not the other way around. In most businesses marketing generates costs, at *Rovio* advertising generates revenues. In marketing you must dare to do things differently if you want to succeed. It's about finding answers to the questions: How can I be even better? How can I do something even more amazing? *Rovio* set out to launch a new brand, an intellectual property with identifiable characters. Walt Disney had the same idea back in the 1950s, using his movies to funnel millions of Americans to *Disneyland*, where they bought untold tonnage of Mickey ears and stuffed Dumbos. Who knows: If Walt Disney were getting his start today, he might have gone with smartphone games instead of cartoons.

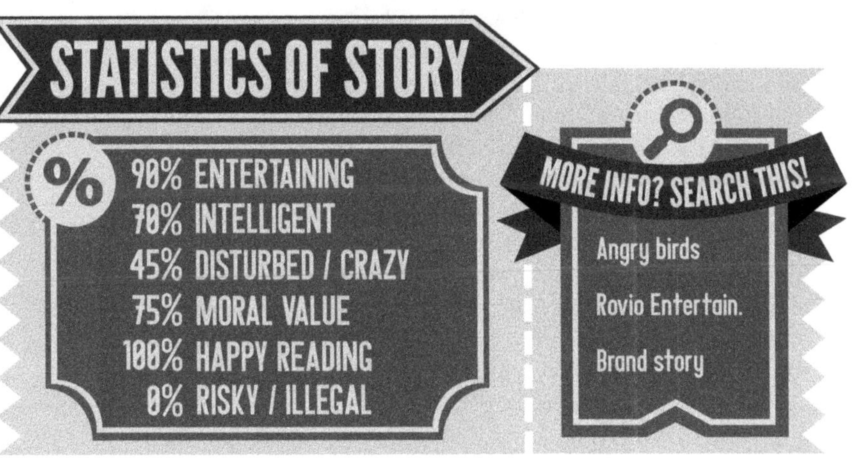

THE GREAT BEER DELIVERY

NEW ZEALAND SPEIGHT'S BAHAMAS
ADVENTURE SHIP OVERSEAS

Tim Ellingham, a kiwi fella (New Zealander) living in London, wrote an email to the *Speight's Brewery* saying he missed being able to order cold *Speight's* beer while in the pub. The employees at *Speight's* felt sorry for Tim, and wanted to help him out but sending this guy a few dozen beers wasn't going to be enough. At the time they received the letter from Tim, *Speight's* was struggling to keep their place of being the best selling beer in New Zealand. The stakes were high, and they knew they needed to do something truly legendary to get people talking about the brand. So together with the creative agency *Mojo* they came up with a brilliant and insane idea: To put a pub on a boat with volunteer crew members and sail them around the world to deliver a fully functional *Speight's Ale House* to London! They called the project *The Great Beer Delivery*. If you wanted to be part of this adventure and were interested in becoming a crew member, all you had to do was to register your application on the *Speight's* website and convince them of your southern ways and values. *Speight's Brewery* and *Mojo* used newspaper advertisements to find recruits. Around 2,000 people turned up to volunteer.

The $300,000 *Speight's Ale House* was to be freighted to London on a 70 meter (almost 230 feet) long chartered container ship sailing from Dunedin in July 2007. With a crew of five people, lots of beer and a full working pub on board, they were now heading towards the United Kingdom. National TV-show *Crowd Goes Wild* joined the crew to document the adventure. The crew sent witty updates of the trip through national TV and kept a live web-log that could be followed on the website. Also the radio network broadcasted daily reports from the crew. The journey took 70 days, with the ship going via Samoa, Panama, the Bahamas and New York on its way to London. Upon arrival in London they got the Ale House on to dry land and there were seven nights of celebrations in the pub itself with free beer, yes that's right – FREE BEER. But only for the local kiwis. All that the New Zealanders living in London needed to do was register their details via the website to become

Sources: "How Speight's crossed the world", Otago Daily Times, Oct 25, 2008. "Work / lion nathan", Publicismojo.com.au.

a "UK Speight's Mate". There were 700 tickets available for the lucky ones. Today the Ale House is, amusingly enough, permanently located in London, so it was not only a costly marketing trick. You can find it above the Temple subway station. Every week 2,000 liters of the famous golden beer are flown in from New Zealand, to support their fellow kiwis and curious Englishmen alike. The trip was also made into a 60 minutes long documentary.

POSSIBLE MORAL

Speight's spent their entire(!) advertising budget on this crazy idea. The PR value alone has been estimated at over $2.5 million dollars, six times the size of the original budget. The fact is that firstly it's a brilliant idea, and secondly, when it's a brilliant idea, people will talk about it. For a long time, the public and media thought that this was some looney idea that the people at *Speight's* would get over, and come back with a script for a regular TV-commercial. But they didn't. They got out there and made it happen. The rest, as they say, is legend.

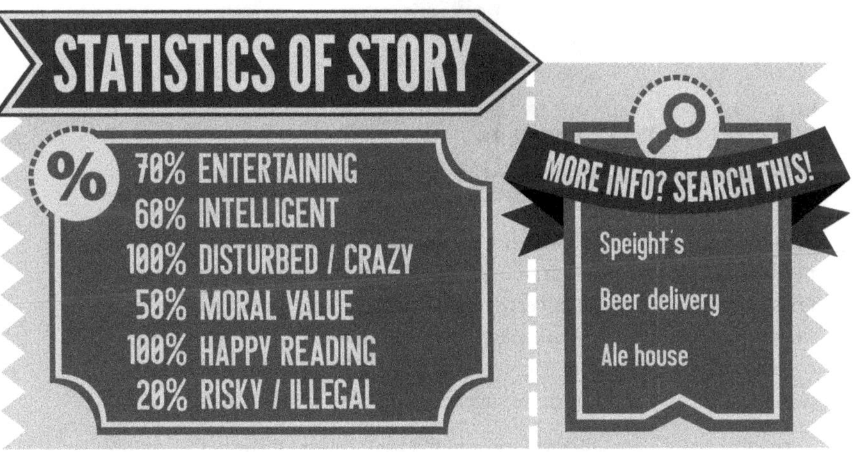

AWESOME MARKETING

THE SOPRANOS

ADVERTISING MAFIA GUERRILLA
TAXI CABS SHOCKING

In 2005 the cable television network *Home Box Office* (*HBO*) advertised their hit show *The Sopranos* by focusing on the crime theme of the show. *The Sopranos* is a television series created by David Chase that revolves around the New Jersey-based Italian-American mobster Tony Soprano.

In this marketing campaign *HBO* definitely broke traditional marketing rules and was effective in attracting a lot of attention. They made a bunch of life-like arms and placed them at the back of several taxis that drove through New York. The arm was sticking out of the trunk, making it look like there was a dead body inside. Next to the arm they had placed a bumper sticker with the series logo saying "The Sopranos – Only on HBO", so people would get the gesture.

POSSIBLE MORAL

This is a great example of the shock value that often accompanies guerrilla marketing tactics. Although one has to wonder if the cab drivers whose taxis hosted the frightful advertisements suffered a drop in business, or if they were more popular than ever. I also wonder if the New York Police received phone calls about arms sticking out of trunks. But if this didn't cause trouble, it's an even more successful marketing stunt in my eyes.

Source: "Killer Examples of Guerrilla Marketing", Betsy Brottlund, Resourcenation, 20 Jan, 2009.

STATISTICS OF STORY
%
55% ENTERTAINING
60% INTELLIGENT
75% DISTURBED / CRAZY
55% MORAL VALUE
50% HAPPY READING
40% RISKY / ILLEGAL
MORE INFO? SEARCH THIS!
Guerrilla marketing
The sopranos
New York

AWESOME MARKETING

UNLEASHING THE IDEAVIRUS

SELF-PUBLISH SPREAD E-BOOK
SETH GODIN GIVE AWAY

Seth Godin, is an American entrepreneur, author and public speaker. In the year 2000 he went to his publisher with his newly written book *Unleashing the Ideavirus* and was asking to publish it on some conditions. Godin needed the book to come out right away, and he also wanted to give it away online for free. The company was unwilling to go along with his marketing ideas, so what did Godin do? He took matters into his own hands and released the book as a free electronic book (e-book) through his website. The whole book, in one PDF file. This turned out to be a very smart move. Handing out *Unleasing the Ideavirus* for free ended up spreading Godin's ideas faster than his previous book *Permission Marketing*, which was a *New York Times* best-seller. The result: *Unleashing the Ideavirus* is today claimed to be the most downloaded e-book of all time.

As the fan base of the book grew fast, many contacted Godin wishing for a real physical book. Through a self-publishing service, the printed version of the book sold for $40 on *Amazon*, and made a ton of money – simply because people had already known about the book from the e-version. Godin completely worked the other way around from the traditional ways. The book has, since the release, been translated into ten languages and published in both hardcover and paperback form.

Sources: "PressPausePlay" documentary, 2011. "Seth Godin...", Anique Gonzalez, MarketingCrossing.

POSSIBLE MORAL

Handing out your creations for free is really a great way to market your product. In today's society many things have become "free". It has almost turned into a public demand. We're streaming movies, TV-shows and music for free. We read news online instead of purchasing the paper. Many games and applications for smartphones/tablets are free. The downside is that we come across more commercials and advertisement, but the good news is that we can be offered more entertainment for no cost. In the early year 2000 this wasn't the case. When marketing his book, Seth Godin was a pioneer in many ways. By offering it for free he pushed the limits and went to the extreme. He proved a valid point and showed the rest of the world that the industry was dead. Godin inspired hundreds of authors to follow his idea. He dared to do something new, bold and different. This story inspires me to contribute with something unique and exciting for my time. Simply not just to follow a trend, but to create it.

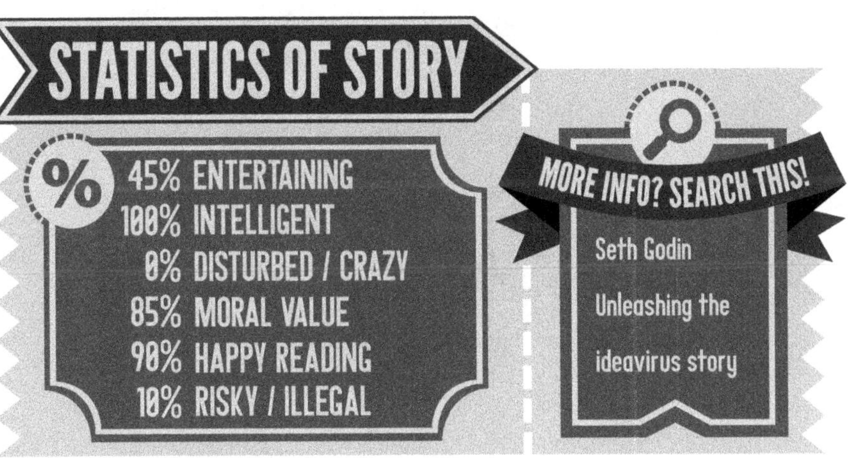

STATISTICS OF STORY
%
45% ENTERTAINING
100% INTELLIGENT
0% DISTURBED / CRAZY
85% MORAL VALUE
90% HAPPY READING
10% RISKY / ILLEGAL
MORE INFO? SEARCH THIS!
Seth Godin
Unleashing the
ideavirus story

ANCHORING

NEGOTIATION DOUCHEY PROPOSAL
FAKING IT AGREEMENT

Anchoring is a smart yet sneaky way of winning a debate. It's a form of negotiation skill. This is how it works: There's a discussion between two parties that has different opinions on a certain topic, but need to meet an agreement. Let's say you're one of those people. First, start off by giving an extreme (almost ridiculous) proposal as if it were your honest opinion. The opponent won't like it. You answer by taking one step back, a rather long one, which if succeeded will lead into an agreement. Now the other person feels like they have won the "debate". But actually it's you who have gotten exactly what you wanted. This because you never really cared for your first, dishonest, proposal. The idea is to simply to try and fool the other opponent with a fake argument that makes them meet you halfway, or at least that's what you make them believe they've accomplished.

Example: A kid wants a bunny as a pet. He knows his parents don't like animals and that they don't trust him to be able to take care of a pet. Though one day he starts asking them for a dog, and they quickly turn him down. He keeps nagging until he reach the point where he gets into a discussion with his parents. Now the kid starts anchoring, and simply says: "Okay, if not a dog – I want a bunny". Compared to the barking, training, price and responsibility of a dog – a bunny sounds like a gift sent from heaven. The parents agree on the boy getting a bunny.

POSSIBLE MORAL

Had the boy only asked for a bunny in the first place, chances are he would have wound up getting only a *Pet Rock* (see page 200). Use this skill wise, and you might well succeed.

Source: "How to Use Spatial Anchors in Persuasion Skills", the nlp company, 26 July, 2012.

STATISTICS OF STORY

20% ENTERTAINING
70% INTELLIGENT
45% DISTURBED / CRAZY
20% MORAL VALUE
20% HAPPY READING
50% RISKY / ILLEGAL

MORE INFO? SEARCH THIS!
Anchoring
Negotiation skill
Method

CLEVER BUSINESS

ARIMUS

GREAT METHOD GUERRILLA OVERACHIEVEMENT
OVERKILLING ADMISSION TEST

Oskar Pernefeldt, a 21-year-old Swede, really wanted to study at the programme *Visual Communications* at *Beckmans College of Design* in Stockholm. He wanted this so badly that he spent seven months creating the fictional country *Arimus*. To be accepted as a student at *Beckmans*, every attendee has to create and submit a piece of artwork as an admission test. The theme for the test is different every year and a jury decides which people are accepted and which are not. In the test, there's always an assignment called "Extra", which allows the attendee to submit some optional work he or she has created. It was especially in this field Oskar's work stood out from the rest. Instead of submitting a logotype, painting or poster; He created the republic of *Arimus*.

Arimus is an island located outside Micronesia. It officially has 12,283 inhabitants, all named Oskar Pernefeldt. *Arimus* is Latin for intellect. Two British scientists found the country and decided to create a country based on wisdom and knowledge. Since much around us is graphic design; creating a country is to create loads of graphic elements for many different areas. Oskar began his work by designing a flag, coat of arms, currency, newspaper, universities, companies with graphical profiles and a military (army, navy, air force).

While working full time as a studio assistant at an advertising agency, Oskar was working night time with the creation of *Arimus*. As he was studying an evening course at *Beckmans*, Oskar could infiltrate and research the kind of information he needed to turn his admission test into perfection. Through friends he found out which people were in the jury (which is almost a secret), and suddenly the republic of *Arimus* started to contact the members in different ways. The first letter looked like it was sent from one of the country's universities. The fake principal explained that they had recently started up a graphic design program and asked *Beckmans* if they wanted to begin an exchange program with them. Oskar went so far that he designed his own postal stamps and a stamp saying "Arimus postal service", making the envelope look like it had been posted from overseas. The letter was then sneaked inside the school. The next letter for another member of the jury was "sent" from the country's bank, asking if he wanted to be an unofficial ambassador of the *Arimus* Bank in the Swedish art world. The letter offered bribes like flight tickets, appliances and pets. The third letter was a parking ticket, asking the jury member to pay 40 Arimusan pounds for improper parking of his Toyota Corolla. The last letter from *Arimus* Intelligence Service was sent to the youngest member of the jury, asking if he wanted to be the official contact for Scandinavia.

In the next step, Oskar took help from a friend to create a website for the Government of *Arimus*. Oskar then faked press releases, speeches, factual texts and statistics – all in bureaucratic English. He even got a friend to compose a national

Sources: "Uppdrag: Övrigt", Oskar Pernefeldt, Vimeo. "Han skapade ett eget land", Helsingborgs Dagblad, 25 May, 2012.

anthem for the country. After hours of work Oskar could finally purchase the internet domain. This opened new doors of possibilities. He could give all the politicians displayed on the website their own email addresses. Instead of spending time faking letters, he could now run the country from his bedroom. Acting as the top politicians of the country, Oskar sent emails explaining their displeasure that *Beckmans* had not replied to one single letter – calling it a political and diplomatic insult. In one email, the Vice President of *Arimus* writes that his son is interested in studying at *Beckmans*, and explains in a harsh tone that it would be most unfortunate if the countries relationship would be hurt by denying him access to the school.

Oskar also wanted the jury to encounter *Arimus* in different situations in their everyday lives. He created posters of a desperate and creepy exchange student from *Arimus*, who was looking for a place to live. The posters were put up in many different locations in Stockholm and at *Beckmans*. Even the man working at the cafeteria at the school got involved in Oskar's project. He collects snow globes from all around the world, and they are all displayed at the desk of the cafeteria. Oskar decided to create one for *Arimus* as well – which is now part of the collection.

Oskar figured the jury probably had seen some really creative stuff in the past, so he went public with his project to increase his odds. Using guerrilla marketing he reached out to newspapers, blogs etc. The feedback was huge. Not surprisingly, Oskar Pernefeldt was accepted at *Beckmans* and he decided to study instead of accepting one of the several job offers he received from the Swedish PR agency elite.

POSSIBLE MORAL

A story that shows that overkilling can be an important method into making a career. Doing that little extra (in this case, a lot extra) can get you ahead in the game. This way of thinking can be applied both in the world of studying and in the world of business.

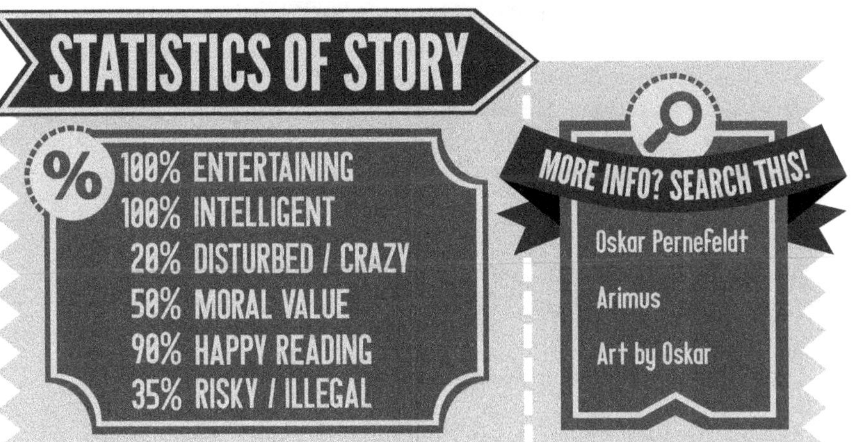

CLEVER BUSINESS

BOLD SPONSOR MOVE

GAMBLING OPENING ICEBAR
PARTNERSHIP ABSOLUT VODKA

Yngve Bergqvist, the founder of the *Icehotel* in Jukkasjärvi in Sweden, was searching for business partners during the early and mid-1990s. He wanted to have *Absolut Vodka*, Sweden's leading vodka manufacturer, as a partner, but they showed no interest. Before the opening of *Icehotel*, Bergqvist therefore took a bold move. He spent a big deal of the hotels budget buying a huge stock of *Absolut Vodka* bottles to the opening party. He then invited the media to join them. The day after the opening, pictures of amazing ice sculptures, people having fun, and the *Absolut Vodka* logotype showing pretty much everywhere spread like wildfire in newspapers. People from all over contacted *Absolut* and gave them credit for participating in such a unique project and congratulated them on their great investment. The people at *Absolut* didn't understand a thing and were, to say the least, caught by surprise. It didn't take long before they contacted Bergqvist and signed a partner contract.

The first *Absolut Icebar* opened at *Icehotel* in 1994. The same year there was an advertising shoot for *Absolut Vodka* in Jukkasjärvi, with photographer Herb Ritts. Models Kate Moss, Naomi Campbell, Mark Findlay and Marcus Schenkenberg were photographed surrounded by ice, wearing creations designed by fashion designer *Gianni Versace*. The concept of the ice bar is that the guests are served vodka in glasses made of ice from the Torne River, often described as a drink "in the rocks". Ice glasses at the bars are brought from the production hall in Jukkasjärvi to the *Icehotel*. Today *Icebar* is a big franchise concept and can be found in the cities Stockholm, London, Istanbul, Copenhagen and Oslo.

POSSIBLE MORAL

A great example how risking something can get you what you search for. Be bold and be brave!

Sources: "Yngve Bergqvist – entreprenör utan gränser!", arvidsjaur.se, 11 Feb, 2010. Icehotel and Icebar's official websites.

STATISTICS OF STORY
%
80% ENTERTAINING
100% INTELLIGENT
60% DISTURBED / CRAZY
45% MORAL VALUE
90% HAPPY READING
65% RISKY / ILLEGAL
MORE INFO? SEARCH THIS!
Yngve Bergqvist
Absolut icebar
Absolut vodka

CLEVER BUSINESS

BUTTON-STORE DISTRICT

IDIOSYNCRATIC TASTE SUBCULTURE
NEW YORK CORRECT FORUM

Subcultures thrive in big cities. If you have idiosyncratic taste, you're much more likely to find others who share those tastes the bigger the city you're in. A store that only sells clothing buttons most likely won't do well in a town of 30,000 people, but in New York City there's an entire button-store district. Maybe not that strange when you consider that the city is inhabited by 8 million people.

A piece of information telling us that there's a time and a place for any idea to thrive. Just make sure to have the correct setting.

Source: "Emerging Technology", Steven Berlin Johnson, Discover Magazine, 9 Sep, 2005.

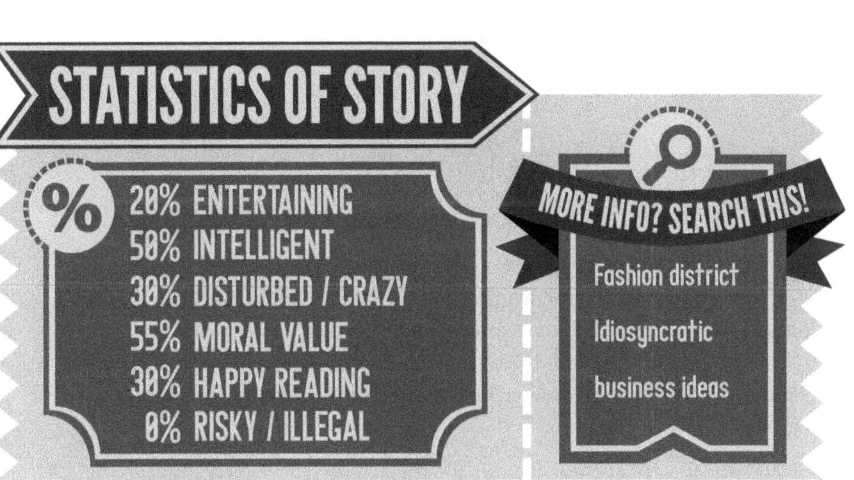
STATISTICS OF STORY
20% ENTERTAINING
50% INTELLIGENT
30% DISTURBED / CRAZY
55% MORAL VALUE
30% HAPPY READING
0% RISKY / ILLEGAL
MORE INFO? SEARCH THIS!
Fashion district
Idiosyncratic
business ideas

CLEVER BUSINESS

COCA-COLA SALESMEN

PERSPECTIVE FACTORY SALES
IMPORTANCE MINDSET

While visiting a *Coca-Cola* factory in Atlanta, sell-coach Tomas Hellgren from *Scenario Sweden* asked a worker what his duty at the factory was – he replied: "I'm a salesman for Coca-Cola". Tomas was a little puzzled because the man was clearly dressed as a factory worker with rubber gloves. It turned out that the man was responsible for checking that the labels on the bottles were looking good and that they weren't crooked or bumpy etc.

It's pretty simple. No customers in the grocery store purchases bottles with torn or ugly labels. I mean, would you? So the man in the factory is indeed a salesperson. In the end he's the guy that makes sure that the bottles will be sold.

POSSIBLE MORAL

Although how cliché it might sound: Everyone is valuable because everyone contributes to the whole. That's why one should not belittle people just because they are wearing overalls instead of suits. This story can teach us to see things with different perspective. The factory worker have a great mindset by not considering himself a drone but a more important employee for his workplace.

Source: Anecdote from lecture with Tomas Hellgren (www.kreatek.se), Piteå Företagarcentrum, 13 Feb, 2012.

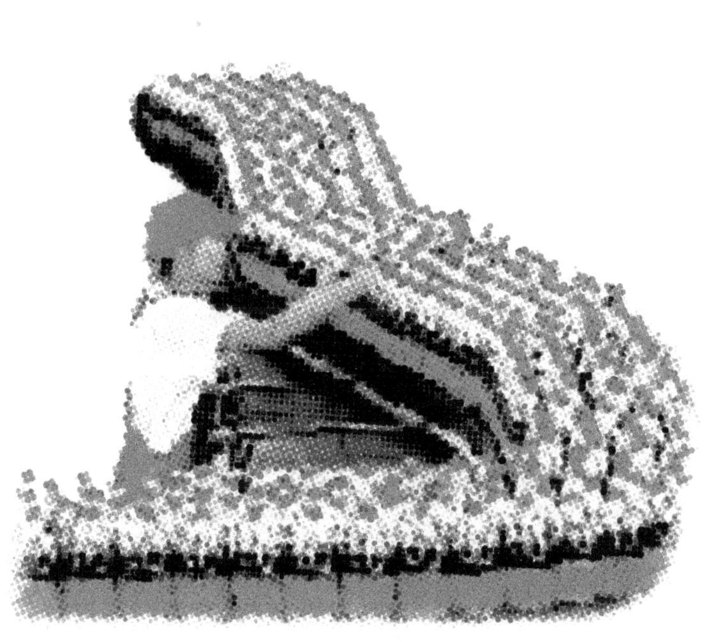

STATISTICS OF STORY
%
60% ENTERTAINING
65% INTELLIGENT
0% DISTURBED / CRAZY
70% MORAL VALUE
30% HAPPY READING
0% RISKY / ILLEGAL
MORE INFO? SEARCH THIS!
Tomas Hellgren
Perspective
Job values

HAVING A MEETING

EYE-OPENER AIRLINE RISKY
LEON NORDIN BAD TREATMENT

Leon Nordin is a Swedish copywriter and creative legend who during the 1960s and 70s renewed Swedish advertising together with art director Alf Mork at the agency *Arbmans*. There are loads of stories about Nordin and his, to say the least, unusual ways of handling clients.

This is one of many stories about him: The agency that he was working with at the time had an ongoing business with a big airline company. One day Nordin had invited the directors and top chiefs to the agency office to discuss their latest advertising plans. On arrival, the airline people had to sit down and wait in a crowded waiting room in uncomfortable chairs. They were served cheap coffee in plastic cups, and had to wait... and wait for the meeting to begin. After 45 minutes they'd had enough and were just about to leave when Nordin walked through the door, upon which one of the directors yelled: "How the hell can you treat us this badly? A crowded and sweaty waiting room, plastic chairs and lukewarm coffee! Who do you think you are?". "Well," said Nordin, "this is exactly how you treat your own customers. Shall we start the meeting now?".

POSSIBLE MORAL

If this story is true, it tells of a risky move that would or could have cost Nordin and his agency their client. However, the moral of this story is clear: Treat others as you yourself want to be treated. The directors of the company hopefully had a major revelation.

Sources: "Uppfinnaren" the audiobook, Alf Mork, 1998. "När kungen hette Leon", Please Copy Me, 30 Jun, 2008.

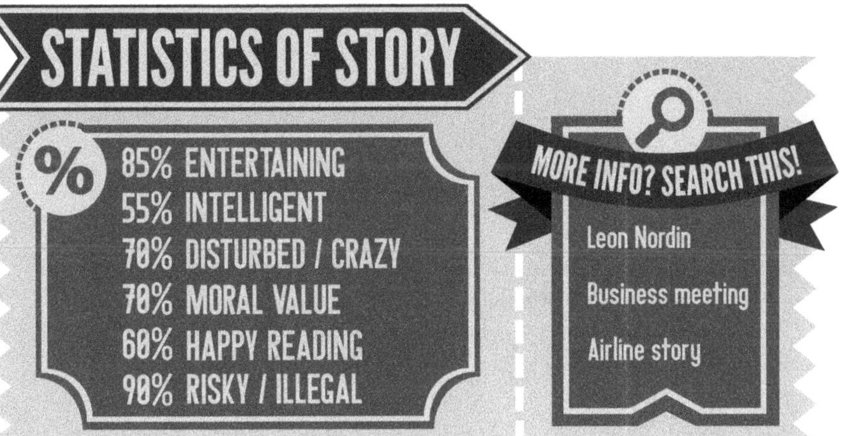
STATISTICS OF STORY
85% ENTERTAINING
55% INTELLIGENT
70% DISTURBED / CRAZY
70% MORAL VALUE
60% HAPPY READING
90% RISKY / ILLEGAL
MORE INFO? SEARCH THIS!
Leon Nordin
Business meeting
Airline story

CLEVER BUSINESS

MARKETPLACE PITEA

FRANCHISING SHOPS NEW MARKET
POPULATION GREAT SOLUTION

Franchising companies have a minimum requirement for the population size of a city for them to open their shops. In Sweden, the smallest figure is usually around 50,000 people for the big companies. The town of Piteå, in northern Sweden, was therefore facing a problem with their 41,000 inhabitants. Piteå is located between the towns of Luleå (75,000) and Skellefteå (72,000) who both meet the requirement and therefore were eligible for these kinds of companies.

One man had a brilliant idea: He created the concept *Marketplace Piteå*. Choosing a radius of 80 km (almost 50 miles) including the three towns (Piteå, Luleå and Skellefteå) and villages outside of the towns, which made a total population of 220,000 people, he was able to launch this as a new marketing area. This area is the most densely populated part of northern Sweden, and by making use of this marketplace, Piteå has been able to open an unusual high number of stores for its population. There is thus a very large range of shopping to choose from for being so few inhabitants.

This is a clever way of getting around a problem. The man created a new market that earlier had not been envisioned. He coined a term with strong power and was literally thinking outside the box. One should not always stare blindly at the municipal and county boundaries. See the solutions, not the obstacles!

Source: Anecdote from lecture with Gunnar Forslund (www.2tango.nu), Piteå Företagarcentrum, 25 Jan, 2012.

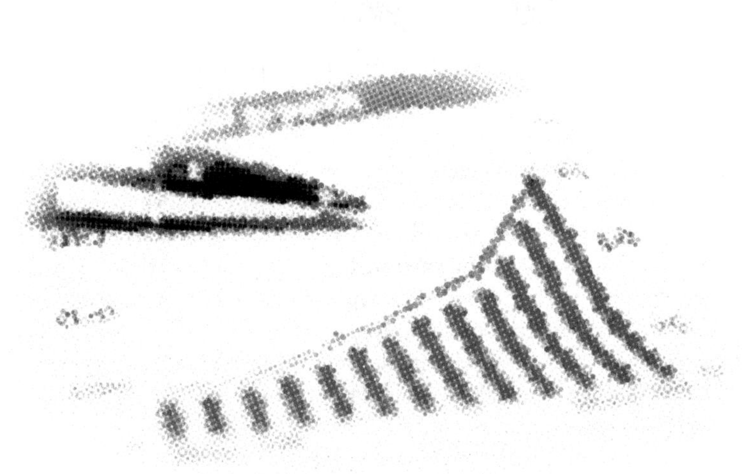

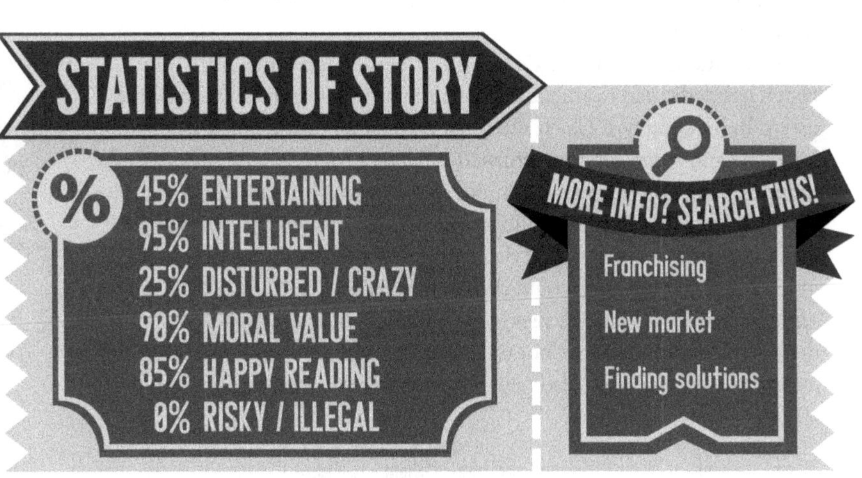
STATISTICS OF STORY
%
45% ENTERTAINING
95% INTELLIGENT
25% DISTURBED / CRAZY
90% MORAL VALUE
85% HAPPY READING
0% RISKY / ILLEGAL
MORE INFO? SEARCH THIS!
Franchising
New market
Finding solutions

CLEVER BUSINESS

SERVICE OF ZAPPOS

ROLE MODEL SHIPPING SALES
FREE PUBLICITY COSTUMER SERVICE

Zappos is a Las Vegas shoe retailer that was founded in 1999, selling shoes online. During a period of over ten years they have expanded to include other products like handbags and sunglasses, and the company has grown to be a $1 billion-per-year-business with very impressive statistics, a good business model and a really good example of how to use social media. Much has been written about how *Zappos* cultivates a culture dedicated to exceptional customer service (they famously offer $2,000 to employees who quit during the mandatory four-week training program for new hires, although few people take the offer).

For *Zappos*, customer service has always been a critical part of the company. Early on, they made the deliberate decision to divert their marketing budget to customer service. They let customers do things like try and return products for up to a year, they only list what is in the warehouse stock, they encourage customers to call them about nearly everything, and invest in "surprise" free overnight shipping for most customers. *Zappos* has thrived, not only by offering free shipping, but by offering free return shipping as well. Also, if you call them and they don't have a particular shoe or product in stock or even offer it, they will actually refer you to their competitors.

What's less known about *Zappos* is just how much time CEO Tony Hsieh has dedicated to spreading the company's vision to anyone who will listen. In his speeches, Hsieh often refers to his so called "pizza story". One night, he and some vendors returned to a hotel room late. Someone in the group was craving pizza and was told room service had closed their service. As a joke, Hsieh suggested calling *Zappos*. Even though they doesn't sell pizza, a surprised customer service employee took his time to find a list of local pizza places that would deliver to the hotel. It's a fun story that seriously reinforces Hsieh's theme of customer service. *Zappos* is one of the biggest companies that not only gets "it" when it comes to exploiting internet technology, but also truly understands the meaning of customer service.

Sources: "Making ideas happen", Scott Belsky, 2008. "Zappos' Tony Hsieh Delivers Happiness...", Briansolis.com, 11 Apr, 2011.

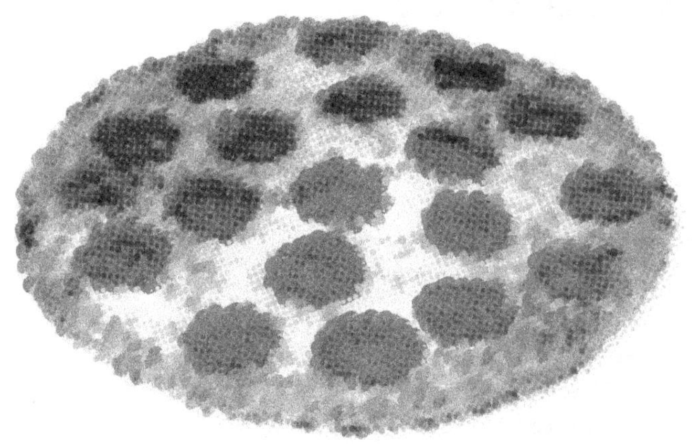

POSSIBLE MORAL

You would much rather support a company that inspires you than one that doesn't. Building positive customer experiences will help create passionate customers who will spread your message on their behalf – almost like an evangelist. Free publicity is worth so much more than a simple lost sale. It's simply not always about selling something to your customers.

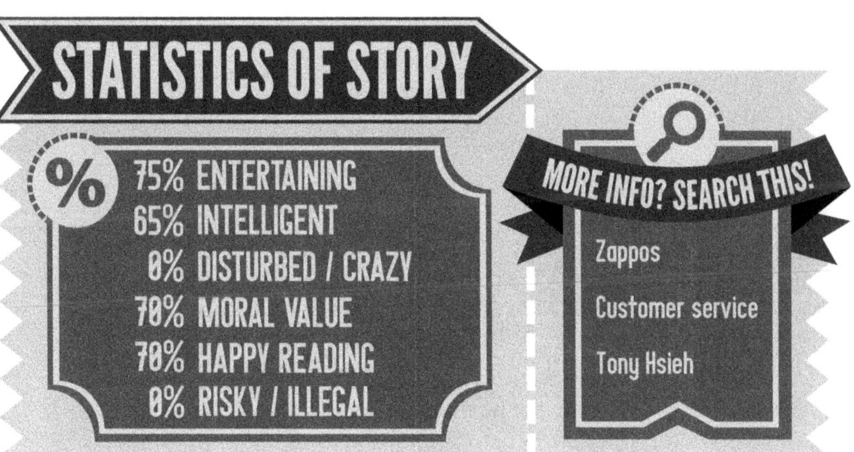

CLEVER BUSINESS

SHARE OWNING CLERKS

INVESTMENT SALES INSIGHT
STOCKHOLDER KNOWLEDGE

Here's a thought for all you people working as clerks for big companies, selling everything from fashion to electronics. There probably aren't many of you who invest in the company you work for by becoming a stockholder or shareowner. Now why's that? It's really a pity. You all have a broad insight into how the collections are received, how sales evolve day by day etc. You have a great starting point for investing in the company you work for. There could be some big money to be earned.

Don't forget that you have knowledge about the company you work for. As we all know, knowledge can be powerful if used in the right way.

Source: From the sane and insane mind of Simon Zingerman.

STATISTICS OF STORY
%
25% ENTERTAINING
75% INTELLIGENT
0% DISTURBED / CRAZY
50% MORAL VALUE
50% HAPPY READING
0% RISKY / ILLEGAL
MORE INFO? SEARCH THIS!
Share owning
Stock market
Investing

CLEVER BUSINESS

TECHNICAL VISITS

EDUCATION TOURISM LECTURES
GAIN ACCESS TECHNOLOGY

A new type of tourism is emerging, and it goes by the name *technical visits*. Today is truly the time of the nerds, and these visits are simply as nerdy as it gets. They are private holiday trips, meant for visitors who are looking to learn a little extra. It's tourism for the curious: Offering small or large groups looking for ways to enhance their experience during their vacation stay.

Through the companies that offer *technical visits*, visitors are able to go deeper into how the specific company or phenomena works and how it is constructed. This can include high-tech technology, aerospace, gemology, entrepreneurship and more. The products under the *technical visits* will provide visitors to, within each activity area, immerse themselves fully in its activities. Visitors can meet scientists, engineers and others who work for real with the product. As a visitor you will gain more access to genuine information and behind-the-scenes-experience than the usual tourist visitors.

In 2009, the construction of the world's most modern symphony organ began in Piteå, Sweden. The *Studio Acusticum Organ* was to be a symphonic instrument for the 21st century, an instrument which combines tradition, artistic renewal and innovative technology, to create a tool for the music of the future and for research in such areas as interpretation. The instrument combines old traditions with new technology. What's unique is that the organ can be played from a distance via online booking. For example, one can book an hour of playing the organ, live from Australia via midi controllers. The construction of this organ created a big hype. Visitors from all over the world came to Piteå to hear tunes played on the organ and to learn more about the technology behind it. At one time a bus of 30 people from Switzerland arrived, with people eager to witness the construction.

Technical visits doesn't offer sunny beaches, crystal clear oceans, cheap beer and parties until 5 o'clock in the morning. What it does offer is in-depth knowledge, entrepreneurship lectures and background stories.

Sources: Lecture with Gunnar Forslund (www.2tango.nu), 13 Feb, 2012. "Out of the ordinary study visits", Kiruna Technical Visits.

POSSIBLE MORAL

A great and enriching way to combine vacation and education. *Technical visits* as private paid vacations are a growing trend that probably will be far more common in the future. As an employee or entrepreneur you can ask yourself today: What kind of working environment am I part of? Could *technical visits* be of any use in my line of business?

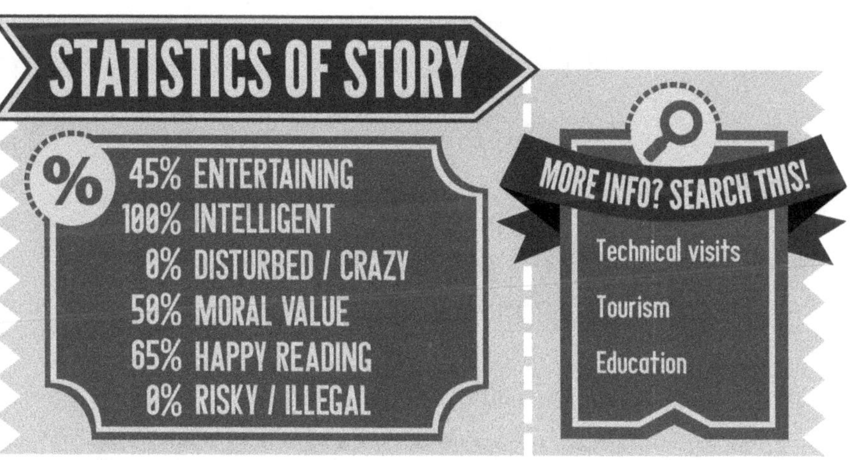

CLEVER BUSINESS

THINK LIKE GOOGLE

TRENDSETTERS SUCCESS PREDICTION
ROLE-MODELS NEXT BIG THING

A small part of the secret of *Google*'s immense success story is that they are sailing with the wind. They are not sitting still relying on some business model or trying to fight their way out of hard economic times by suing their customers. *Google* tries to figure out what's going to happen and plans to be standing there when it does. They do not force things to happen their way.

What is fascinating is that if you look back in time you will see that many business ideas that have become really successful have not been written in the investment banks' reports, which means that projects and ideas that have been predicted to be successful many times don't make it big. Former professional ice hockey player Wayne Gretzky had the right idea: "A good hockey player plays where the puck is. A great hockey player plays where the puck is going to be", which leads us back to *Google*. When *Google* was founded, search engines were unpopular. The large search-engine companies of that time was rather looking to become big web portals, with services such as; email, news, stock prices, and entertainment.

See if thinking like *Google* can help you figure out what the next big thing will be, then head over there and create/invest.

Sources: "The Secret To Google's Success", Bloomberg Businessweek, 5 Mar, 2006. "Google at 10", BBC, Tim Weber, 4 Sep, 2008. Quote: From "Gretzky: An Autobiography", Ricky Reilly, 1990. Drill with his father, on the fundamentals of smart hockey.

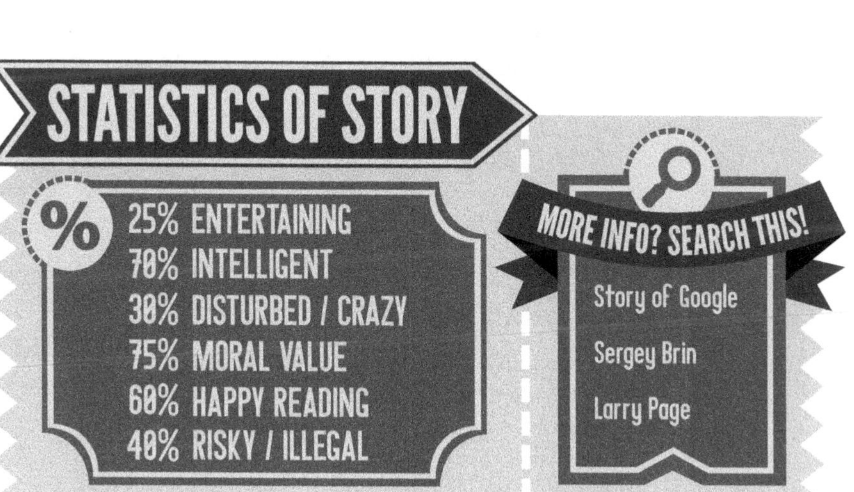
STATISTICS OF STORY
25% ENTERTAINING
70% INTELLIGENT
30% DISTURBED / CRAZY
75% MORAL VALUE
60% HAPPY READING
40% RISKY / ILLEGAL
MORE INFO? SEARCH THIS!
Story of Google
Sergey Brin
Larry Page

DUMB BUT BRILLIANT

CHEVY PUBLICITY

NEGATIVE ADS PROMOTE TOOL COMMERCIALS ACTIVISTS

In 2006, *General Motors* (*GM*) launched a contest to promote its *Chevy Tahoe* Sport utility vehicle (*SUV*). At *chevyapprentice.com*, viewers were given video and music clips with which to create their own 30-second commercials. The website allowed visitors to select backgrounds, video shots, and input text in an attempt to win prizes ranging from a *Jackson Hole Getaway* to a trip to the *Major League Baseball All-Star Game*. The visitors could save the videos and send the links to their friends. Because the *SUV* does roughly half a mile to the gallon, it didn't take long before environmental activists were filling the site with attack-commercials. Among the new Tahoe-commercials that soon proliferated across the web were ones with taglines like "Yesterday's technology today" and "Global warming isn't a pretty SUV ad – it's a frightening reality".

To the surprise of everyone, *GM* let the negative commercials stay online. Maybe they were afraid to lose credibility if they removed them? During this campaign, the apprentice-website got more visitors than the total amount of search hits for "Chevy" and "Tahoe" generated on both *Google* and *Yahoo* together during the same period. The *SUV* ended up selling pretty well. The campaign was, maybe unexpectedly, a success. This even though the top search results for "Chevy Tahoe" on *Google*, even to today's date, consist of negative commercials.

POSSIBLE MORAL

Chevy Apprentice turned into an activism tool and became a strange example of showing that all publicity can be good publicity. If *GM*'s decision of keeping the attack-commercials on their site were intentional this was a brilliant move by them.

Source: "Chevy Tries a Write-Your-Own-Ad Approach, and the Potshots Fly", The New York Times, 4 Apr, 2006.

because you hate
mother nature

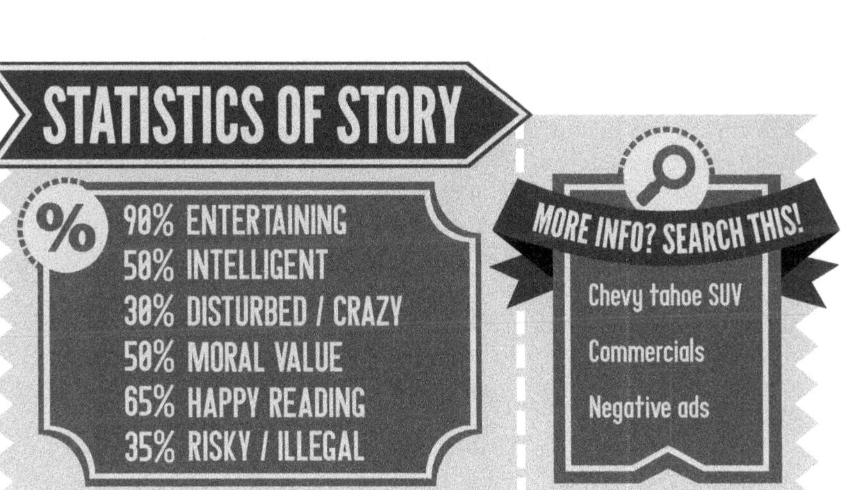
STATISTICS OF STORY
90% ENTERTAINING
50% INTELLIGENT
30% DISTURBED / CRAZY
50% MORAL VALUE
65% HAPPY READING
35% RISKY / ILLEGAL
MORE INFO? SEARCH THIS!
Chevy tahoe SUV
Commercials
Negative ads

MILLION DOLLAR HOMEPAGE

PIXEL SPACE STUDENT ADVERTISING
INNOVATION PAY FOR SCHOOL

Take one college-bound student with an overdrawn bank account and one twenty-minute brainstorming session on how to raise money to pay for school, and what do you get? A million-dollar idea that's had people around the world slapping their foreheads and muttering "Why didn't I think of that?" ever since.

We're back in year 2005. With only one month to go before he was to begin university and no money in his bank account, Alex Tew was determined to find a way to avoid student debt. Armed with a notebook and pen, Tew stayed up late one night brainstorming ways to make some quick cash. To help jumpstart his creativity, he wrote down just one question on his notepad: How can I become a millionaire? Twenty minutes later, he had his answer: Sell one million pixels of advertising space on a website for $1 each.

Tew already had some experience with website design, so with $100, he quickly bought a domain name and some basic web hosting services and had his website, *MillionDollarHomepage.com*, up and running in two days. The concept was simple. Businesses could buy 10x10 or larger blocks of advertising space for a $1 per pixel and place their logos and links on his site. Tew knew that no one would be interested in buying pixel space if he didn't get the ball rolling, so he convinced some family and friends to chip in to buy the first 1,000 pixels. He also thought it would be a good story for the media to pick up, so Tew took the money he made from the first 1,000 pixels he sold and used it to write and send out press releases to the local media near his hometown of Cricklade, England.

Four months and 2,000 customers later, including *The Times* and *Orange*, the million dollars was almost surpassed. Two million people had accessed the site. On the 1st of January 2006, the final 1,000 pixels were put up for auction on *eBay*. The auction closed on January 11th with a winning bid of $38,100 that brought the final sum to $1,037,100 in gross income.

Sources: "The Million-Dollar Home Page", Entrepreneur, Sarah Pierce, 13 Jan, 2006. "FAQ", milliondollarhomepage.com.

POSSIBLE MORAL

The secrets of Alex Tew's success story comes down to two important factors: The power of word of mouth and the story of a student making a million, which enchanted the media. Others eager to learn from him should have faith in their creative mind, take calculated and affordable risks, and treat "failure" in a positive way, as a learning process.

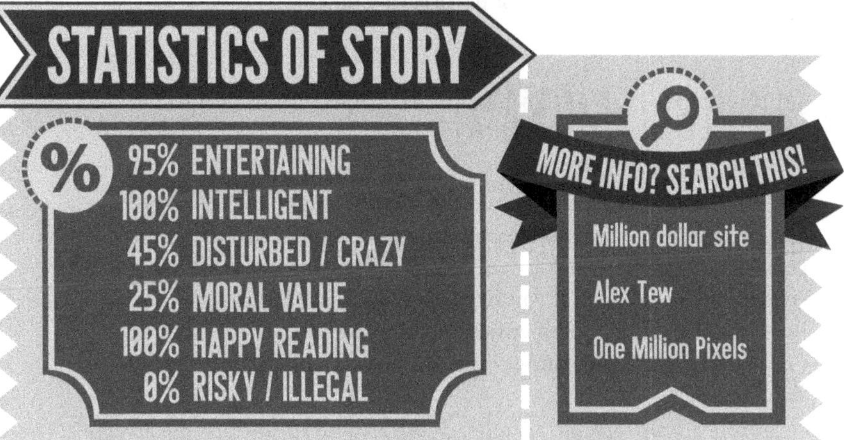

DUMB BUT BRILLIANT

SANTA MAIL

POSTCARDS ALASKA STRONG VISION
GREETINGS PERSONALIZED LETTERS

Okay, how's this for a brilliant idea. Get a postal address at the North Pole, Alaska, pretend you're Santa Claus and charge parents $10 for every letter you send to their kids? Well, address-owner Byron Reese has sent over 300,000 letters since the start of his business, *Santa Mail*, in 2001, which makes him a couple million dollars richer. Parents who want their children to have a personal greeting for Christmas just need to make an order online, and they will receive a letter in the mail. The company sends out fully personalized letters all across North America, and they're even postmarked from the North Pole, which gives them an authentic feeling.

The magic of Christmas is a serious business for Reese. He has implemented a rigorous quality-control program that has multiple people (his elves) checking each letter, ensuring complete accuracy for each one, as well as Birthday cards from Santa and the post-Christmas "Greetings from Hawaii" postcard from a tanned, beach-bound Santa. Reese started out with low expectations, but sold 10,000 letters the first year.

Reese's childhood Christmas memories include installing 200 strings of Christmas lights and decorating dozens of Christmas cookies each year, and today he loves the look on the postman's face when he goes to buy 40,000 Santa stamps at the post office each Christmas.

POSSIBLE MORAL

An idea that at first glance seems really stupid – might just be in need of some polishing. The more details, depth and thought you put into your ideas the more valuable they become. What you also need is to believe in your product. If you lack belief, it will show through. Byron Reese may have met a lot of criticism against his "stupid" idea, but due to his determination he put his idea into practice and has become rich along the way.

Source: "Home Based Business Millionaires, Part I (Santa Letters Millionaire)", Ezine Articles, John Deprice, 16 July, 2006.

STATISTICS OF STORY
70% ENTERTAINING
90% INTELLIGENT
45% DISTURBED / CRAZY
35% MORAL VALUE
60% HAPPY READING
0% RISKY / ILLEGAL
MORE INFO? SEARCH THIS!
Santa mail
Byron Reese
Self-belief

FOOD FOR THOUGHT

CLOSED DUE TO SUN

WELL-BEING SIGN SABBATICAL
TIME OFF BEHAVIOR

The summer had just arrived in the city of Stockholm. With long and cold winters, the summer time is holy in Sweden – and the sunny days can be few. On one of those perfect days without a cloud in the sky, a handwritten sign could be found hanging on the door of a store in the city, it read: "Closed due to sun".

POSSIBLE MORAL

To me, this sign is hilarious. It's such a cocky thing to do as an owner of a store. It makes me think about time, and the ability to be trapped by opening hours. I believe that the value of taking time off is often overlooked. With this story I want to encourage people to weigh the consequences of making similar actions in your life. Like the owner of the store you sometimes need to prioritize what feels good instead of what is "right". Don't always care for what is expected of you, but what is best for your well-being.

I once had a lecturer that, in the start-up of her own business, decided that she should always have at least three months of vacation every year. Even through her first tough years she kept that promise to herself, thought financially she really would've needed to work more. Another example is the legendary graphic designer Stefan Sagmeister. Every seven years he closes his New York studio for a yearlong sabbatical to rejuvenate and refresh his and the other employees creative outlook. Sagmeister himself travel and pursue experiments that he finds difficult to accomplish during the regular working year.

Sources: From the sane and insane mind of Simon Zingerman. TEDTalks, "Stefan Sagmeister: The power of time off", 2009.

Sorry We're
CLOSED

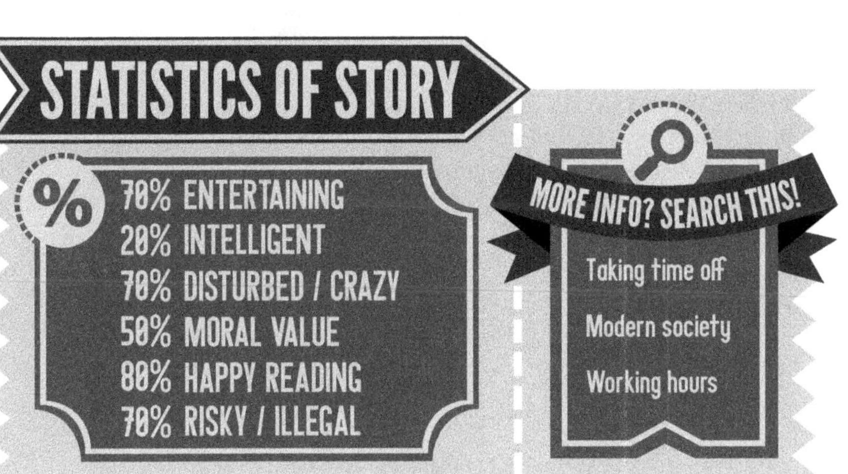
STATISTICS OF STORY
%
70% ENTERTAINING
20% INTELLIGENT
70% DISTURBED / CRAZY
50% MORAL VALUE
80% HAPPY READING
70% RISKY / ILLEGAL
MORE INFO? SEARCH THIS!
Taking time off
Modern society
Working hours

FOOD FOR THOUGHT

DISNEYLAND CLEANERS

PERSPECTIVE HEROES EMPLOYEE VALUE APPRECIATION STRONG VISION

From the very start it's been a hallmark of *Disney* to keep their parks clean. When the original *Disneyland Park* in California opened in 1955, a journalist told Walt Disney how he believed that the park was beautiful that day but would quickly become dirty as the crowds continued to enter. Walt vigorously disagreed. He said: "We're going to make the park so clean that people are going to be embarrassed to throw anything on the ground". Walt Disney himself led the early efforts, insisting that attractions, gates and benches were to be repainted on schedule, even if a touch-up would've been enough. He made sure that light bulbs were replaced even before they burned out and that trash cans were emptied before they were full. The *Disney* culture was simple: Everyone had a part in keeping the park clean.

At *Disneyland* the cleaners have one of the highest status of all employees. They have good looking uniforms, shiny name badges and working equipment of high quality. They play an important role in reflecting *Disney*'s values. The park should always be clean and tidy. In this respect, the cleaners are the real heroes of *Disneyland*. Those who keep the parks looking fresh are rightfully the most important. Details like these are key elements in the park's success. It's most likely one of the many reasons why the number of visitors at *Disneyland* increased by 8 percent in 2009, despite the economic downturn, while the crowd numbers dropped at Southern California competitors like *Universal Studios Hollywood, Six Flags Magic Mountain* and *Knott's Berry Farm*. Worth mentioning is that the cleaners of *Disneyland* collect approximately 30 tons of trash during a busy day – that's a lot of trash!

Sources: Anecdote from lecture with Tomas Hellgren (Piteå Företagarcentrum), 13 Feb, 2012. "Mouse Planet" article.
Quote: Recalled by Jack Lindquist, former Disney executive and legend.

FOOD FOR THOUGHT

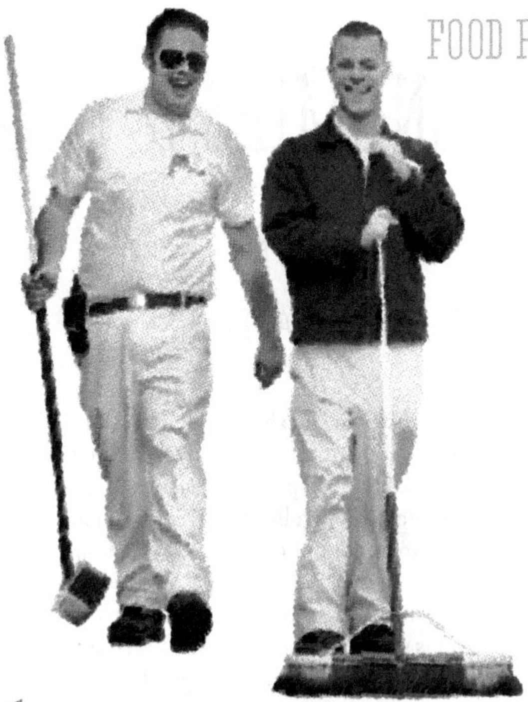

POSSIBLE MORAL

Walt Disney truly understood the importance and value of his employees. Far too many of us look down on other people's work, whether it's the taxi driver taking us to work or in this case the cleaner of an amusement park. Learn to appreciate the work of others and your character will grow.

STATISTICS OF STORY

%

90% ENTERTAINING
100% INTELLIGENT
0% DISTURBED / CRAZY
100% MORAL VALUE
100% HAPPY READING
0% RISKY / ILLEGAL

MORE INFO? SEARCH THIS!

Disneyland cleaner

Employee value

Disney's values

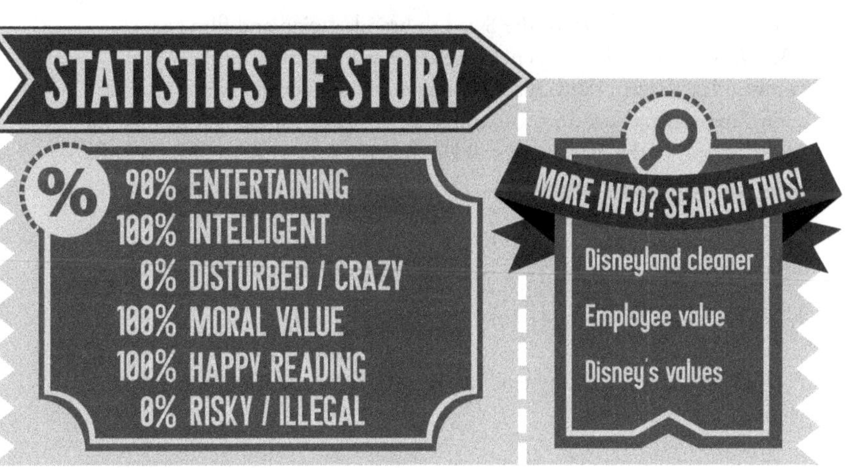

FOOD FOR THOUGHT

MAKING ENEMIES IS GOOD

MOTIVATION GROWTH EGO
FUEL FOR FIRE REALITY CHECK

Competition is part of life as we know it. It exists not only as a part of our human nature, but as something that can be seen in everything in existence, even molecules and bacteria "compete" for balance. We humans are faced with competition through life, privately, in school and at workplaces. This story serves to honor our competitors, or *enemies* as I would like to call them.

If you have no enemies, you may fall victim to the "Yes-people" that surround you. A "Yes"-person is someone who agrees with everything and never goes against the flow. This person will never point out flaws, question decisions, or add any input to a situation that contradicts what the person of power wants. You can learn from everything, even the bad things. That is why enemies can be great motivators. They serve as fuel for your fire. Enemies are just as important to us as our friends are, but with a completely different effect. While friends are there to motivate us and keep us pleased. Our enemies are there to annoy us, which makes us work harder to beat them. These people may also serve as a reality check from time-to-time. To knock us down when our ego becomes too large and help us face reality.

Fredrik "Freddie" Öst of the Swedish brand, design and film agency *SNASK* once said: "Having enemies means you're distinct in how you communicate your brand. Also, having enemies probably means you have some fans and ambassadors too, unless you've gone too far. You can be the nicest person in the world and still have enemies. Having enemies is both good and necessary".

POSSIBLE MORAL

Haven't you heard? Making enemies is good! So, get out there and make yourself some enemies.

Sources: "Why You Need Enemies", The Future Buzz, 12 Apr, 2010. "Stop being so boring", Freddie Öst, Computer Arts, Feb, 2012.

45% ENTERTAINING
80% INTELLIGENT
65% DISTURBED / CRAZY
65% MORAL VALUE
25% HAPPY READING
50% RISKY / ILLEGAL

MORE INFO? SEARCH THIS!
Making enemies
Motivators
Reality check

FOOD FOR THOUGHT

MONKEY BUSINESS

EXPERIMENT MONEY ANALYSTS
PURE GAMBLE STOCK MARKET

Stock market and fund analysts sell their services on the assumption that they possess knowledge that allows clients to earn more money. The concept is simple: Wise management and knowledge equals profit. But here's the thing: No one has sufficient knowledge to predict the stock market. That's right – nobody.

In the late 90's some people designed an experiment to see if monkeys could make a larger profit than stock market analysts. They allowed a monkey to operate a fund by selecting the shares that should be bought or sold (by selecting yes or no when the shares were held up to him). The results were pretty disappointing for all professional analysts. The monkey beat most of them, even the ones who bragged about beating the stock market index each year (which many of them, the year after, didn't). This shows that being a success on the stock market is more about pure chance than anything else.

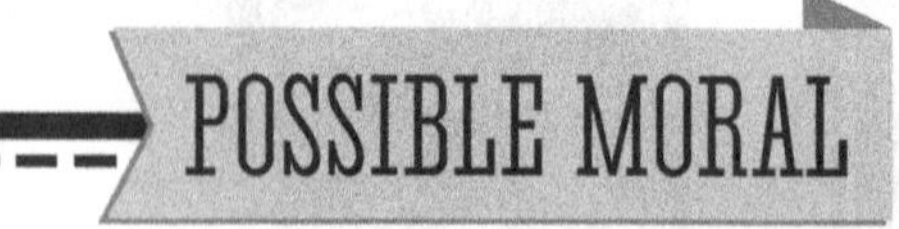

Monkey fund next?

Sources: "Can A Monkey Beat A Hedge Fund? New Study...", KapitallWire, 25 Jan, 2012. Lecture with Gunnar Forslund, 30 Jan, 2012.

STATISTICS OF STORY
%
65% ENTERTAINING
50% INTELLIGENT
30% DISTURBED / CRAZY
45% MORAL VALUE
60% HAPPY READING
0% RISKY / ILLEGAL
MORE INFO? SEARCH THIS!
Stock market
Monkey analysts
Selecting shares

FOOD FOR THOUGHT

GOOD NEWS ONLY

PSYCHOLOGY REACTION TWIST
MEDIA STUDIES POSITIVE ANGLE

In 2003, Germany's best-selling newspaper *Bild* managed to find a positive angle to every news development in Germany and around the world in the past 24 hours, treating its 12 million readers to a Christmas edition that was filled with nothing but good news. *Bild* columnist Peter Bacher said there was always plenty of good news around, even if it was "sometimes overshadowed by evil, horror and terror".

They dropped the normal content of crime, violence and scandals for stories about tax cuts, falling petrol prices and accelerating economic growth. "There's only good news today", *Bild* wrote in two-inch high letters at the top of page one, where the giant headlines are usually devoted to sex scandals, murderers, adulterers or dishonest politicians. Skipping its usual "loser of the day" entry, *Bild* picked two "winners of the day", of which one was rock star Ozzy Osbourne who was released from intensive care in hospital after an accident in Britain. Even a story about a Berlin celebrity who broke up with her boyfriend took a positive approach: "Great news, Djamila Rowe is single again".

Sources: "Paper bans bad news on Christmas...", Reuters, 28 Dec, 2003."German paper prints only good...", ABC News, 25 Dec, 2004.

POSSIBLE MORAL

Bild's action made people react and it started a discussion about the way bad news stories are overshadowing the good ones. Is the media negative? Media studies show that articles about bad news outnumber those with good news by as much as seventeen to one. Why is this? The answer may lie in the findings of evolutionary psychologists and neuroscientists. These experts say that our brains evolved during our hunter-gatherer stage in evolution, where anything novel or dramatic had to be attended to immediately for survival. So while we no longer defend ourselves against saber-toothed tigers, our brain development hasn't caught up. Our brains are wired to be far more sensitive to negative triggers than positive ones, and that's why humans seek news of dramatic, negative events.

So, according to psychology – being positive about things in general and reading or publishing good news is somewhat against our human nature (read more about the topic on page 226). If that really is the case, I say we keep on fighting against those negative triggers!

FOOD FOR THOUGHT

STOP AND LISTEN

PERCEPTION VIOLINIST INCOGNITO
JOSHUA BELL SOCIAL EXPERIMENT

In 2007, a man stood in a subway station in Washington D.C. playing the violin. It was a cold January morning. He played six Bach pieces for about 45 minutes. During that time, which was rush hour, it was calculated that thousands of people passed, entered or exited the station, most of them on their way to work. No one knew this, but the violinist was Joshua Bell, one of the top musicians in the world. He played one of the most complex pieces ever written, on a violin worth 3.5 million dollars. Two days before playing in the subway, Joshua Bell sold out at a theater in Boston. Seats averaged $100 each.

Joshua Bell playing incognito in the metro station was organized by the *Washington Post* as part of a social experiment about people's perception, taste and priorities. The aim were to make people reflect on questions such as: In a commonplace environment at an inappropriate hour, do we perceive beauty? Do we stop to appreciate it? Do we recognize talent in an unexpected context?

One of the possible conclusions from this experience could be: If we don't realize that one of the best musicians in the world is playing some of the most impressive music ever written on our way to work, how many other things around us are we not noticing?

Source: "Pearls Before Breakfast", The Washington Post, Gene Weingarten, 8 Apr, 2007.

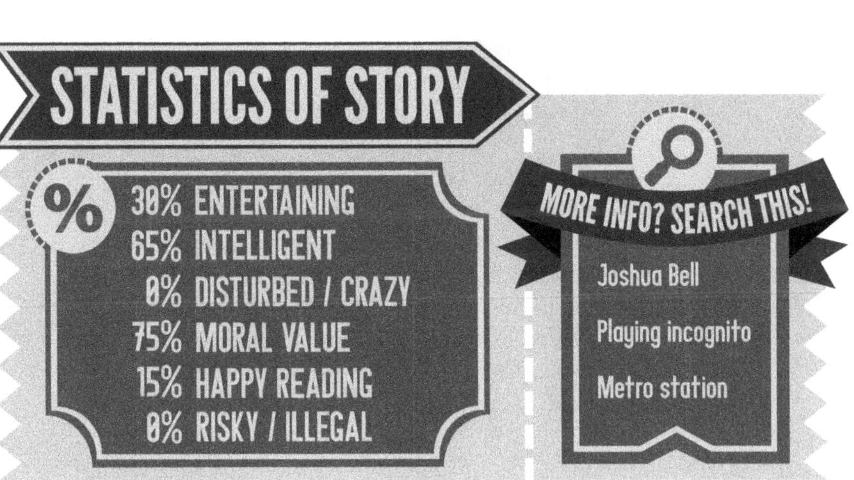
STATISTICS OF STORY
%
30% ENTERTAINING
65% INTELLIGENT
0% DISTURBED / CRAZY
75% MORAL VALUE
15% HAPPY READING
0% RISKY / ILLEGAL
MORE INFO? SEARCH THIS!
Joshua Bell
Playing incognito
Metro station

FOOD FOR THOUGHT

WHOPPER SACRIFICE

AMASSING BURGER FACEBOOK
FRIENDSHIP APPLICATION

In 2009, *Burger King*, together with advertising agency *Crispin Porter + Bogusky*, introduced a *Facebook* application called the *Whopper Sacrifice*. The concept was essentially this: Delete ten of your *Facebook* friends and received a coupon for a free *Whopper*. Each time you remove someone, it's posted in your news feed.

The application was used by 82,000 people, who together ended over 230,000 friendships on *Facebook* in just seven days. According to the developer however, a week after the *Whopper Sacrifice* made the news for its creative (and aggressive) use of *Facebook* friend removals as a way to spread the application, *Facebook* forced *Burger King* to disable the application's functionality.

POSSIBLE MORAL

With social networks like *Facebook* taking the term "friends" to new levels in the digital world, it's easy to wonder what a friend is, by today's measure. The obsession of amassing "friends" creates the impression that some users are wildly more sociable than others. But while we may be able to count 5,000 friends on the online social networking site, scientists have shown that humans brains are capable of managing a maximum of just 150 friendships. That means people with more friends than that must have many that can be sacrificed. So, at the end of the day – who would you delete for a burger?

Source: "Delete 10 Facebook friends, get a free Whopper", CNET News, Caroline McCarthy, 8 Jan, 2009.

YOU LIKED ADAM.
YOU LOVE
THE WHOPPER.

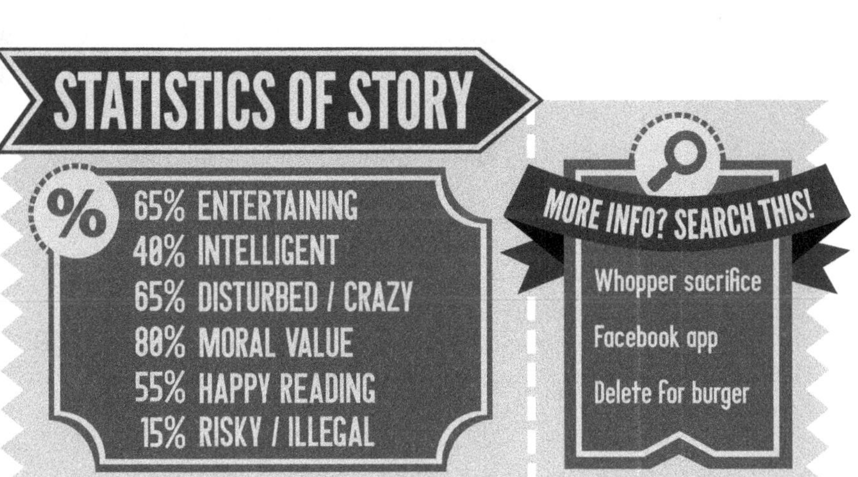
STATISTICS OF STORY
%
65% ENTERTAINING
40% INTELLIGENT
65% DISTURBED / CRAZY
80% MORAL VALUE
55% HAPPY READING
15% RISKY / ILLEGAL
MORE INFO? SEARCH THIS!
Whopper sacrifice
Facebook app
Delete for burger

FOOD FOR THOUGHT

YAKUZA KOBE RESCUE

EARTHQUAKE MAFIA JUDGEMENT
HOMELESS GOVERNMENT FAILURE

In 1995, a 7.5 magnitude earthquake killed over 6,000 people, injured 30,000 and left 300,000 homeless struck Kobe, Japan. With billions of dollars' worth of destroyed buildings covering the streets, the only way in and out of the city was by helicopter or foot. Unfortunately, in the immediate aftermath of this disaster the national and local governments got stuck in debates, resulting in an extremely slow official response. It would take as long as four days before there was a build-up of emergency rescue people from outside the city. Therefore thousands of stranded victims had to fend for themselves.

Enter the *Yakuza*, the Japanese mafia, which mobilized and sprung to action while government officials were still debating. The *Yakuza* got thousands of its members into Kobe to distribute food, water, medicine and baby diapers. That's right: The mob got together and passed out diapers. Then, as if to prove that there's no crisis that can't be solved, these gangsters descended into Kobe from their helicopters and gave thousands of blankets to the homeless.

POSSIBLE MORAL

It may seem puzzling that the *Yakuza*, an organized crime group, which receives their revenue from illegal activities such as collecting protection money, blackmail, extortion and fraud would show this type of civility. In this moment of crises, the slow response by the government was in my eyes a pure act of crime. If the response had been quicker, lives probably could've been saved. I don't support the *Yakuza* in any way, and there might very well have been criminal intentions behind their rescue act. Though one can't hide from the truth: They still did more for the people of Kobe this time than the Japanese government. Moral of story? I guess you shouldn't always judge a book by its cover, no matter how awful.

Source: "Yakuza to the Rescue", The Daily Beast, Jake Adelstein, 18 Mar, 2011.

ヤクザ

STATISTICS OF STORY
45% ENTERTAINING
70% INTELLIGENT
45% DISTURBED / CRAZY
60% MORAL VALUE
60% HAPPY READING
0% RISKY / ILLEGAL
MORE INFO? SEARCH THIS!
Kobe earthquake
Yakuza rescue
Distribute food

GOOD HEARTED

ETERNAL REEFS

ENVIRONMENT DIVERS UNDERWATER CREMATION BUSINESS IDEA

Eternal Reefs is a company started by Don Brawley. The idea is quite simple: His business combines cremation, permanent underwater urns and ash scattering into the deep blue ocean. Those who purchased his service can mark their eternal reefs with their name, flag, death date or with a quote. On one hand his business is profitable and on the other hand, it helps the underwater environment and habitats.

The *Eternal Reefs* story began in the late 1980's with a pair of college roommates from the *University of Georgia*, who often went diving off the Keys in Florida during school breaks. Over the years of diving they saw significant deterioration and degradation of the reefs they visited. Brawley realized the reefs needed help so they made a decision to do something about it. Once the friends were out of school they began to talk about what contributions they could make that would help protect and restore these fragile ecosystems. They decided to develop a material that would substitute the reef that supports coral and microorganism. The solution was an environmentally friendly concrete formula that attract microorganisms to make the new reefs, and thus, the concept of the *Reef Ball* was invented.

They faced two primary design challenges. First, stability was crucial. The design needed to be capable of absorbing and dissipating energy in the marine environment without moving. It would need to withstand not just the normal tidal and current flows, but also major storms and the dynamic energy impacts that accompany them. Second, the material would also need to be friendly to the marine environment. It had to be made of natural materials that would attract and encourage microorganisms to settle and propagate on the reefs. Patented mold systems were developed to create reefs that closely mimicked natural reef formations. Special design features were included to make it easy for sea life to attach and grow on these designed reef structures.

Sources: "About Eternal Reefs", eternalreefs.com. "Reef Balls Help You Save the Environment...", Eventective, 29 Oct, 2008.

POSSIBLE MORAL

This business idea is great on so many different levels. Military veterans, environmentalists, fishermen, sailors, divers and other people who have been active around water are comforted by the thought of resting in the place that meant the most to them. At the same time, their underwater urns do good use to the environment. Their act in death gives life to other life forms.

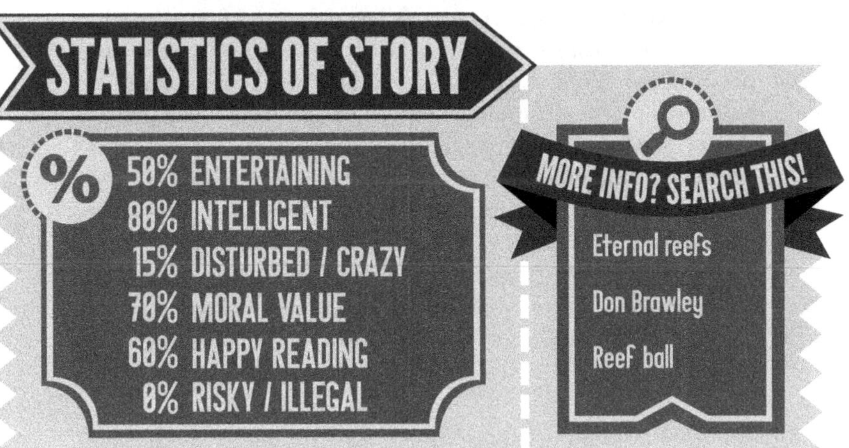

GOOD HEARTED

FOCUS ON THE DISABLED

DEVELOPMENT ACTOR OPPORTUNITY
EMPLOYMENT TV-COMMERCIALS

ICA Group is one of the leading retail companies with around 2,300 own and retailer-owned grocery stores in Sweden, Norway and the Baltic. In Sweden, the TV-commercials for *ICA* are some of the most appreciated to watch. While combining great storytelling with focus on humor, and at the same time showing us their latest offers – they have become a great success that appeals to the audience. Since 2001, featuring the staff and customers of a fictional *ICA* grocery store, approximately 320 commercials have been aired.

In 2009, *ICA* decided to bring a new character into the "series". They brought in Mats Melin, an actor active at *Glada Hudik Theatre*. Melin was to play the character of Jerry, a new intern at the *ICA* store. The thing that created a big fuss around this commercial when it was first aired, was not whether or not Melin did a great performance – it was about him having Down's syndrome. The commercial plays on the prejudices that exist and was meant to spark debate. The Swedish Association for children, youth and adults with developmental disabilities, *FUB*, have been involved in encouraging the commercials. Melin worked together with *ICA* until 2012; in his last commercial he says good-bye to his fellow workers.

Over the next three years, *ICA* stores will provide 500-1,000 disabled people with employment. The project is called *Vi kan mer* (*We can do more*) and runs in partnership with *Samhall*, the leading Swedish company in providing development opportunities for people with disabilities through employment, and a number of Swedish municipalities.

Some 50 *ICA* stores (the number is still increasing) have disabled employees, and they are working to expand and develop this collaboration. Through the venture, *Vi kan mer*, all *ICA* stores will continue to increase the understanding towards people with disabilities by making them more visible to others, and at the same time learn from these new perspectives. The goal is to help build a society where everyone can participate and achieve their full potential – even if the conditions are varied.

Sources: "På Ica är handikapp inget hinder", Dagens Nyheter, 8 Jan, 2011. "Det hade inte varit möjligt utan Samhall", samhall.se.

POSSIBLE MORAL

The moral is to believe in people and give everyone the opportunity to be seen, heard and valued. *Vi kan mer* has also been a successful advertising project. Other companies have followed the same path and are now creating similar concepts.

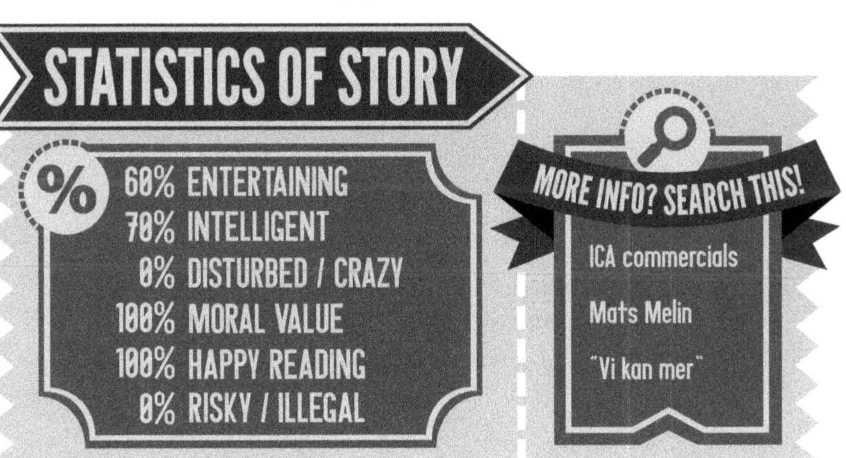

STATISTICS OF STORY
%
60% ENTERTAINING
70% INTELLIGENT
0% DISTURBED / CRAZY
100% MORAL VALUE
100% HAPPY READING
0% RISKY / ILLEGAL
MORE INFO? SEARCH THIS!
ICA commercials
Mats Melin
"Vi kan mer"

GOOD HEARTED

GAMING MARATHONS

ENTERTAINING CHARITY INTERACTION
AWARENESS RAISING MONEY

A video-gaming marathon is just that – a marathon of video-gaming. Two examples are *GameToAid* and *Lame Game Marathon*. Over an extended period of time, the hosts broadcast themselves over the internet (streaming) playing either much-loved (or hated) video games in the hopes that people will pay to be entertained. The money that's raised is given to a specific charity. The hosts of the marathons try to keep things interesting by conversing with people in the designated chat room, and run various audience interaction activities such as polls and contests.

Australian based *GameToAid* is operated by two 19-year-olds, and in 2011 they fought the water crisis in Africa by video-gaming for 60 hours in a row, only playing what have been deemed the worst video games in history. The marathon helped raise $10,637 to bring fresh drinking water to Ethiopia and Malawi! The money was used to build and rehabilitate fresh water wells and provisions for the people in need. It was also used to start teaching communities about safe hygiene practices and to form local water committees to look after the projects after completion.

The *Lame Game Marathon*, also Australian based, raised over $5,000 for the *The UN Refugee Agency* (*UNHCR*). That's enough to provide over 700 meals to refugee children, over 100 therapeutic feeding kits or over 55 survival kits.

POSSIBLE MORAL

These Aussies have found a great way to raise money for good. These types of live-events are in fashion. They're a form of entertainment that don't cost much to set up, and you can reach out to the whole world; a winning concept! Now who says video games make young people stupid and unaware?

Sources: "Marathon Gaming for Charity", ABC News, 18 Feb, 2011. "About", lamegamemarathon.com.

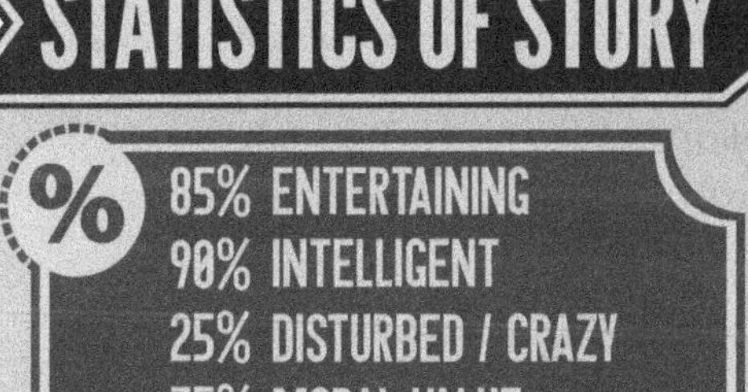

85% ENTERTAINING
90% INTELLIGENT
25% DISTURBED / CRAZY
75% MORAL VALUE
70% HAPPY READING
0% RISKY / ILLEGAL

MORE INFO? SEARCH THIS!
Gaming marathons
Game to aid
Lame game

GOOD HEARTED

REAL LIFE SUPERHEROES

COMMUNITY CHANGE GOOD INTENTIONS
ACTIVISM PUBLIC APATHY

Real Life Superheroes (*RLSH*) is an online community of people who engage in different forms of activism using the thematic device of the costumed superhero, many of them adopting pseudonyms and wearing custom-made outfits. They perform services that they believe benefits the community in a variety of ways, fighting what they consider their biggest enemy: Public apathy. Some *Real Life Superheroes* hand out supplies to the homeless, raise money for charity or just lend an ear so someone in trouble knows they care. Others seek to combat crime through community patrols and neighborhood watch, in which suspicious activity is identified and reported to the proper authorities. Some in the *RLSH* community try to resolve issues on their own, contrary to the wishes of the police.

They call themselves superheroes, and with names like *Dark Guardian*, *Red Dragon* and *Viper*, they would fit perfectly among the pages of comic books. However, unlike their ink-and-paper counterparts, they can't fly, vanish into thin air or outrun a speeding locomotive. They are usually armed with nothing more than good intentions – and maybe a camera and a cell phone. They come from all walks of life, have all sorts of body types and range in age from 6 to over 60. Many share a love of comic books and superhero movies and a passion for bringing the superhero virtues of trustworthiness, bravery and selflessness to the real world.

The Vigilante Spider, who has spent 11 years performing acts of kindness around San Diego, is a member of the *Real Life Superheroes*. The group has nearly 60 members, who wear tights, cloaks etc. and to spread the message that "everybody can make a difference".

Sources: "Costumed crusaders taking it to the streets", NBC News, Jim Gold, 14 Feb, 2011. "About", reallifesuperheroes.org.

GOOD HEARTED

POSSIBLE MORAL

What does it take to be a superhero? What powers must you possess to do what is right and help others? If you ask any of these "superfolks" who help out their community around the world, I bet they would say: "Just be a neighbor. Reach out to those in need. Stand up for what you know is right. If you have the power and the ability to change the surrounding social environment, do so". Everyone wants the world to change, but who out there will try?

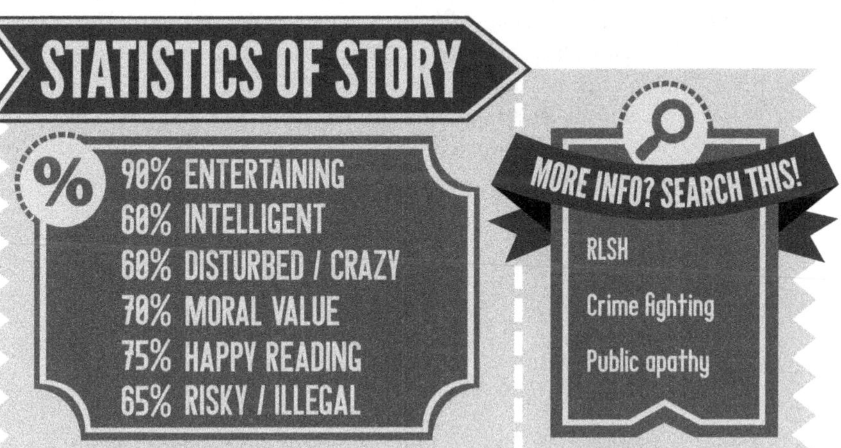

GOOD HEARTED

THE GAP SAVIOR

ENGAGEMENT RESCUE CARING
LISTENING COMMUNICATION

Donald "Don" Ritchie is an Australian who is said to have prevented at least 160 people from committing suicide over a 45 year period. He lives across the street from the most famous suicide spot in Australia: A cliff known as *The Gap*. Most people would move, but Ritchie has lived there for almost 50 years and has, in doing so, saved a lot of people. The house might be situated on the worst piece of real estate ever: Roughly one person per week commits suicide at *The Gap*. Despite its legendary reputation as a suicide spot dating back to the 1800's, the ledge is marked only by a small, one-meter fence. In an interview with *The Christian Science Monitor* Ritchie says he doesn't feel burdened by the fact that people are always contemplating jumping to their deaths outside his house. In fact, he and his wife Moya see it as a blessing: "I think: isn't it wonderful that we live here and we can help people? I used to sell kitchen scales and bacon cutters, at The Gap, I'm trying to sell people life".

Ritchie wakes up every morning and looks out the window for "anyone standing alone too close to the precipice". If he sees someone who looks like they might be contemplating to jump, he walks over and strikes up conversation. Richie just gives them a warm smile, asks if they'd like to talk and invites them back to his house for tea. Sometimes, they join him. He says he does his best with each person and if he looses one, he accepts that there was nothing more he could have done. In 2006, Ritchie was awarded the *Medal of the Order of Australia* for his rescues.

Sources: "An angel walking among...", The Sydney Morning Herald, 1 Aug, 2009. "Suicide watchman...", The Independent, 13 Jun, 2010.
Quotes: From interview by "The Christian Sceince Monitor", Article: "He invites suicide jumpers for a cup of tea", 18 Oct, 2010.

POSSIBLE MORAL

At a time of grief or despair, small gestures that show you care can be of definitive value. What Don Ritchie does is to lend people an ear and the prospect of friendship. By inviting them in for tea, he invites them to talk and he offers to listen. There are a lot of people wandering around who are in need of someone to talk to. It's important to be a good listener. I believe good things will come to those who are willing to listen (read more about the topic on page 96).

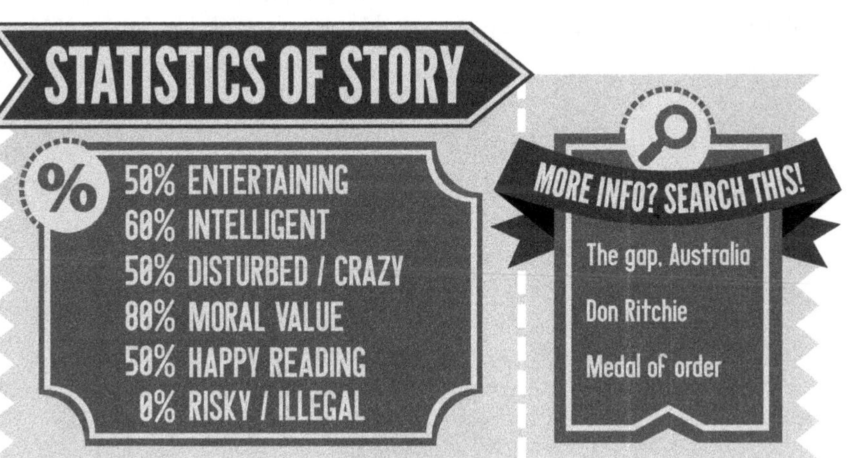

THE BUBBLE PROJECT

INSPIRATIONAL MESSAGE PUBLIC DIALOGUE
REACTIONS PERSONAL PROJECT

Bored with his advertising agency gig and the uninspiring work he was producing, Ji Lee decided to take matters into his own hands in 2002. The result was his ad-spoofing *Bubble Project*, in which Lee placed blank speech bubbles on advertisements around New York City. These cartoon "thought bubbles" were originally printed in 30,000 copies and began appearing on print advertisements in the subway. Inspired passers-by started to fill them in, initiating a dialogue about the advertisement, its message, the city, American culture, and between each other. Lee then went back to photograph the results and later posted them on the project website.

Lee's low-tech *Bubble Project* needed no instructions, no moving parts, no planning, and almost no investment – and yet it yielded a rich set of commentaries from and about the people of New York. More Bubbles meant more space for expression, more sharing of personal thoughts, more reactions to current events and most importantly, extended possibilities of showing imagination and having fun. People responded positively and the project spread like a virus over the city.

Since its launch, the *Bubble Project* has become a global project. Bubblers all around the globe are bubbling their own towns. The results of the project gained Lee recognition and ultimately forwarded his professional career.

POSSIBLE MORAL

This project really shows the power and the importance of personal projects. It's an interesting way to get a feel for the public social environment of today. What do people have to say? What are people thinking? In the *Bubble Project*, the public spaces were in a way returned back to the public. This project instantly transforms the intrusive and dull corporate monologues into a public dialogue.

Sources: "Manifesto", thebubbleproject.com. "The Transformative Power of Personal Projects", Behance 99U, 2010.

On one poster of a young model someone wrote: "What am I gonna do when I'm 23?".

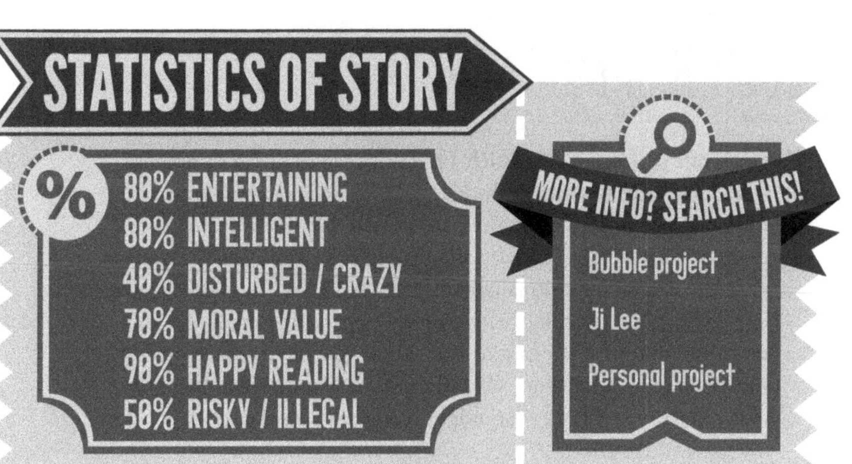

HIDDEN MESSAGES

THE FREE LECTURE

PRODUCER VALUE PRICE TAG
TEACHING PRINCIPLES

The programme in Audio Technology at *Luleå University of Technology*, Piteå in Sweden, were looking to hire a famous music producer for two days of lectures for their students. When discussing the price, the producer said he wanted a payment of 200,000 Swedish Kronor (around $29,000) per day (!). After a moment of silence, the teacher told the producer that they didn't have that amount of money. That kind of budget just didn't exist. He then answered: "Yeah, really? Well then I'll do it for free instead".

POSSIBLE MORAL

How can one go from having such a big price tag to doing something for free? I interpret the music producer's act to be about sticking to your principles. If not his price tag, then none at all. He doesn't try to lower his price as if his services were on sale. Could it be a question of honor/character, or did he intentionally make it look like he's the "good guy"? Whatever his reason was, in the end the students could enjoy two days of lectures from one of the best in their field. Possible moral: Don't sell yourself short, be true to yourself and do more work for free (see page 188 for a crazy example of what might happen if you do).

Source: Anecdote from "Karriärdagen" at Luleå University of Technology, 2011.

FREE
SPEECH

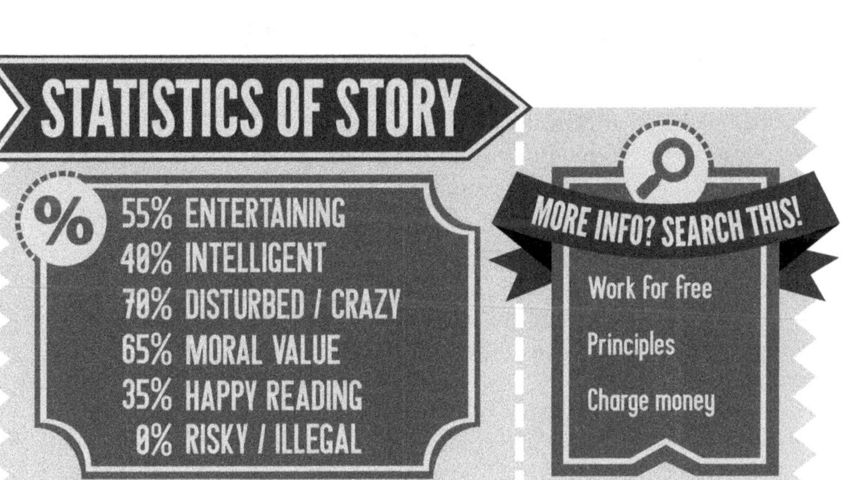
STATISTICS OF STORY
55% ENTERTAINING
40% INTELLIGENT
70% DISTURBED / CRAZY
65% MORAL VALUE
35% HAPPY READING
0% RISKY / ILLEGAL
MORE INFO? SEARCH THIS!
Work for free
Principles
Charge money

HIDDEN MESSAGES

THE POWER OF LISTENING

INTERVIEW CAREER APPRECIATION
JOB OFFER COMMITMENT

I recently learned and understood a new side of how powerful listening to others truly can be. In the search of stories for this book I met up with some people for interviews. I simply wanted to hear what different entrepreneurs and creative directors had to say, and what kind of stories they'd come across, or created themselves – during their careers.

One day I met up with a man who'd worked most of his life at an advertising agency, but was now into interior design and architecture. I started my interview by briefly presenting myself and the book I was planning to write. Then I asked my first question and began to listen. As soon as I heard something interesting, I noted it in my notepad. When my interviewee came to a pause or lost track, I asked for more information about the notes I'd made. I never interrupted when he was talking and the story got more and more interesting as time went. I kept listening carefully and showed interest in what he was telling me.

What was supposed to be a one-hour interview ended up to be a two and a half hour long chat. My interviewee was so committed he almost missed a meeting with a client. In the end of the interview, he showed me what he was working with at the moment. He was building a set-scenery for a company selling floors. "Do you have any experience in building scenery?", he asked me. "Nope, but I'm pretty creative when it comes to concept design", I answered. He looked at me and said "You seem like a really nice guy. What do you say about to coming here next week to brainstorm some ideas for this project? I'm not promising anything, but I've been looking for someone to help me with this kind of work". At first I thought he was kidding, but apparently he was dead serious. I said yes to his offer.

After leaving his office my mind was filled with thoughts and questions. I was seeing this man for an interview, and then ended up going home with a possible job offer. I hadn't really seen that one coming. What struck me was that I never told him about my skills. He had never seen any of my previous work. I was a student he had just recently met. What had

Source: From the sane and insane mind of Simon Zingerman.

I done that made him so fond of me? Then I started to figured it out. The one thing I had done, and done well, was to listen. My interviewee was digging up stories from his past and with my simple questions I brought up great memories and nostalgia. Other than listening, I was also sending out signals of confidence, but at the time unaware of them and the role they played. If you were to compare this to a regular job interview, it's a lot different. The advantages being that you're not the center of attention. I was relaxed and natural. In a job interview you would likely not be as true to yourself because of the need to impress.

POSSIBLE MORAL

In our society, the power is given to those who talk – loud and often. What if the exact same power can be found in listening? Most people do not realize the power of just sitting down, listening and paying attention to what someone has to tell you. I think good listeners will always be appreciated. I myself had no intentions what so ever of getting a job offer through this interview. Could this perhaps be a new way of getting a career? See others until they see you? Apparently, even on a small scale, taking time and listening to others can lead to success. I wonder how many businesses are failing because managers and leaders don't listen effectively to others?

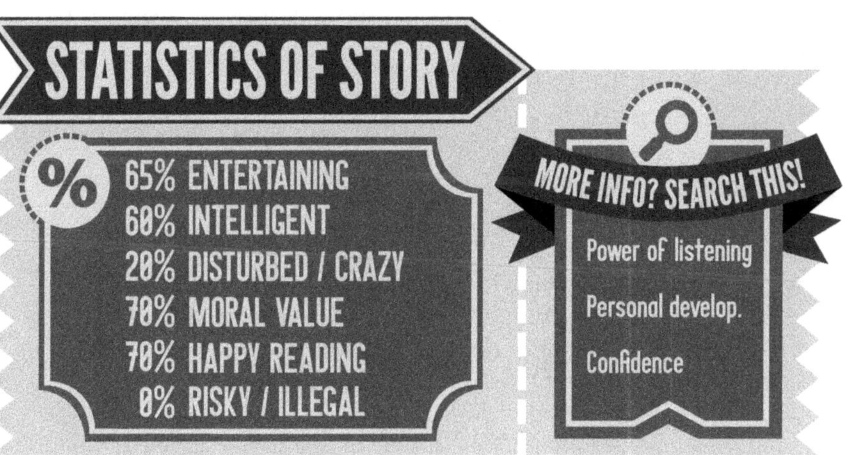

STATISTICS OF STORY
%
65% ENTERTAINING
60% INTELLIGENT
20% DISTURBED / CRAZY
70% MORAL VALUE
70% HAPPY READING
0% RISKY / ILLEGAL
MORE INFO? SEARCH THIS!
Power of listening
Personal develop.
Confidence

WI-FI CLEVERNESS

NETWORKS GUERRILLA MESSAGE
STICKING OUT ADDED VALUE

At the airport in Hamburg, Germany, there are more than five different care rental agencies to choose from, and more car rental advertisements than one can consume. The walls, floors and even the ceilings are covered with them. So how do you stand out in a sea of commercials? This was the issue that car rental company *SIXT* was troubled with because nobody seemed to be reached by their latest airport special car-deal.

To solve the problem, their German advertising agency came up with a really clever idea. They simply put their offers everywhere. How? By installing three very strong wireless networks at the *SIXT* counter of the airport and then naming the different networks into parts of a sentence (their advertising message). The first one said: "Stop surfing. Start driving", the second: "The SIXT airport special:", and the third: "A BMW 3 Series from 159 Euro". When the people at the airport browsed through the wireless networks to log onto using a computer, tablet or cell phone, they would see this sentence together with all the other networks. Listed after each other, they created the full sentence so people got the message. After they connected to one of the networks and launched their web browser, they were met by a special *SIXT* offer website, with a location plan. This clever guerrilla marketing idea was also installed at the airports of Munich, Cologne, Frankfurt and Berlin.

POSSIBLE MORAL

What makes this so innovative isn't just making very affordable use of an existing platform, the Wi-Fi network, but that its target audience was arguably the group most likely to be accessing that platform. Besides being a case study in clever guerrilla marketing, this is a great example of using tools that are already at your disposal.

Sources: "SIXT Car Rental – guerilla marketing...", The Blog of Bullseye, 12 Oct, 2010. "SIXT WI-FI GUERILLA IDEA", YouTube.

STATISTICS OF STORY
45% ENTERTAINING
65% INTELLIGENT
10% DISTURBED / CRAZY
65% MORAL VALUE
50% HAPPY READING
0% RISKY / ILLEGAL
MORE INFO? SEARCH THIS!
SIXT car deal
Airport wi-fi
Clever marketing

FAMOUS YET ANONYMOUS

STREET ART BANKSY IDENTITY
PUBLICITY CONTROVERSIAL

Banksy is probably the most infamous street artist alive. To some a genius, to others a criminal. Always controversial, he inspires admiration and provokes outrage in equal measure. Since *Banksy* became famous with his trademark stencil-style "guerrilla" art in public spaces – on walls in London, Brighton, Bristol and even on the *West Bank barrier*. His work has sold for hundreds of thousands of pounds. He also has dozens of celebrity collectors including Brad Pitt (together with Angelina Jolie) and Christina Aguilera. What is unique about *Banksy* is that he prefers to keep his identity under wraps and shies away from publicity. He has struggled for years to maintain the secret of his identity, and even today it remains shrouded in mystery.

Banksy's talent isn't limited to painting and the occasional pencil drawing. He has been responsible for a number of social commentaries. In 2006 he replaced hundreds of Paris Hilton CD's with CD's of his own creation. He has also been sneaking his own work into several art museums, including a prehistoric-looking piece at the *British Museum*, which the museum decided to add to its own permanent collection. Some of *Banksy*'s most high-profile and memorable graffiti was done in Palestine. The 425-mile-long barrier separating Israelis and Palestinians looked like social injustice and a huge blank canvas to the guerrilla artist. He created nine paintings there in 2005, most of which were ill-received by the local population. When he was working on one of the pieces, an old man approached him and said that his paintings had made the wall look beautiful. *Banksy* thanked the man, but the man responded: "We don't want it to be beautiful, we hate this wall. Go home". Another of his controversial stunts was made in California. He had a *Guantanamo Bay* prisoner inserted into the landscape of a ride at *Disneyland*. The figure remained in place for an hour and a half before the staff of the park removed it.

The growing fame of *Banksy* and his work has resulted in a huge following of people who have extensively documented his art with

Sources: "Banksy Paradox: 7 Sides of...", Web Urbanist. "Graffiti artist Banksy unmasked...", The Daily Mail, 12 July, 2008.

photographs, collected prints and custom tattoos of his work. Along with his fame, *Banksy* appears to have accumulated quite a fortune, with his work being shown in famous galleries around the world and purchased by collectors at astonishing prices.

In England, graffiti removing squads are being ordered to restore destroyed *Banksy* art while removing regular graffiti. This has started up debates on the different values of street art and graffiti. When asked to comment on being given preferential treatment, *Banksy* answered: "If you think my graffiti is overrated you'd be right. I only hope that one day I get the lack of recognition I deserve". Love him or hate him, *Banksy* is without a doubt one of the most influential artists working today. He has affected the art world across the globe.

POSSIBLE MORAL

Any form of art is a form of power. With street art, *Banksy* found a way to express his social and political opinions to the world. His art talks about the environment, war, human rights, giant corporations etc. Combining dark humor with facts, his art moves the audience. It tells a story that hopefully will enlighten the viewer. His art has started debates about the *Israeli West Bank barrier*, the *Guantanamo bay prison* and the *2012 Summer Olympics* in London to name a few. At the Olympics his artwork served to remind the world that outside the glossy bubble of the event there was real impact issues – including the legal and moral dilemmas of using military drones.

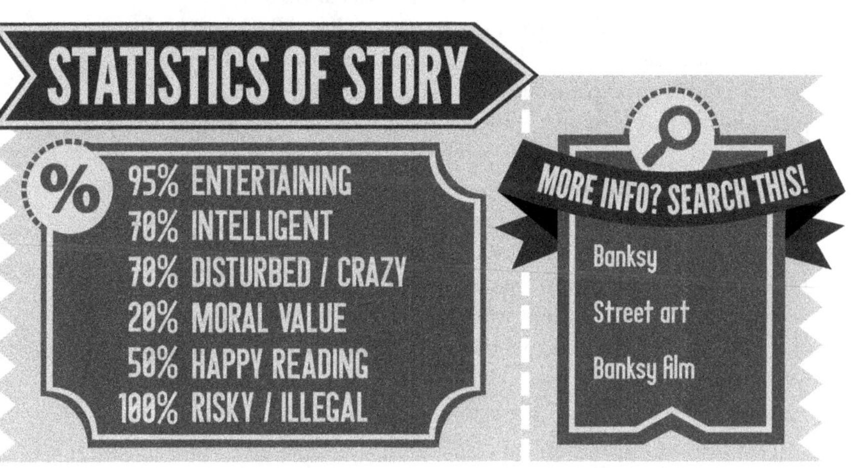

SMASHED PORCELAIN

GAINING FANS ORDERS INSANE METHOD BASEBALL BAT CUSTOMER SERVICE

This is the story about an American company that manufactured and sold porcelain products such as mugs, bowls and vases among others. They were sold exclusively online. When receiving orders, the workers packaged the products in boxes, neatly and professionally. There was nothing special about this, except that, for about every 20th order, they did something quite unexpected. The employees took a baseball bat and hit the box, breaking the products inside. This was all done very strategically and with great precision. They intentionally broke half or two thirds of what was inside, and allowed the rest to remain intact. The box was then sent off as usual, like nothing had happened.

On the company's website it said that complaints about the goods could only be done over the phone. This was because they wanted to have direct contact with their customers. Not surprisingly, the phone rang at regular intervals, with dissatisfied and sometimes angry customers on the line. The company received word about the "accident" with the broken goods and explained how sadden they were and pointed out how much they care for their costumers. Of course the customers were going to be compensated. The company offered them completely new sets of what they'd ordered, despite the fact that all the products weren't broken. "But three of them are whole…", the customers could sometimes object, but it didn't matter, they were to receive a complete new set of shiny porcelain products. The new products was packaged and posted with express delivery with a enclosed sorry card and a bag of sweets. The customer thus went from being angry or sad to being satisfied and happy.

This company turned angry customers, who never wanted to buy from them again, into people who loved the company and chose to come back for future orders. They made haters into ambassadors (fans). With this insane (and I think also slightly criminal) method they created customers "for life". They would remember this fake "rescue" and appreciate the outstanding customer service. Apparently, the customers exposed to the "smashed porcelain attack" chose to come back.

Source: Anecdote from lecture with Gunnar Forslund (www.2tango.nu), Piteå Företagarcentrum, 25 Jan, 2012.

POSSIBLE MORAL

I guess I wouldn't recommend using a similar approach in your own business, but I do think there's some good moral to be found here. True or not, this story serves to illustrate what great customer service can result in (even though the company used a shady method), and why having ambassadors of your business or brand is important. Regardless of how strong your marketing is, how amazing your product is, or how incredible your service is, you still need to get people talking about you. It's crucial to build real passion and engagement surrounding your business. Reaching people is one thing, but getting people to tell other people about you is the next level (see page 52 for more on customer service).

STATISTICS OF STORY
%
90% ENTERTAINING
15% INTELLIGENT
90% DISTURBED / CRAZY
55% MORAL VALUE
60% HAPPY READING
80% RISKY / ILLEGAL
MORE INFO? SEARCH THIS!
Smashed porcelain
Baseball bat
Customer service

TEACHERS REVENGE

COMPLAINTS SCHOOL RESPONSIBILITY
OFFENSIVE ANSWERING MACHINE

The story goes as follows: A high school in Queensland, Australia, had quite a special answering machine message. The message came about due to the implementation of a policy requiring students and parents to be responsible for their children's absences and missing homework. The sarcastic message presented callers with a list of options that outline a range of possible complaints about school services or teachers.

The outgoing message said:
"Hello! You have reached the automated answering service of your school. In order to assist you in connecting to the right staff member, please listen to all the options before making a selection:

- To lie about why your child is absent – *Press 1*
- To make excuses for why your child did not do his homework – *Press 2*
- To complain about what we do – *Press 3*
- To swear at staff members – *Press 4*
- To ask why you didn't get information that was already enclosed in your newsletter and several flyers mailed to you – *Press 5*
- If you want us to raise your child – *Press 6*
- If you want to reach out and touch, slap or hit someone – *Press 7*
- To request another teacher, for the third time this year – *Press 8*
- To complain about bus transportation – *Press 9*
- To complain about school lunches – *Press 0*

If you realize this is the real world and your child must be accountable and responsible for his/her own behavior, class work, homework and that it's not the teachers' fault for your child's lack of effort: Hang up and have a nice day! If you want this in another language, move to a country that speaks it".

This offensive message became a big internet hit and spread quickly on

Sources: "School phone message hoax", Sunshine Coast Daily, 17 Sep, 2009. "Funny Answering Machine", YouTube, 26 Sep, 2009.

sites like *YouTube*. It didn't take long for the school to react, and explain that this message was a hoax and not connected with them in any way. The truth is that the *School Answering Machine* message was a long running joke that had been falsely associated with a number of schools in several countries.

POSSIBLE MORAL

Hidden in sarcasm, there's a message here about teachers and other employees in schools and what they have to endure on a day-to-day basis. Though the message is fake, school employees worldwide suffer from many of the things that are mentioned in the message. In both Europe and the United States, there are numbers of schools and teachers being sued by parents who want their children's failing grades changed to passing grades. This even though these children are absent and do not complete enough school work to pass their classes. Although this specific message above might seem a bit extreme, it makes me think – is it so wrong to demand more from the children and their parents?

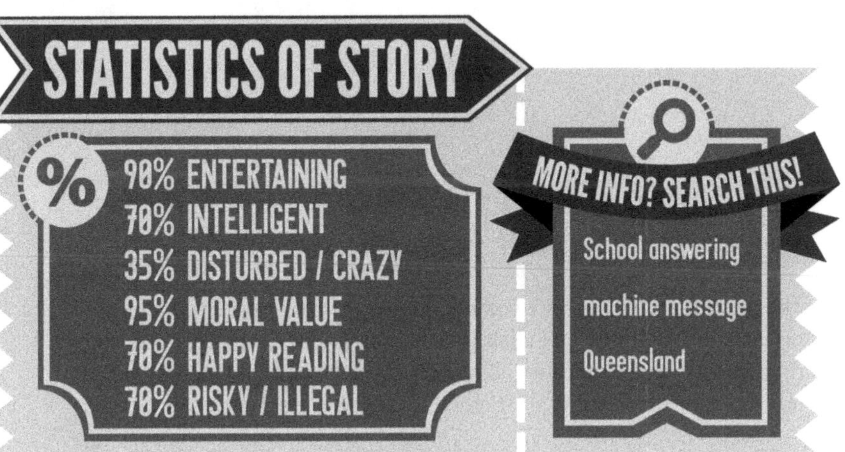

STATISTICS OF STORY
%
90% ENTERTAINING
70% INTELLIGENT
35% DISTURBED / CRAZY
95% MORAL VALUE
70% HAPPY READING
70% RISKY / ILLEGAL
MORE INFO? SEARCH THIS!
School answering
machine message
Queensland

THE LOVE LETTER

CAMPAIGN DIVORCE ENVELOPES
POLICE REPORT SECRET LOVER

An envelope company sent out advertising messages in the form of love letters to its customers. The letters were designed to look like a sheet of paper from a physical notepad, with only hand-written text. The purpose of this advertising campaign was for the advertising agencies and printing companies who received the letter to know that the envelope company missed having them as customers. "Long time since I heard from you" basically meant: Please order more envelopes.

This was a great and funny advertisement. The only problem was that the letter looked so real, that it resulted (among other things), in the divorce of a couple where the woman thought that the letter was from her husband's secret lover. The whole thing, of course, received major attention in the media. The husband reported the envelope company to the police and it ended up with a full page in the newspaper. Over one million readers took part of the story. Afterwards, there have been speculations that the envelope company was purposely looking for this outcome of the campaign, to gain media attention.

POSSIBLE MORAL

The twist: Although his wife was referring to the fake love letter and knew nothing about the real love affair that her husband was having at the same time, he admitted to cheating, obviously thinking that his wife had found out about it. The irony! A great moral ending to a fun story.

Source: Anecdote from lecture with Gunnar Forslund (www.2tango.nu), Piteå Företagarcentrum, 6 Feb, 2012.

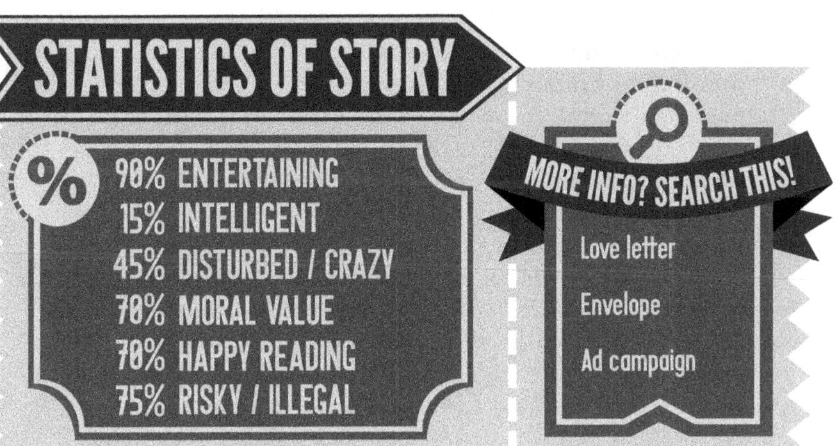
STATISTICS OF STORY
%
90% ENTERTAINING
15% INTELLIGENT
45% DISTURBED / CRAZY
70% MORAL VALUE
70% HAPPY READING
75% RISKY / ILLEGAL
MORE INFO? SEARCH THIS!
Love letter
Envelope
Ad campaign

NEVER GIVE UP

COLONEL SANDERS

TRADEMARK RETIRED NEVER TOO LATE
REJECTIONS FIGHTING SPIRIT

The Colonel Sanders' story about founding *Kentucky Fried Chicken* (*KFC*) is truly inspiring. Harland Sanders was born on September 9, 1890. He was the oldest of three, and had a younger sister and brother. His father died when he was six years old. By the age of seven, his mother taught him the art of cooking because she was forced to go to work, and he had to feed himself and his two siblings. He quickly learnt to master many dishes, and the skill he acquired would change his life in the future. Sanders dropped out of school in seventh grade. When his mother remarried, he ran away from home because his stepfather beat him.

During his early years, Sanders had many jobs, including being a steamboat pilot, insurance salesman, railroad fireman and farmer. At the age of 40, Sanders took up cooking as a profession. He began cooking chicken-based dishes and other meals for people who stopped at his service station in Corbin, Kentucky. Since he did not have a restaurant, he served customers in his adjacent living quarters. Locally, his popularity grew, and Sanders eventually bought and moved into a motel that had a 142-seat restaurant. Over the next nine years he developed his "secret recipe" for frying chicken, using a pressure fryer that cooked the chicken much faster than pan frying would. In 1935, he was made into an honorary Colonel by the governor of Kentucky for his cooking skills.

At the age of 65, Sanders had to shut down his motel-restaurant because of plans to build a new highway where it was located. At that point he decided to retire from the tough life he had led and the hard work he had done. A while later he received his first social security check, which was for only $105, and he started to wonder how he was going to survive financially. This was the beginning of his journey to open *KFC*.

As an elderly, Sanders did not just sit back and wait for things to happen. He decided to franchise his fried chicken at the not so young age of 65. Sanders traveled around by car, offering his fried chicken to restaurant owners. He cooked the chicken on the spot and let the owner try it. If the owner liked the chicken, he hoped it would result in

Sources: "Stories", colonelsanders.com. "Colonel Sanders – Story of Perseverance & Entrepreneurship", Articlesbase, 4 Feb, 2007.

an agreement to sell his fried chicken. How many times do you think Sanders heard "no" before getting the answer he wanted? It's said that he was refused 1,009 times (!) before he heard the first "yes". He spent two years driving across North America in his old, beat-up car, sleeping in the back seat in his rumpled white suit, getting up each day, eager to share his cooking with someone new. After he got his first positive answer, the success story of *KFC* had begun. By 1964, Colonel Sanders had 600 restaurants selling his trademark fried chicken. Sanders sold the entire *KFC* franchising operation the same year for $2 million ($14,987,124 by todays standards). He died at the age of 90 (allowing him to enjoy his success for more than 15 years), and had up until then traveled 250,000 miles every year visiting all the *KFC* outlets he'd founded. The Colonel became the still famous company icon, identified by his glasses, white mustache and beard, black string tie and walking stick.

POSSIBLE MORAL

It seems it's never too late to turn your dreams into reality. Colonel Sanders' story has become a symbol of great entrepreneurial spirit. He truly had a "Never-Give-Up" attitude. It's common for entrepreneurs to face failure in their first business(es). The lesson to be learned is that every time you do something, you learn from it, and you find a way to do it better next time. Instead of feeling bad about the last restaurant that had rejected his idea, Sanders immediately started focusing on how to tell his story more effectively and get better results from the next restaurant.

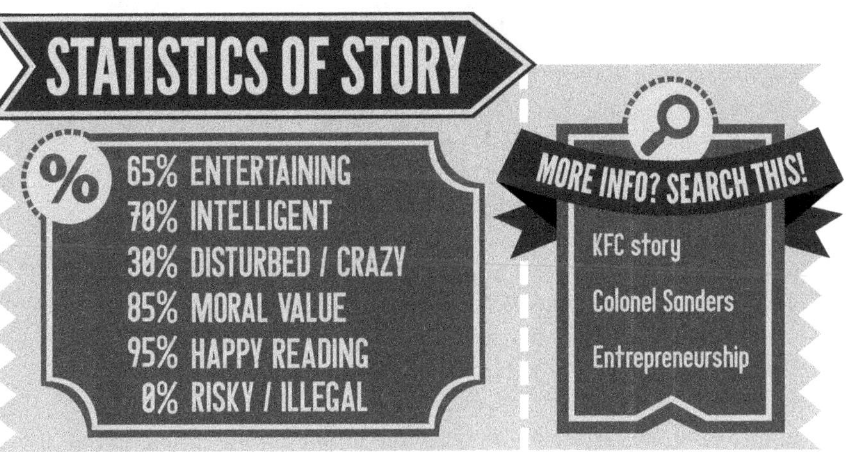

NEVER GIVE UP

HOMELESS TO FASHION KING

ODD MOLLY BELIEF REHAB SKATEBOARD SECOND CHANCE

In the year 2002, Per Holknekt and Karin Jimfelt-Ghatan founded *Odd Molly* in Stockholm, Sweden. *Odd Molly* is a clothing brand which tries to highlight different female qualities in the garments. Seven years later their brand became an international success story with almost 2,000 retailers' worldwide. Supermodel Helena Christensen fronted the international brand campaigns. *Odd Molly* was nominated designer of the year (*Guldknappen*, 2008) and has won numerous awards on top of this. What this success story doesn't tell us is that only two years prior to the start of his business, Per Holknekt was homeless with a rehab institution as his only shelter.

Born in the small city Falun, Holknekt was a top student raised under the best of circumstances, a young wild-minded and independent entrepreneur always eager to bring his ideas into reality. A big hobby of his was freestyle skateboarding. So he moved to California to skateboard professionally. He stayed for five years, became world champion, designed skate clothes and started a skateboard magazine. Holknekt got involved with product development with his sponsors in 1981 and this was also the birth of his involvement in fashion. Unfortunately, the destructive lifestyle of partying and drug taking got the best of him, and he moved back home in 1985 after a couple of close-call overdoses. This was not how he intended to live his life.

In 1988 Holknekt got more involved in the clothing side of skating. He started the company *Streetstyle* which sold and distributed skateboards. His business was going great and the profits were able to finance his drug abuse, which once more started to get the upper hand. In 1997 Holknekt founded the clothing brand *Svea*. It became the winner of the *Elle Rookie of the year*-award. In late 1999 he chose to give the brand up when his life fell apart over night. He went from having everything to absolutely nothing, and ended up on the streets. Holknekt lost his home, money, relationships and self-respect, spending cold winter nights by himself in a forest in the southern outskirts of Stockholm. His life was now very far

Sources: "Från uteliggare till innedesigner", Dagens Nyheter, 9 Mar 2008. "Far from Odd", Inside Retail, 18 Jan, 2012.

away from the previous glamour, money, friends and family.

On the night of April 4, 2000, Holknekt decided to turn his life around, get sober and straighten up his life. Thanks to a social worker who believed in him, he received money for rehabilitation. The rest is as they say, history. Holknekt started *Odd Molly* in 2002, and in 2007 he had a fortune of millions. In 2010 he celebrated his comeback 10th year sober.

POSSIBLE MORAL

Life came back in quality style for Holknekt. For me, this is a story of giving people a second chance, but also about taking good care of those chances. I admire the social worker that believed in him. It doesn't matter whether it's parental, personal or work related – everyone deserves a second chance to prove their worth and their commitment. Never waste a second chance. Per Holknekt's story is a great example of what can happen if you don't.

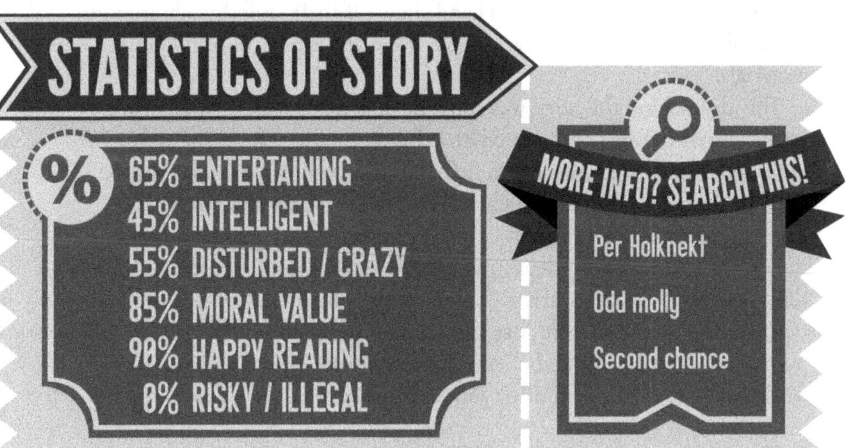

NEVER GIVE UP

THE ICEHOTEL

VISIONARY ARTISTS DOER
SCULPTURES WORLD'S FIRST

In one of the country's coldest and darkest places, above the Arctic Circle, lies one of Sweden's most famous modern tourism attractions: The *Icehotel.* Existing each year between December and April in the village of Jukkasjärvi, about 17 km from the city of Kiruna, founder Yngve Bergqvist has created the world's first ice hotel. He had an idea and a vision that very few believed in. If it's possible to build a hotel of ice in a small village 200 km inside the Arctic Circle, which strikes the whole world with amazement, then anything is possible. The story of the *Icehotel* is indeed a fairy tale come true.

The entire hotel is made out of snow and ice blocks taken from the Torne River. Even the glasses in the bar are made of ice. Each spring, around March, tons of ice are harvested from the frozen Torne River and then stored in a nearby production hall with room for over 10,000 tons of ice and 30,000 tons of snow. The ice is used for designing an ice bar (see page 42) and for creating ice glasses, holding ice sculpting classes, events and product promotions all over the world, and the snow is used for building a strong structure for the building. About 1,000 tons are used in the construction of the next *Icehotel.* Every year the most creative artists all over the world visit Jukkasjärvi and show off their sculpting abilities. As the ice from the Torne River is unique, none of the artists use any other materials.

The idea behind the hotel was thought of in 1989, when Japanese ice artists visited the area and created an exhibition of ice art. In the spring of 1990, French artist Jannot Derid held an exhibition in a cylinder-shaped igloo in the area. One night there were no hotel rooms available in the town, so some of the visitors asked for permission to spend the night in the exhibition hall. They slept in sleeping bags on top of reindeer skin; they were the first guests of the "hotel". Today, the hotel has three different types of rooms, a restaurant, bar and lounge, an ice church (where it's popular to get married) and of course plenty of sculptures and other works of art to admire. Some of you might think that there's nothing

Sources: "Icehotel: cuisine...", Lars Magnus Jansson, 2002. "The Complete Guide....Northern Lights", The Independent, 21 Aug. 2004.

special about a hotel built of ice and snow as there are several of them now. But when it comes to the first and the biggest one in the world, there is nothing to be proved. The *Icehotel* is simply a art masterpiece which gets better with every winter that passes.

POSSIBLE MORAL

If you look at any of the most successful people in history, they all have the following in common: They would not be denied. They wouldn't take no for an answer. They wouldn't allow anything to stop them from transforming their vision, their goal, into reality. Walt Disney is said to have been turned down 302 times before he got the financing he needed to create "The Happiest Place on Earth". All the banks thought he was crazy. He wasn't crazy; he was a visionary and, more importantly, he was committed to making that vision a reality. Today, millions of people have shared, "the joy of Disney", all thanks to the stubbornness of one man.

Yngve Bergqvist shares that same spirit. He had a dream and made it into reality. No matter what other people called him, no matter what they were thinking. The *Icehotel* is not only a great idea, but also a great combination of human effort and natural wonders. There are few people in the world that have managed to make such an unknown place world-famous in such a short period of time. The next step for Yngve is to, in the near future, make it possible to go on a one hour journey into space from Jukkasjärvi; 300 tickets have already been sold. For this man there seems to exist no limits of what's possible.

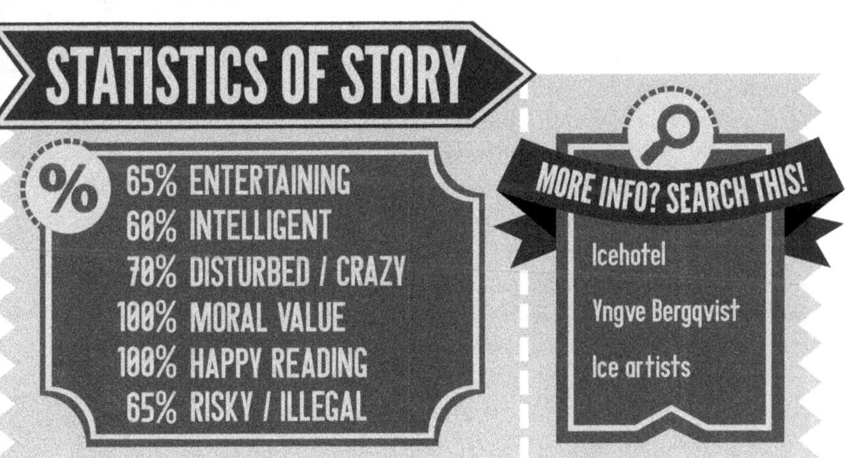

NEVER GIVE UP

THE ROCKY STORY

PERSISTENCE ACTOR SETBACKS
REJECTED STARRING ROLE

In the 1970's, film star Sylvester Stallone was nearly broke and living in New York. With barely $50 to his name, he sold his script for the movie *Paradise Alley* for $100. Stallone had his first starring role in the soft-core pornography feature film: *The Party at Kitty and Stud's* (1970). He was paid $200 for two days work. Stallone later explained that he had done the film out of desperation after being evicted from his apartment and finding himself homeless for several days. He has also said that he slept three weeks in the New York City Port Authority bus station prior to seeing a casting notice for the film. With no money for food or electricity, he had to steal his wife's jewelry and sell for $25 what he loved most in life; his dog. His life was full of setbacks, which would have made most people give up, before he finally broke through with his film *Rocky*.

Sylvester Stallone was born in New York in 1946. From birth, parts of his face was paralyzed, resulting in his characteristic slurred speech. Stallone knew deep within that he wanted to be an actor in the movie business, but because of his paralyzed face he received constant rejections at auditions. He went to every agent in New York several times each.

Despite his poverty, he refused to take a regular job, as he did not want to lose his motivation and his will to succeed. Two weeks later he saw a movie which inspired him to write *Rocky*. When visiting the different producers, Stallone said he wanted to sell the script, but on one condition, he was to play the lead role. The companies liked the script, but due to his demands he received countless rejections. It came to a point where he was offered $325,000 for the script, but he kept refusing their offer. Eventually, one company agreed to give Stallone the starring role in *Rocky* and paid him $35,000. He couldn't have been happier. The same day he went to buy his dog back, but the man who bought him didn't want to sell. Stallone then offered him $1,500 for his dog, plus a small role in the movie. The man agreed, and both he and the dog were featured in the film.

When *Rocky* was released in 1976, the film became a huge success. It brought in $225 million and won three Oscars awards. At the award

Sources: "Sylvester Stallone", Below Zero to Hero, 23 May, 2011."Sylvester Stallone, The Rocky Road to the top" doc, 1997.

ceremony Stallone read out some of the rejection slips from those who said the film would be sappy, predictable and a film that no one would want to watch.

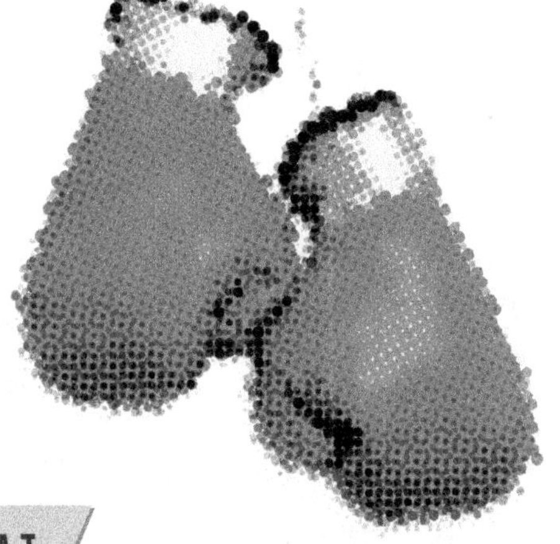

POSSIBLE MORAL

This story is about the power of persistence and self-belief. Sylvester Stallone was offered $325,000 for his script, but still declined. Was he nuts? I mean, the man was poor, he could barely pay for food. He was certain that he was an actor and that was it, there was no room for compromise. True persistence and self-belief pays off every time in every circumstance. Persistence will fight off failure faster than skill or luck ever could. Just ask Stallone, he persisted and knew his outcome.

NEVER GIVE UP

TREEHOTEL

ARCHITECTS NATURE EXPERIENCE
ADVENTURE SELF-BELIEF

If I told you: "let's build a hotel in the middle of nowhere in the forests of northern Sweden" – you'd call my idea a failure. If I told you: "it will be a huge success, win prizes and have visitors from all over the world" – you'd call me crazy! But of course, this has been done and the result is the unique and inspiring *Treehotel.*

Why not create a hotel that gives people a chance to experience nature amongst the tree-tops, while also providing a uniquely designed housing experience? In 2009, these questions led to the creation of *Treehotel* in Harads – a place where nature, ecological value, comfort and modern design are combined for an exciting experience. At the hotel, visitors are offered high-standard accommodation in a harmonious setting where your daily stress melts away. Guests can relax and renew their energy while being surrounded by unspoiled nature.

The hotel is run by a couple who began by renting out a tree-hut built for the movie production of *Trädälskaren* (*The Tree Lover*), a documentary made by Jonas Selberg Augustsen. The movie, which has inspired *Treehotel,* tells a tale of three men from the city who want to go back to their roots by building a tree house together. *The Tree Lover* is a philosophic story about the significance of trees for us human beings.

Together with some of Scandinavia's leading architects, the people of *Treehotel* created uniquely designed "tree-rooms". The rooms are suspended 4-6 meters above ground – all with spectacular views of the Lule River. The five rooms are designed for a total of twelve guests. They each have a different theme and were designed by different architects. Each room is unique. Not only the architecture but also its furniture, lighting and fabrics are custom designed. They include running water, sanitation and a sauna. One of the most impressive rooms, *The Mirrorcube,* is a lightweight aluminum structure hung around a tree trunk. A 4x4x4 meters box clad in mirrored glass. The exterior creates a feeling of space and weightlessness. By reflecting its surroundings with mirrors, *The Mirrorcube* remains more or less invisible wherever it's mounted. To prevent birds from flying into

Sources: "About" treehotel.se, "Treehotel – Sweden", The Coolist, "Wood you believe it!", The Daily Mail, 12 Jul, 2010.

the cube an infrared film, invisible to humans but highly visible to the birds, has been installed into the glass.

POSSIBLE MORAL

Never give up on your ideas. Believe in them. If you don't believe in your ideas how can you expect anyone else to believe in you? The power of ideas lies in getting others to believe in them and to take action. The people behind *Treehotel* fearlessly built a handful of rooms a few meters height on a forest slope in the middle of nowhere, far away from big roads, cities and airports. They created a unique hotel with finesse and style and put a huge amount of time and energy on the architecture and the design. This because they truly believed in their idea: Finding the important balance between small size, simplicity, closeness to nature and exclusivity. The hype has spread internationally and others have fallen in love with their idea. Soon there will be no country left in the world that has not reported about the hotel.

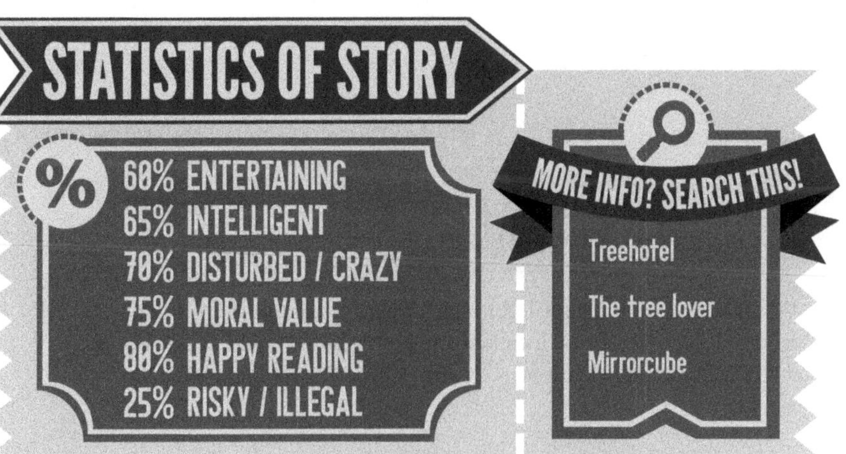

PLAY WITH SENSES

CHOCOLATE WEBSITE

STOUT BEER SAGRES ANALOG
QUALITY GOES DIGITAL

In the year 2010, *Sagres* (Portugal's number one beer brand) released their new *Preta Chocolate*, a stout beer with chocolate flavor. They also launched an amazing idea to bring attention to their new product: The world's first website made out of chocolate. What could have been a more suitable way to launch their new brew, than a site made entirely out of chocolate?

With the help of *Maître Chocolatier*'s Victor Nunes, renown in Portugal for his chocolate sculpturing, they designed and produced an interactive website ready to be launched in 2011. All the buttons and links were carved out into minute detail before being shown off at a trade fair. The chocolate was then photographed in high resolution and turned into the website. When the site went online, *Sagres* offered their first online visitors pieces of the real chocolate site, and sent them directly to their homes together with a six-pack of chocolate beer.

The analog meets the digital, through a clever yet simple idea. What were the advantages for *Sagres*? It caused a huge stir in the media, it set records and it exemplified the company's values – believing in quality over mass production.

Source: "The World's Coolest Website Made Entirely from Real Chocolate", Odditycentral, 1 Jun, 2011.

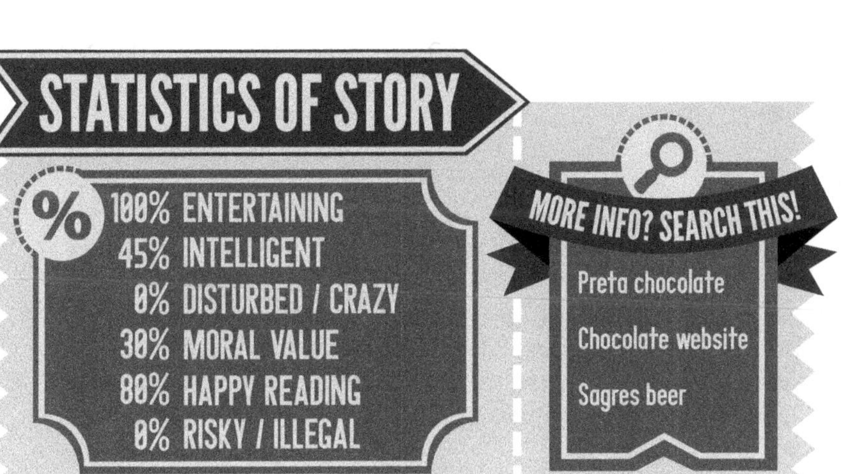
STATISTICS OF STORY
%
100% ENTERTAINING
45% INTELLIGENT
0% DISTURBED / CRAZY
30% MORAL VALUE
80% HAPPY READING
0% RISKY / ILLEGAL
MORE INFO? SEARCH THIS!
Preta chocolate
Chocolate website
Sagres beer

PLAY WITH SENSES

EYE OF THE BEHOLDER

AWARENESS QUESTION EXPERIENCE
PERSPECTIVE DIFFERENT NEEDS

It's strange how the meaning of things can change so dramatically depending on how you choose to see them. Imagine for example how the description of the human body can vary from context to context. Sex advisors divide the body into erogenous zones. Surgeons see them as operational areas. Athletes see them as different muscle groups. Fashion designers perceive the body more like a mannequin. They all give different descriptions and different meanings. It's sometimes hard to believe they're talking about the same thing.

A man and a woman may share a moment. To her, it's a gesture of romantic interest, but to him it's just a friendly conversation. A mother may discipline her teenage son. To the mother, it's good parenting, but to her son, it's oppression. Two website developers may work tirelessly to design a new social networking platform. To one, the project is about helping people communicate more effectively. To the other, it's about breaking new technological ground. We all have different needs, different perspectives, and thus different ways of understanding and describing our experiences. This is why we rarely have the same exact interpretation of a shared experience.

POSSIBLE MORAL

We see things differently. It's all about perspective. To actively question and analyze the perspectives of those around you will make you realize that your way is not the only way. This will give you a whole new awareness and appreciation for the world around you, which can help you in business as well as personal situations.

Sources: "Different Perspectives", Get.gg, Carol Vivyan. "Gaining Fresh Insight By ...Different Perspective", Watt Works.

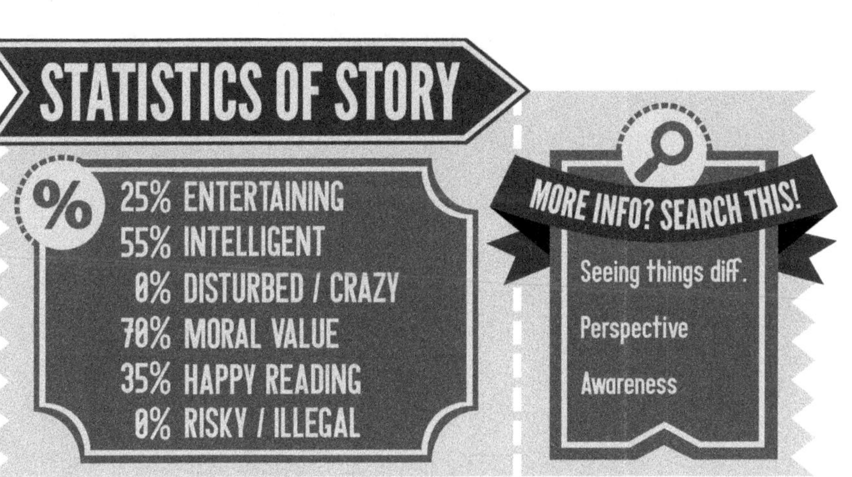
STATISTICS OF STORY
%
25% ENTERTAINING
55% INTELLIGENT
0% DISTURBED / CRAZY
70% MORAL VALUE
35% HAPPY READING
0% RISKY / ILLEGAL
MORE INFO? SEARCH THIS!
Seeing things diff.
Perspective
Awareness

FOR HUMANS ONLY

DISTRICT 9 REALITY FICTION
SEGREGATION RACISM

In 2009, the marketing team at *Sony* came up with a truly clever advertising campaign for Peter Jackson and Neill Blomkamp's science fiction movie *District 9*. The plot behind the movie: 28 years ago, aliens landed in Johannesburg, South Africa. A powerful private military corporation known as *Multi-National United* (*MNU*) moves all the aliens into a concentration camp called *District 9*. After years of protest from civilians, *MNU* finally decides to evict the aliens from *District 9* and move them to a more controlled area. The movie's setting echo the real-life conditions of poverty and prejudice.

Before anyone had heard of the film, signs forbidding non-humans from using benches and restrooms could be seen in major cities such as Los Angeles. Messages including phone numbers were also put up on billboards, shelters and inside comic book stores, asking people to report non-humans. If you called the number listed to "report" the aliens you reached the fictive *MNU*. The message of the advertisements was simple: Keep the aliens out.

During two weeks time, *MNU* received over 33,000 phone calls and about 2,500 people left voice messages about alien sightings. Of these, 92 percent came from cell phones, indicating that people were reacting, on the spot, in the streets.

Sources: "'Alien' bus-stop ads create a stir", LA Times, 19 Jun, 2009. "When tight-lipped...", Moviechoshop, 17 Aug, 2009.

POSSIBLE MORAL

These advertisements blurred the line between the real and the fictional world created by the filmmakers. What's important about this campaign is how it copies the civil rights movement for a generation of young people who don't have first-hand experience with segregation and overt racism. I admire those who dare to make a statement about the world or even want to change it – by using metaphors. The parallels not only with South Africa's apartheid history but with the attitude to refugee asylum seekers or "illegal aliens" in the west can be found in both the movie and in the advertisements. The campaign really brought out the essence the movie. In the era of "skipping commercials" this idea was sure to survive. In short, a great marketing campaign by *Sony* that made people react.

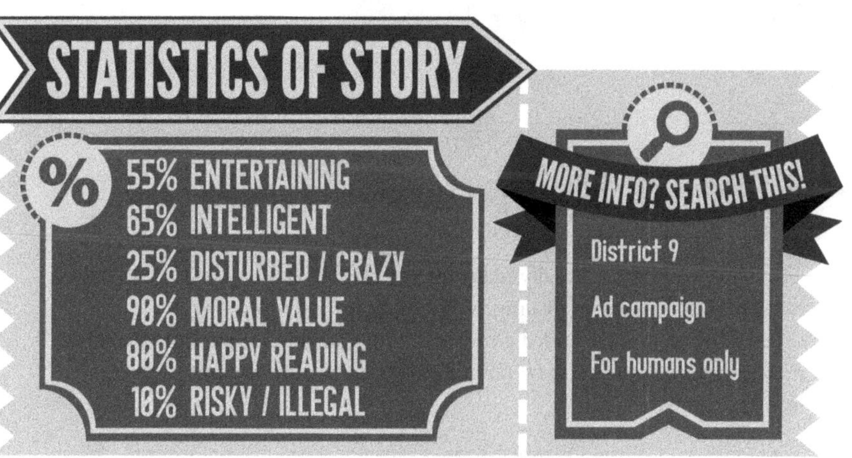

PLAY WITH SENSES

GOING BIG IN A SMALL WAY

BILLBOARDS TWIST STEALING
VIDEO GAME MARKETING

Some billboard ads don't have to be gigantic to draw attention. Video game *LittleBigPlanet* launched a fitting campaign of tiny billboards, which were scaled miniatures of their larger comrades. One would now have to look down instead of up to see them. Touting the message "Little is the New Big", these cute advertisements popped up everywhere, seemingly overnight. The message about *LittleBigPlanet* was quickly and effectively spread through this viral marketing gimmick.

The game's advertising agency *Deutsch* and *Sony* created around 1,000 of these billboards which were put up in New York, Los Angeles and San Francisco. These weren't your average flyers, though, the billboards where real-life miniatures and even had working lights and ladders.

Sony was comfortable with the idea that the signs would likely be stolen. In fact, a spokeswoman went as far as to wish for the thefts, so *LittleBigPlanet*-fans could help spread the word. One man auctioned one of these tiny billboards on *eBay*; it sold for $260.

POSSIBLE MORAL

Tiny signs wouldn't normally make for the best advertisements, but since they got people talking, stealing and bidding for them it can truly be called a success. *Deutsch* used a classic outdoor advertising structure, and made a fun twist on it – incorporating the theme and meaning of the game into the campaign.

Sources: "Be Careful Not to Step on the Tiny Billboards", Adweek, 26 Aug, 2008. "eBay auctioning off...", Quickjump, 8 Sep, 2008.

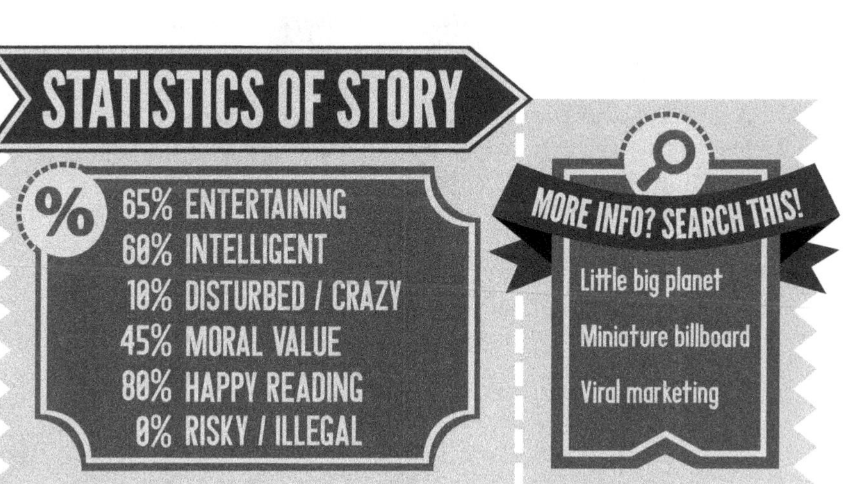
STATISTICS OF STORY
%
65% ENTERTAINING
60% INTELLIGENT
10% DISTURBED / CRAZY
45% MORAL VALUE
80% HAPPY READING
0% RISKY / ILLEGAL
MORE INFO? SEARCH THIS!
Little big planet
Miniature billboard
Viral marketing

PLAY WITH SENSES

SIGHT THROUGH SOUND

PASSION BLIND TAKE CONTROL
DANIEL KISH ECHOLOCATION

Echolocation is the process by which certain animals (such as bats and dolphins) use a sort of built in sonar in order to "see" their environment with the help of sound. They send out sound waves, which bounce off the objects and creatures around them. They then interpret the echo and use it to get a reading of what's in the vicinity. This technique can be used for locating prey and navigating through dark areas. We may not consider it too remarkable when animals do it, because we've all heard about bats catching food without being able to see well, but what's interesting is that humans can reproduce this effect as well. It's not incredibly common, but a number of people have practiced the art of human echolocation to such an extent that it effectively replaces their need for vision.

Daniel Kish is completely blind. He lost sight in both eyes at 13 months of age. Now he uses his ears to see. When he walks around unfamiliar places (for example when hiking) he clicks his tongue and then listens as the sound bounces off nearby objects. Kish has also found a technique using a walking cane combined with echolocation to further expand his mobility.

Kish is the president of *World Access for the Blind*, a non-profit organization founded in 2001 to facilitate "the self-directed achievement of people with all forms of blindness" and increase public awareness about the strengths and capabilities of blind people. He teaches teenagers how to hike and mountain-bike through the wilderness and how to navigate new locations safely.

Sources: "Blind man uses his ears to see", CNN, 11 Nov, 2011. "Human echolocation: Using tongue-clicks...", BBC, 12 Sep, 2012.
Quotes: "World Access for the Blind", worldaccessfortheblind.org, 2012.

POSSIBLE MORAL

This shows a person's will to take control of his environment rather than letting it take control of him. Daniel's insight reaches far beyond his blindness, and I feel it's something we could all learn from. I admire his passion for life and wanting others to share his dream of "helping people reach beyond their limits through creativity, writing, and music". Daniel Kish has proven that a person (blind or otherwise) can do anything he or she puts their mind to, and because he took the time to finely hone this ability, he's able to live a very capable life that very few of us would be able to replicate if we were to go blind tomorrow.

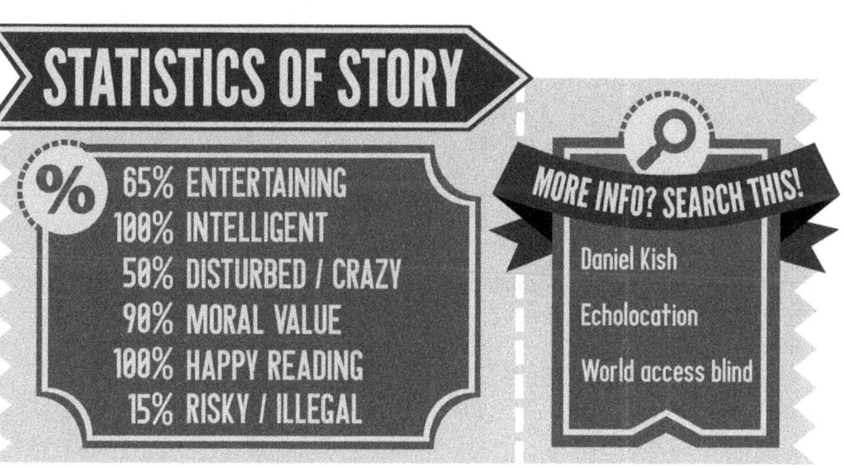

THE POWER OF NAMES

REBELLIOUS FCUK ACRONYM
CONTROVERSY REACTION

French Connection is a retailer and a wholesaler of fashion clothing and accessories. The company was founded in 1972 by Stephen Marks and is based in London. It was one of the first British companies to address the market for well-designed accessible men's casual wear.

French Connection soon expanded into both formal and informal clothes for men, women and children. After near bankruptcy in the late 1980s, the company was able to get on their feet and once again become one of the hottest and fastest growing brands in Britain during the late 1990s and early 2000s. How was this possible? In large part it was thanks to the controversial and suggestive marketing campaign launched in 1997, rebranding under the "fcuk" logotype. The letters represented the company's initials (*French Connection UK*). Reportedly, they first discovered the acronym when a fax was sent from their Hong Kong store, entitled "FCHK to FCUK". Though they insisted it was an acronym for "French Connection United Kingdom", its similarity to the word "fuck" caused controversy.

French Connection exploited the controversy of the name, producing an extremely popular range of t-shirts with messages such as "fcuk fashion", "fcuk this", "hot as fcuk", "mile high fcuk" and "too busy to fcuk".

POSSIBLE MORAL

French Connection went from anonymous dullard to an exciting rebellious brand. They created a huge reaction. The idea behind "fcuk" is either a brilliant piece of marketing or a badly disguised euphemism. Love it or hate it, the acronym that represents *French Connection UK* is set to stick around. Showing us the power of names, indeed.

Sources: "International Directory of Company Histories", Vol. 41, 2001. "Can The Wrong Name...", Marketing Magazine, 13 Jul, 2008.

fcuk

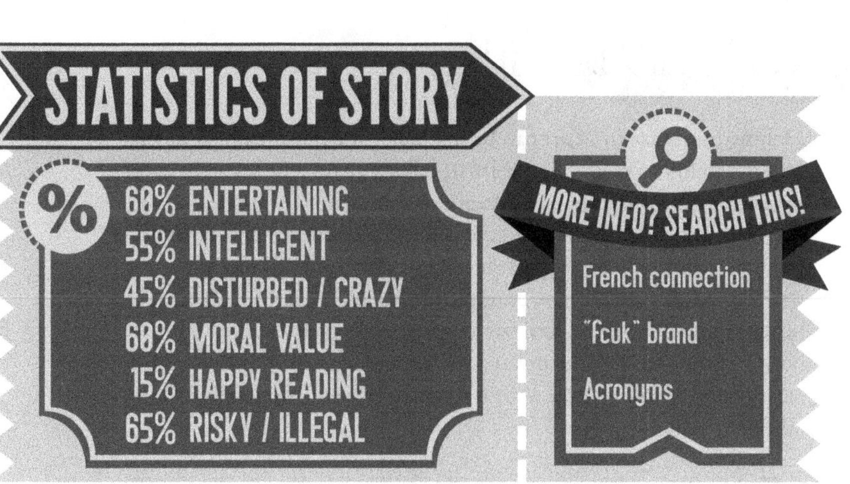
STATISTICS OF STORY
60% ENTERTAINING
55% INTELLIGENT
45% DISTURBED / CRAZY
60% MORAL VALUE
15% HAPPY READING
65% RISKY / ILLEGAL
MORE INFO? SEARCH THIS!
French connection
"fcuk" brand
Acronyms

RE-INVENTIONS

DESIGN THAT SURVIVES

LISA LARSON CERAMIC DESIGNER
STAY TRUE GUSTAVSBERG

Lisa Larson is a Swedish ceramic designer whose career started out at *Gustavsberg Porcelain Factory* in 1953. During her time there she created several hundred different designs – many of which became design classics and sought after by antique dealers and private collectors. She became an important public relations (PR) personality for the company during the 1960's and 70's as her products were immensely popular. Larson was employed at the factory until 1980. Since then, she has worked as a freelance designer and sculptor artist. She is best known for her humorous and friendly figures, generous shapes and artfully drawn incised decoration.

In 1965 she launched her design of a lion, which in Swedish spells "Lejon". The figure became a huge success and can be found in homes all around the world. Over the years it has turned into a classic art piece. The figure is still being produced today, and the design has been the same for almost 50 years. Talk about doing it right from the start!

POSSIBLE MORAL

Making business out of art can be difficult. One must really trust in a persons ability to create. Some artists believe that being an artist is only reserved for a select few, but if creating your art makes you feel alive, then you are an artist. It's ever so important to believe in what you do, trust your ability to create and show yourself worthy. Never sell yourself short. A simple yet effective example of this is Lisa Larson's *Lejon*. She believed in her art form, and has kept the concept for almost 50 years. The bottom line is that if you are an artist who believes in your worth and your creations, you will become a great business person. "Follow your heart, but take your brain with you".

Sources: "Lisa Larson: bland lejon och änglar", Gisela Eronn, 2006. "The Film About Lisa Larson" documentary, 2010.

60% ENTERTAINING
30% INTELLIGENT
0% DISTURBED / CRAZY
70% MORAL VALUE
80% HAPPY READING
0% RISKY / ILLEGAL

MORE INFO? SEARCH THIS!
Lisa Larson
Ceramic designer
Gustavsberg

RE-INVENTIONS

FOLKDRAKT 2.0

ENGAGEMENT FASHION CULTURE
IDENTITY YOUNGER AUDIENCE

Founded in 1885, the *Swedish Tourist Association*, *STF*, aims to promote outdoor life and knowledge about Sweden among tourists as well as Swedes. It's a nonprofit organization that depends on its members to survive. Like many other associations *STF* is faced with the challenge of reaching a younger audience. In 2010, celebrating 125 years, the members began a search of a project that would appeal to the younger generation. They wanted to find a solution that would display *STF*'s history and the unique knowledge the association possesses about Sweden, both past and present. They found the solution in the Swedish national folk costumes, the *folkdräkt*.

Folk costumes have a long history, for many it's a forgotten phenomenon, but for others it's almost holy. Furthermore, it's about fashion – a topic that could attract young people. What would happen if they took part in breathing new life into the costumes? Together with *Syrup Sthlm* and Sweden's leading design schools, *STF* created *Folkdräkt 2.0*: A contest to re-design the Swedish folk costume.

Sweden has 25 provinces and they have no administrative function, but remain historical legacies and the means of cultural identification. Long ago, every province had its own style of clothing, and every village displayed its history and culture through their outfits. The competing students were asked to choose a respective province, they then had to travel there and stay at *STF*'s facilities to discover and experience the local culture. On site they gathered inspiration, met people and after some inspiration-hunting they could begin their work to develop a new and updated costume. The participant's blogged about the event, and on the *Folkdräkt 2.0* website visitors could follow the participants and vote for a top-10 list. On the last day of the competition, all the creations were showcased in a fashion show that was live-streamed on the website.

Sources: "Om Folkdräkt 2.0", Svenska Turistföreningen. "Om Folkdräkt 2.0", YouTube, stfturist, 13 Sep, 2010.

POSSIBLE MORAL

Sweden is full of culture and influences from both yesterday and tomorrow. Just as anywhere else on the globe, clothing reflects your identity. A suit or baggy clothes, are a reflection of who you are. *STF* believes that one of the most exciting garments of all time is the folk costume. But before *Folkdräkt 2.0* the costume appeared almost exclusively at midsummer celebrations, in a specific region of the country called Dalarna, or in museums. For many Swedes, the folk costumes was outdated and didn't reflect the Sweden of today, but *STF* succeeded changing that. *Folkdräkt 2.0* shows that with the right concept, a 125-year old association can have both 18-year-old costume designers and "folk costume-fashion cops" to engage in their country and its tourism.

STATISTICS OF STORY
%
70% ENTERTAINING
70% INTELLIGENT
0% DISTURBED / CRAZY
65% MORAL VALUE
80% HAPPY READING
0% RISKY / ILLEGAL
MORE INFO? SEARCH THIS!
Folkdrakt 2.0
Swedish folk
Costume design

RE-INVENTIONS

KHAN ACADEMY

MINI-LECTURES ONLINE FUTURE
SALMAN KHAN VIDEOTAPED

In 2006, Salman Khan started educating people across the globe for free. From his closet in Mountain View, California, he videotaped mini-lectures on topics ranging from simple addition to vector calculus and Napoleonic campaigns. He's a math, science and history teacher for millions of students, yet none of them have ever seen his face.

The idea behind *Khan Academy* was born when Khan was tutoring his cousin Nadia in mathematics using *Yahoo!'s Doodle* notepad. When other relatives and friends sought similar help, Khan decided it would be more practical to distribute the tutorials on *YouTube*. His lectures became a huge success. Every day, the videos were viewed around 70,000 times – double the entire student body of *University of California, Berkeley*. His viewers were diverse, ranging from rural preschoolers to Pakistani engineers.

Three years later the students prompted Khan to quit his job in finance, and asked him to focus full-time on the tutorials. Khan did as they pleased, and turned *Khan Academy* into a full-time occupation. Today, the academy has a video library with over 3,000 videos in various topic areas and over 140 million delivered lessons. Since its launch, the *Khan Academy* website has recorded more than 16 million page views.

Mark Halberstadt discovered the *Khan Academy* in 2007. He watched all the videos on calculus, trigonometry, physics and arithmetic, and in 2010 he decided to go back to school and get a degree in Electrical Engineering. Previously a self-described "straight C student" whose original *Grade Point Average* (*GPA*) was in the 2.0 region, Mark now got a 4.0 *GPA* (the best grade) for the entire year. He even got perfect scores on both his calculus final exams and chemistry. He says he couldn't have gotten the same help from anywhere else.

Is *Khan Academy* showing us the future of education? Backed by *Google* and Bill Gates among others – Khan wants to improve education worldwide, and his work has already made a huge impact on many peoples lives.

Sources: "Salman Khan: Let's use video...", TEDTalks, Mar, 2011."Sal Khan's 'Academy' sparks...", USA Today, 30 May, 2012.

POSSIBLE MORAL

The biggest weakness in many countries school system is that it's standardized, so students who are not suited to learn from the pedagogy used are being left behind. *Khan Academy* is amazing, not because it replaces teachers but because it bridges the gaps that teachers can't possibly fill within the constraints of standardized teaching. The students of *Khan Academy* have the ability to watch the videos repeatedly, instead of having to ask the same questions over and over to a teacher, which may make them feel embarrassed or stupid. They also have the ability to review things they "should have" learned weeks, months or maybe even years ago. As a supplement to regular teaching, I hope these tutorials make it into every classroom.

STATISTICS OF STORY

RE-INVENTIONS

MYTHBUSTERS

TV-SHOW SCIENCE INITIATOR EXPERIMENTS ENTERTAINMENT

MythBusters is a science entertainment TV-show created and produced by Australia's *Beyond Television Productions* for *Discovery Channel* in 2003. In each episode, hosts Adam Savage and Jamie Hyneman focus on two or more popular beliefs, Internet rumors, or other myths, and try to prove them scientifically through the use of experiments..

Can a skunk's smell be neutralized with tomato juice? Can a sunken ship be floated with the help of Ping-Pong balls? Can a car stereo be so loud that it blows out the windows? The myths tested in the series come from many different sources, including the personal experiences of the cast and crew as well as suggestions from fans of the show (such as those posted on *Discovery Channel*'s online *MythBusters* forums). Mr. Savage and Mr. Hyneman, who produce Hollywood special effects and gadgets for a living, come up with ways to challenge each hypothesis and build experiments with the help of a small crew. By the end of each episode, the myths are rated "busted", "plausible" or "confirmed".

MythBusters typically test myths in a two-step process. In early episodes, the steps were described as "replicate the circumstances, then duplicate the results" by Savage. This means that first the team attempts to recreate the circumstances that the myth alleges, to determine whether the alleged result occurs. If that fails, they attempt to manipulate the circumstances to the point that will cause the described result. Occasionally the team will hold a friendly competition between one another to see which of them can devise the most successful solution to recreating the results. This is most common with myths involving building an object that can accomplish a goal (for example, rapidly cooling a beer, or finding a needle in a haystack).

Sources: "The Best Science Show on Television?", The New York Times, 21 Nov, 2006. "MythBusters", Internet Movie DataBase.

POSSIBLE MORAL

In a way, *MythBusters* have taken physics and chemistry and made it cooler. Savage and Hyneman are popularizing science. It's really a smart concept that combines teaching science and entertaining the audience They combine their curiosity-driven hypotheses with inventive testing methods, producing results that always surprise their viewers and oftentimes, themselves. I believe *MythBusters* can work as an initiator/ gateway for people who have difficulty finding an interest in physics and chemistry. If these people start watching this show, they will likely be watching other science-related shows in the near future, and who knows: Maybe get inspired for their future careers?

REVOLUTION OF KNOWLEDGE

ENCYCLOPEDIA VISION WIKIPEDIA
VOLUNTEERS FREE KNOWLEDGE

Imagine a world in which every single person on the planet is given free access to the sum of all human knowledge. That was Jimmy Wales vision when he started working on *Wikipedia*. Since its launch in 2001 as "the free encyclopedia that anyone can edit", it has blossomed to contain explanations to more than a billion words spread over ten million articles in 250 languages, including 2.5 million articles in English.

All the entries has an "Edit this page" button on it, available to all. Every one of us is an expert at something, and on *Wikipedia* no subject is too narrow to have an entry. However, experts can be wrong, historians don't always agree on the developments of passed events and scientists don't always agree on the specifics of physics and chemistry. Also, *wiki* entries are sometimes written by experts, and other times written by amateurs. They can be a great form of quick reference, but before you rely too much on an entry it can be a good idea to verify the information. In other words: While relying on a *wiki* to provide you with more information on actor Morgan Freeman is fine, but relying on a *wiki* for the possible drug interactions between your heart pressure medicine and your cholesterol medicine is probably something you want to verify somewhere else.

Source: "History of Wikipedia", en.wikipedia.org, Sep, 2012.
Quote: Jimmy Wales, from "Wikimedia Founder Jimmy Wales Responds,"Robin "Roblimo" Miller, Slashdot, 28 Jul, 2004.

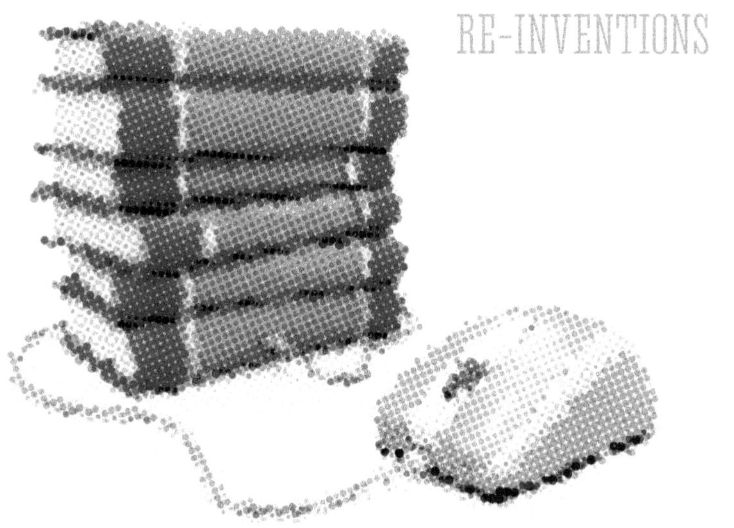

POSSIBLE MORAL

Before *Wikipedia*, the availability of knowledge was a matter connected to financial means. Everything from education, encyclopedias or library cards – cost money. *Wikipedia* on the other hand is free and can be used by anyone. What's the most amazing part however, is that this online encyclopedia with millions of articles was put together by volunteers. It wasn't their job and they didn't get paid. *Wikipedia* is a great example of what amateur user contributors can achieve. It's fascinating that *Wikipedia* doesn't collapse into anarchy. It's constantly being improved on and the employees and users work together to heal it from hackers and spammers.

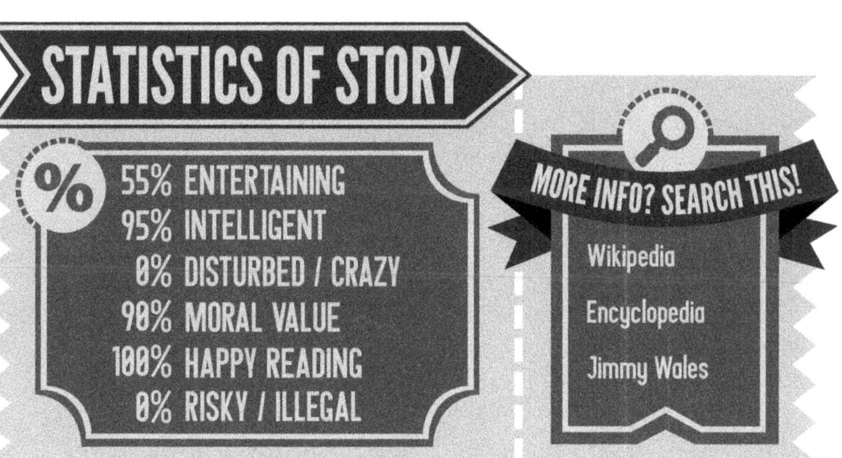

ROVIO AND NASA STORY

ANGRY BIRDS ENGAGE CO-BRANDING
YOUNG KIDS SPACE STATION

The *National Aeronautics and Space Administration* (*NASA*) has trouble making itself heard, especially with the younger crowd, and interest in space technology has therefore decreased. In 2009, the Finnish computer game developer *Rovio Entertainment* created the video game *Angry Birds* – a phenomenon with a gigantic fan base of children of all ages. *Rovio*'s fourth game in the series, *Angry Birds in Space*, is set in outer space instead of planet Earth as the previous games. The idea for the game actually originated in a challenge *NASA* made to *Rovio* in 2011 on *Twitter*. *NASA* said it would help *Rovio* launch birds if "pigs could fly in space". One thing led to another and in 2012 it was announced that *Rovio* was releasing the game, in a collaboration with both *NASA* and *National Geographic*. *NASA* scientists actually helped out in designing the physics-engine in the game.

The announcement of *Angry Birds in Space* was truly ambitious. It wasn't just the launch of a game: It was the launch of a huge franchise. The launch was bigger than most movie launches in Hollywood. *Rovio* managed to send stuffed animals and toys symbolizing the game's characters and scenery into space, for real! A teaser for the game was actually filmed on the *International Space Station*, featuring a live *Angry Birds* demonstration and physics lesson from astronaut Don Pettit. Search for the video and be astonished. *Angry Birds in Space* is also supported by a book on physics and mathematics (with the colorful birds from the game of course) published by *National Geographic*, aiming to increase interest in the subjects. Imagine that this book was also handed out in schools in the United States – crazy but true.

This is an example of how three very different companies can work together in order to jointly achieve the things they couldn't have achieved alone. There will always be a need for people to work at *NASA* or similar working fields in the future, but the problem they face are the low interest in the subjects that are central, mathematics, physics, chemistry, astronomy, etc. Through this partnership, *NASA* can at least hope that the game's audience will become more interested in physics and astronomy,

Sources: "NASA Works with Rovio to Launch...", Daily Tech, 8 Mar, 2012. "'Angry Birds Space' Launches...", NBC News, 22 Mar, 2012.
Quote: Rovio Mobile's official Twitter (@RovioMobile), post by NASA (@NASA), 27 Mar, 2011.

and that they want to learn about *NASA*'s work. The key to this successful co-branding was that *Rovio* had the people and *NASA* the technology. With this marketing campaign *Rovio* used outer space as their billboard, which of course would have been impossible without the help of *NASA*. We thus have a win-win situation!

POSSIBLE MORAL

Together equals stronger. This is an extraordinary example of co-branding. Suddenly *Angry Birds* had taken over space, without greater effort and with a marketing budget of $0 for *Rovio*. There are many examples where brands seek to benefit from each other's image, such as *McDonald's* and *Disney*, *H&M* and *Versace*. Although the story of *Angry Birds in Space* takes it to a whole new level, it's a big time re-invention of classic co-branding.

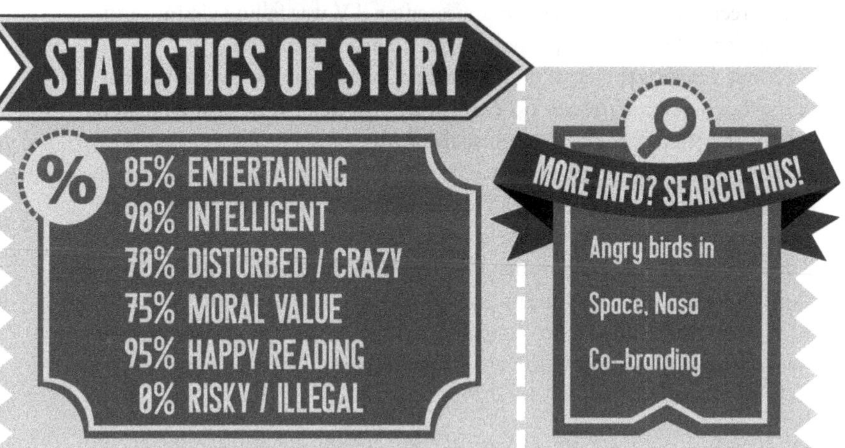

THE FORGOTTEN PLATFORM

TELETEXT REVISIT LITAGO AWARENESS LIMITED BUDGET

Litago is the most popular chocolate milk in Norway. With a very limited budget, advertising agency *Dist Creative* was asked to create awareness and buzz around the company's new flavor, *Litago Mocca*. Since the new flavor contained more and darker chocolate, they created the concept: "A new darker side of Litago". *Dist Creative* wanted to create a interactive campaign that allowed the audience to do some mischief. They found that the perfect medium for this was teletext: An obsolete (but still used) television information retrieval service, offering a range of text-based information like news, weather and TV-schedules.

This is how it worked: You turned your TV on, went to teletext-mode and entered the number that then transferred you to the *Litago Mokka* page. To clarify: Every TV with teletext has a remote control with a *Mix*-button. If you push this button, the teletext background disappears, and only the text will be visible on top of the TV-picture. This allows the user to watch TV while reading. Instead of text, *Dist Creative* had created ten different teletext pages only displaying a static pixel-drawing of glasses and a moustache. With it, you could do some funny mischief: By switching through the pages, you'd move the moustache and glasses across the screen. Soon, everyone that appeared on TV was falling victim to the campaign: The royal family, politicians, actors and athletes.

Since *Litago* is the most popular chocolate milk in Norway, it had a huge fan base on *Facebook*. So *Dist Creative* started by spreading the news about the teletext pages through social media and newsletters, reaching thousands of their target audience. It didn't take long before people started posting their own pictures of TV-celebrities with moustaches and glasses. Although teletext is impossible to track, *Dist Creative* could see some really great results by their use of social media. The campaign also got picked up by *Waschera*, a popular youth program that airs on Norwegian national TV. They made the teletext campaign a part of their editorial content by launching a competition. The viewers could send their best pictures and win great prizes.

Sources: "LITAGO ON TELETEXT", Advertolog, 2009. "TINE Litago – Mocca on teletext (casefilm)", YouTube, distcreative.

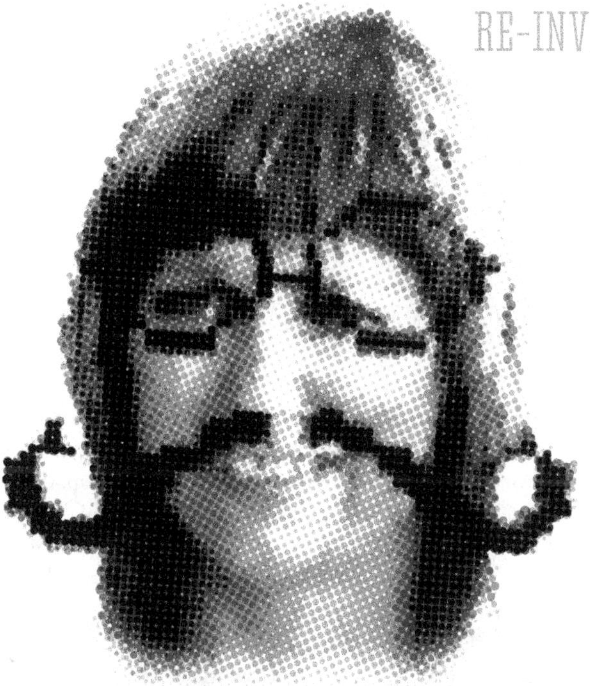

POSSIBLE MORAL

By using a "forgotten" platform, *Dist Creative* made television interactive in a completely new way. This is a great way of showing how one can achieve new and interesting solutions by using old techniques. Tip of the day: Go and revisit the past to find inspiration.

STATISTICS OF STORY

%

70% ENTERTAINING
65% INTELLIGENT
15% DISTURBED / CRAZY
70% MORAL VALUE
80% HAPPY READING
0% RISKY / ILLEGAL

MORE INFO? SEARCH THIS!

Litago mocca

Teletext

Dist Creative

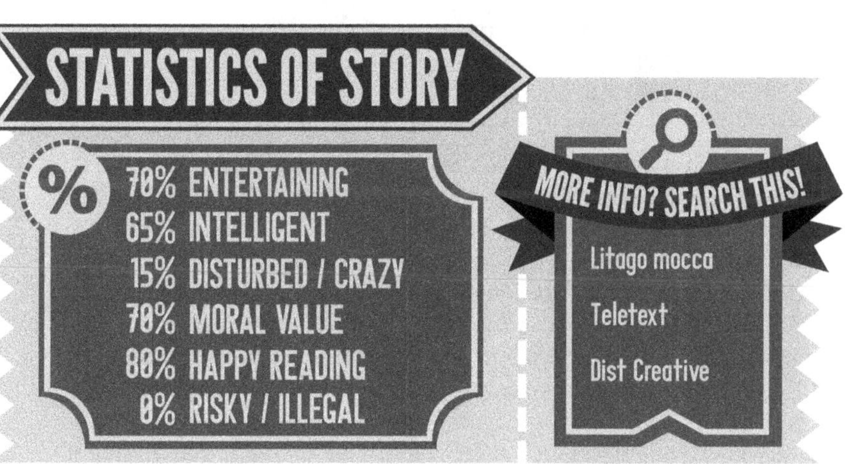

RE-INVENTIONS

WORDFEUD

SCRABBLE WORDS REVIVAL
DIGITAL GAME BOARD GAME

Scrabble is one of the best-loved board games of all time. For those of you who don't know, it's a word game in which two to four players score points by forming words from individual lettered tiles on a game board marked with a 15-by-15 grid. The players take turns trying to form the highest scoring words out of the letters they have been dealt. The words are formed down or across in crossword fashion and must be included in a standard dictionary. The first versions of the game came out in the 1940's.

In 2010, Norwegian Håkon Bertheussen released a game for smartphones and tablets called *Wordfeud*. It is essentially *Scrabble* by another name, except only two players at a time can compete against each other. A player can play several games simultaneously, with same or different players. In order to play, each participant needs a phone or tablet, and access to the internet.

Wordfeud has become a huge success and has been downloaded over ten million times, making Håkon Bertheussen a very rich man. Interesting fact: The success of *Wordfeud* has actually increased the sales of the classic board game. In Sweden, *Scrabble* sales increased with 70 percent in 2011.

POSSIBLE MORAL

You don't have to be a genius, but it's important to be first! In Europe, Håkon revived a game that many of today's youth didn't even know existed. This is a great way of creating a business idea. I recently saw that you can download the old *Snake* game for your smartphone, with the classic cell phone "skins" for a more authentic feel. I think that's hilarious. We have the greatest of technology, but we still want to re-live the memories from the late 90's. It says a lot about how we people function, and the power of nostalgia. Something that was big in your time might have been forgotten today – maybe it's time to revive it?

Source: "Pengaregn över Wordfeud...", Svenska Dagbladet, 23 Sep, 2011. "Alfapet blir pop...", Svenska Dagbladet, 3 Oct, 2011.

W
1

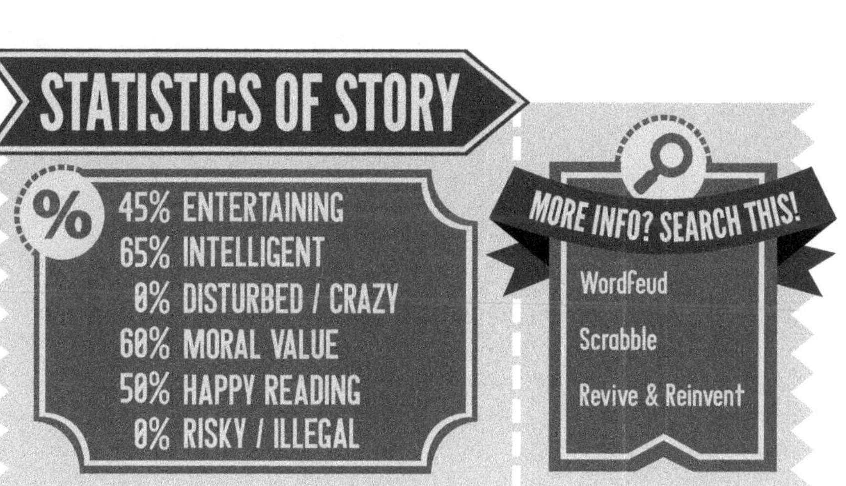
STATISTICS OF STORY
%
45% ENTERTAINING
65% INTELLIGENT
0% DISTURBED / CRAZY
60% MORAL VALUE
50% HAPPY READING
0% RISKY / ILLEGAL
MORE INFO? SEARCH THIS!
Wordfeud
Scrabble
Revive & Reinvent

SIMPLE SOLUTIONS

AMMO WITH FLAVOR

SEASON SHOT HUNTING MEAT
INJECTION INVENTION

The *Season Shot* is a revolutionary form of ammunition invented by Brett Holm in 2005. It's strong enough to kill an animal (pheasant, quail, duck or turkey) on impact and it's shell is filled with spices designed to "shoot, kill and season". The *Season Shot* is made of tightly packed seasoning covered with a fully biodegradable outer shell. The seasoning is actually injected into the bird on impact, seasoning the meat from the inside out. When the bird is cooked the seasoning pellets melt into the meat, spreading the flavor to the entire bird. So forget worrying about accidently damaging your teeth from shot left in the bird, and start wondering about which flavor shot to use. Choose from seasonings like Cajun, Lemon Pepper, Garlic, Teriyaki and Honey Mustard.

A morbidly hilarious product! Brett Holm's idea spurred a new one in my head: This could be an easy way to season meat from your local supermarket. It doesn't need to be used exclusively for hunting. Buy a chicken or a steak, bring it to your backyard, load your rifle with *Season Shot* and fire – this could make cooking fun again.

Source: "How it works", seasonshot.com, 2006.

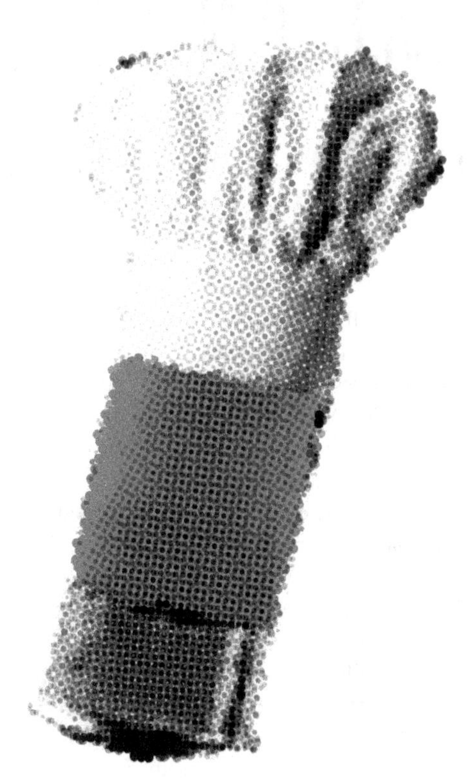

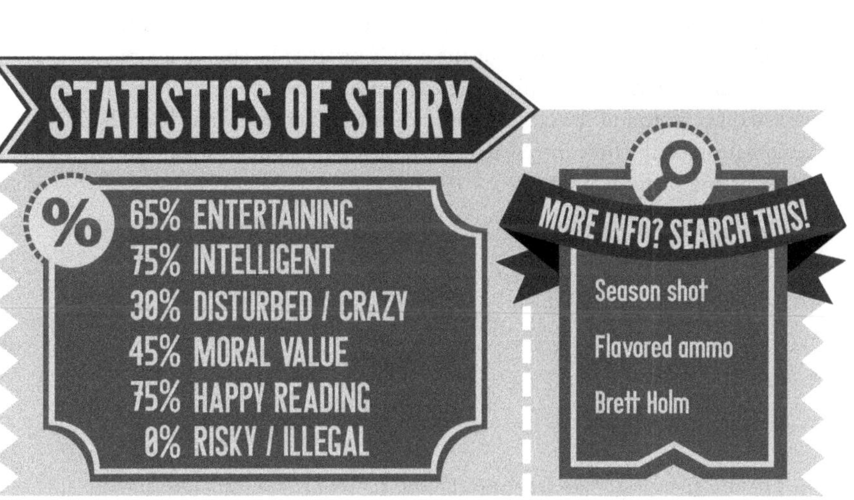
STATISTICS OF STORY
%
65% ENTERTAINING
75% INTELLIGENT
30% DISTURBED / CRAZY
45% MORAL VALUE
75% HAPPY READING
0% RISKY / ILLEGAL
MORE INFO? SEARCH THIS!
Season shot
Flavored ammo
Brett Holm

CRIME AND DONUTS

NEW YORK ROUTINE SMALL DETAILS
CRIME RATE COFFEE SHOPS

As the crack epidemic hit New York in the 1980s, the city's crime rate rose. During the 1990s the crime rates dropped dramatically, even more than in the United States as a whole. Violent crimes declined by more than 56 percent in New York. Lots of efforts were made to fight crime, for example: Increasing the number of police officers and mapping crime with the organizational management tool *CompStat*. There's been many debates about which of the efforts has had the biggest crime preventive effect. Some say that the increase in crime was an epidemic and a small increase of the number of police officers was enough to tip the balance back (*The Tipping Point, Malcolm Gladwell*). Other people argue that the crime drop was due to the legalization of abortion, they suggest that many would-be neglected children and criminals were prevented from being born (*Freakonomics, Steven D. Levitt and Stephen J. Dubner*).

A less heard of, alternative explanation, that might have made a bigger impact than it's been given credit for was an extremely simple yet effective measure. It's said that during this time, all police stations in New York City were strictly ordered to inform their officers never to buy coffee and donuts at the same place during a day at work. So every single day, a new route was set out. The aim was for the public never to be able to figure out the officer's pattern during shifts. This also created a wider distribution of police officers around the city. The effect was that criminals now had a hard time figuring out where the cops where located. They couldn't learn their patterns and plan accordingly.

Sources: "The Tipping Point", Malcolm Gladwell, 2000. "Freakonomics", Steven D. Levitt and Stephen J. Dubner, 2009. "Why Did Crime Fall in NYC?", NY Times, 13 Aug, 2007.

POSSIBLE MORAL

Regardless of whether the implementation of this strategy had an effect on crime or not, it still gives an example of how small and simple means can have an impact on the bigger picture. We're all human after all. I can really understand how many of the officers in New York have their favorite coffee shops and food chains after years of service and it's definitely not a strange thing that they want to return to the same place every day. However, as told in this story, their behavior was predictable and could easily be monitored by those out to commit crime. It's the little details that are vital. Little things can make big things happen.

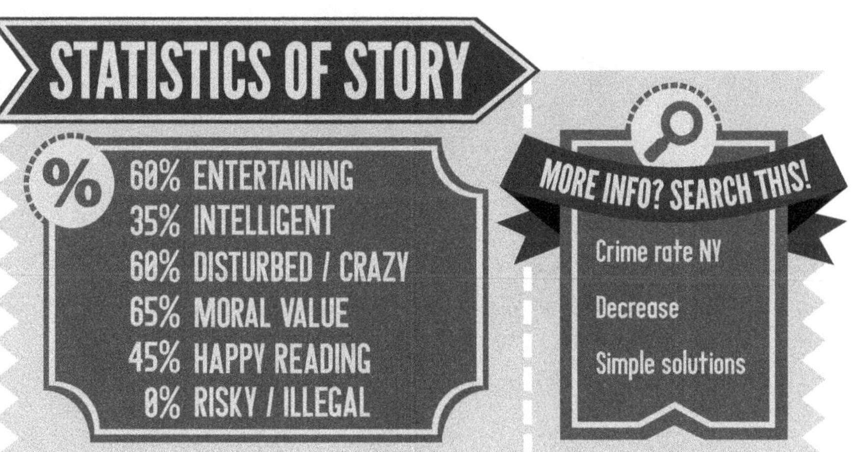

SIMPLE SOLUTIONS

EMPTY BOXES

ECONOMIZE ISSUE SOLUTION INDUSTRIAL PACKAGING

One of the biggest cosmetic companies in Japan received a complaint from a customer about receiving an empty perfume box. A huge technical and management meeting was called to investigate how an empty box could've reach the market. They were able to figure out that the mistake had been made in the packaging sector, and so they invoked the efforts of technical engineers to make such a robust and reliable system that not even a single box would end up empty during packaging. In order to do this, the engineers had to redesign the entire system that was in use and implemented a surveillance system costing millions of Yen.

The same problem was experienced by a small soap manufacturing company in India. They too, received complaints about empty boxes. The manufacturer in India however, solved this problem in a thousand fold simpler way and at a cost of almost nothing. He just bought a large industrial fan and placed it facing the conveyor belt that the soap boxes travelled along. The empty boxes flew away and the soap carrying boxes would move ahead for storage.

Always look for simple solutions and avoid complicated ones in order to economize your resources.

Sources: "Corporate Lessons", ajmalbeig.addr.com, M. Ajmal Beig Naz. "Keep It Simple" article, Entrepreneur magazine, Feb 2006.

STATISTICS OF STORY
%
70% ENTERTAINING
65% INTELLIGENT
10% DISTURBED / CRAZY
80% MORAL VALUE
85% HAPPY READING
0% RISKY / ILLEGAL
MORE INFO? SEARCH THIS!
Simple solutions
Japanese business
Indian factory

SIMPLE SOLUTIONS

RE-WRITE LYRICS

UNFITTING SINGING VOCAL DEVOTION
EDUCATION RE-THINK

Caroline Törnberg runs the company *Vocal Devotion*, a company that helps peoples' singing voices through vocal training, voice treatment and wellness choirs. The idea is to offer lessons for both businesses and individuals, with "everyone can sing" as their mantra.

One day while teaching a group of children, Törnberg encountered a problem. The children wanted to sing popular music, such as songs by *Lady Gaga* and Swedish pop-singer *Erik Saade*. Many of Gaga's lyrics can be considered inappropriate for the younger audience and Saade's biggest hit is all about being popular, like it's the most important thing in the world. So, the problem was not in the music itself but in the inappropriate lyrics. The solution? Törnberg wrote new child-friendly lyrics to the songs, which included stories about candy, ghosts and pirates instead. Smart thinking.

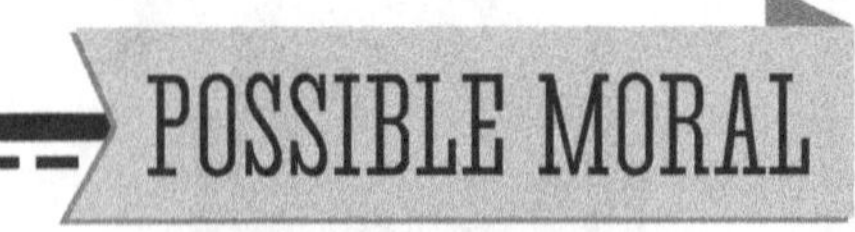

It's still the music that the kids love, but with a more appropriate lyrical content. A simple, clever and intelligent way of working around a problem.

Source: Anecdote from lecture with Caroline Törnberg at "Karriärdagen", Luleå University of Technology, 19 May, 2011.

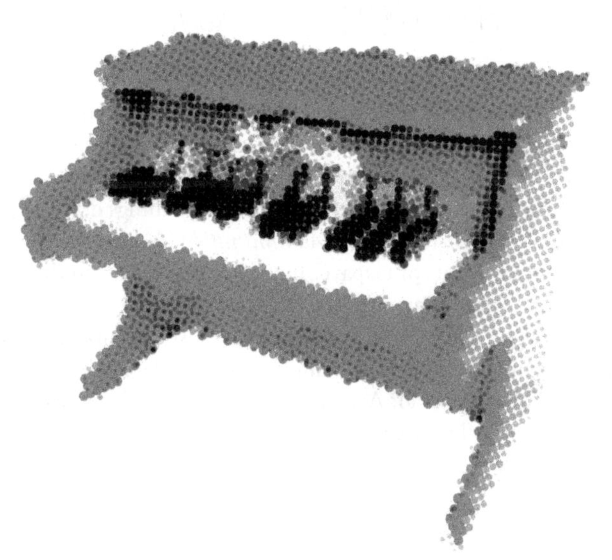

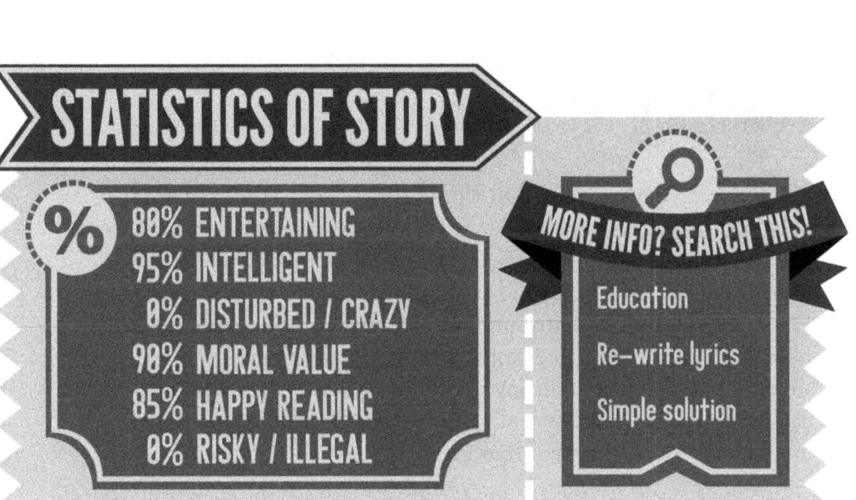
STATISTICS OF STORY
%
80% ENTERTAINING
95% INTELLIGENT
0% DISTURBED / CRAZY
90% MORAL VALUE
85% HAPPY READING
0% RISKY / ILLEGAL
MORE INFO? SEARCH THIS!
Education
Re-write lyrics
Simple solution

SIMPLE SOLUTIONS

RUSSIAN SPACE PEN

COSMONAUTS SOVIET NASA
RIGHT FOCUS EXPENSIVE INVESTMENT

During the space race in the 1960's the United States and Soviet both had a problem that needed a solution. They realized that the ballpoint pen wouldn't work in zero gravity, and that they needed to figure out another way for the astronauts/cosmonauts to be able to write things down.

The *National Aeronautics and Space Administration* (*NASA*) spent two years and millions of dollars of taxpayer money to develop a pen that could put ink onto paper without gravity. The result was the perfect pen that could write in weightlessness, upside down, on almost any surface and at temperatures ranging from below freezing to over 300 degrees Celsius.

So what did the Russians do? According to the legend, they solved the same problem – simply by using graphite pencils.

POSSIBLE MORAL

The Russian cosmonauts used an old, effective, cheap and tested solution. Why spend millions when you already have technology that works? Most of us tend to try and solve challenges by trying to hard, either to impress others or ourselves. I want you to try and perform the act of simplification. Eliminate all but the essential until you find the real issue and the basic need, and you are likely to discover a great yet basic solution. For me, to simplify is to also step inside my comfort zone. Thinking inside the box can many times be more rewarding than trying to achieve something original, expensive and mind-blowing.

Source: "Fact or Fiction?: NASA Spent Millions to Develop...", Scientific American, Ciara Curtin, 20 Dec, 2006.

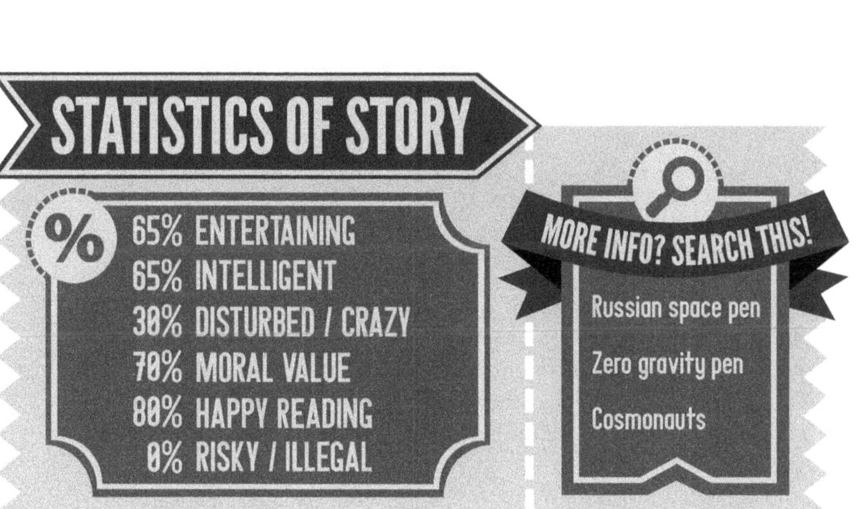
STATISTICS OF STORY
65% ENTERTAINING
65% INTELLIGENT
30% DISTURBED / CRAZY
70% MORAL VALUE
80% HAPPY READING
0% RISKY / ILLEGAL
MORE INFO? SEARCH THIS!
Russian space pen
Zero gravity pen
Cosmonauts

SIMPLE SOLUTIONS

SPOONACHOS

NEW SHAPE CONCEPT SCOOP
BUSINESS IDEA RE-DESIGN

In 2010, young designer Denis Bostandžić from Belgrade shared his concept of *Spoonachos* with the world. As you might guess by the name Bostandžić combined a regular nacho with the shape of a spoon. The idea behind the design was to make it easier for the user to scoop up salsa and dip. Although there are scoop shaped nacho chips already out there (called *Tostitos*), the *Spoonacho* adds a new dimension of cleverness. While the *Tostitos* was a momentous moment in the history of dipping, it has one conclusive flaw: Your thumb takes up half the scoop. *Spoonachos*, however, have a handle, which is a simple yet critical improvement on the design. Although *Spoonachos* are not yet available on the market, the idea will most likely be picked up and ready for sale in the near future.

The ordinary nacho simply isn't curved enough to do the job the *Spoonacho* can. With the *Spoonachos*, your salsa to-chip-ratio will get way better. In this case the improvement was to add a feature rather than to reduce one. The finished product on the other hand removes the need for extra cutlery and therefore helps to simplify. I'm seriously looking forward for these to hit the market.

Source: "Spoonachos™", Denis Bostandzic Blog, Oct, 2010.

STATISTICS OF STORY
50% ENTERTAINING
70% INTELLIGENT
0% DISTURBED / CRAZY
35% MORAL VALUE
45% HAPPY READING
0% RISKY / ILLEGAL
MORE INFO? SEARCH THIS!
Spoonachos
Denis Bostandzic
Concept design

SIMPLE SOLUTIONS

SWAN VESTA

NEW IDEA MATCH PRODUCTION COSTS SHARES INSIGHT

At the British match company *Swan Vesta*, an employee got a great yet simple idea while working. He went to the senior management and told them that he had thought of a way they could save themselves millions of pounds in production costs. He would reveal his idea to them if they agreed to give him a large share of the savings they were to make. They got the whole thing agreed with a solicitor, so that if they indeed were able to save millions, he'd be entitled to a share of the profits. His idea? He told them to only put a striking strip on one side of the matchbox instead of both sides (as they currently had). His suggestion was adopted and he retired a very wealthy person.

Never be afraid to present new ideas to the company for whom you work. After all, you probably have great insight about lots of things involving their products or production: Which parts that are the most expensive for the business, where the competitors are ahead of you etc. You might also be the one in contact with the customers themselves. In that way you know what people are missing or are unsatisfied with. Use this knowledge!

Sources: "Should we trust the wisdom of crowds?", BBC, 5 Jul, 2010. "Blue collar innovation", Wave, Katarina Ždraljevi, 17 Sep, 2011.

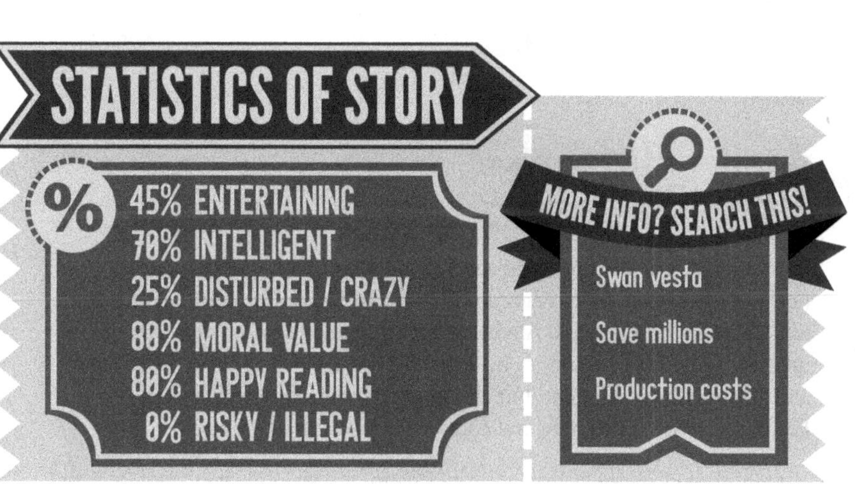
STATISTICS OF STORY
45% ENTERTAINING
70% INTELLIGENT
25% DISTURBED / CRAZY
80% MORAL VALUE
80% HAPPY READING
0% RISKY / ILLEGAL
MORE INFO? SEARCH THIS!
Swan vesta
Save millions
Production costs

SIMPLE SOLUTIONS

THE MEANING OF KODAK

NEOLOGISM RANDOM PIONEER
CONFIDENCE GEORGE EASTMAN

In 1888, a man named George Eastman started a photo business. He chose to call it "Kodak", a strange choice during this time as the word didn't mean anything. No one gave random names to reputable products or companies in those days. Eastman said that there were three principal concepts used when creating the name: It should be short, difficult to mispronounce and it shouldn't resemble or be associated with anything else.

The name *Kodak* is a so-called neologism, a completely made-up word or a newly coined term or phrase that may be in the process of entering common use, but has not yet been accepted into mainstream language. Neologisms are often directly attributable to a specific person, publication, period, or event.

In today's society, naming companies randomly or with names meaning nothing is probably more common than the other way around. Eastman was a pioneer in this sense. A rebel of brand standards, as he did what no one else was doing. Lessons to be learned: Dare to swim against the stream and do something different, but also believe in your ideas while doing so. Eastman had both meaning and confidence in his chosen name.

Source: "Where the Brand Name "Kodak" Came From", Today I Found Out, Daven Hiskey, 30 Dec, 2011.

STATISTICS OF STORY
55% ENTERTAINING
65% INTELLIGENT
0% DISTURBED / CRAZY
25% MORAL VALUE
60% HAPPY READING
45% RISKY / ILLEGAL
MORE INFO? SEARCH THIS!
The name kodak
George Eastman
Neologism

THE POWER OF SLEEP

MISTAKES SPEECH WAKE-UP CALL
HEALTH ISSUE SLEEP DEPRIVATION

Arianna Huffington is the co-founder and editor-in-chief of *The Huffington Post*. In 2011 she shared a fundamental idea at *TED* (online conferences on technology, entertainment and design) that has the potential of awakening much bigger ones: The power of a good night's sleep. Lack of sleep is one of the most intellectually and physically damaging of a number of underestimated problems facing people in modern age. Instead of bragging about our sleep deficits, she urges us to shut our eyes and see the big picture: We can sleep our way to increased productivity, happiness and smarter decision-making.

In 2007, Huffington understood that she was suffering from sleep deprivation. One day she suddenly passed out from exhaustion and banged her head in the fall. The result was a broken cheekbone and five stitches under her eyebrow. That's when Huffington knew she needed to renew her estranged relationship with sleep. They'd had a great relationship in the past, but as time went on and responsibilities piled up, they grew apart and took each other for granted. When sleep was back in Huffington's life, she pretty much became obsessed with it. She started to study about it, and found out that America as a nation had become deeply sleep deprived. Lack of sleep has for some reason become a sort of symbol for endurance and something to brag about.

Lack of sleep is bad for us in a number of different ways: It can lead to an increased risk of high blood pressure, obesity, diabetes, a weakened immune system, anxiety, depression and heart disease – and the risks are higher for women than for men. The damage can also have effects on other bedroom activities, nearly 25 percent of Americans say they have less sex or have lost interest in it because they are too sleepy. In the United States, sleep deprivation is also involved in one of every six fatal car crashes. As if this wasn't enough, sleep deprivation also severely affects relational memory, which task is to help us see the big picture and solve problems with creative and innovative breakthroughs.

Sources: "Women, It's Time to Sleep...", Huffington Post, 1 Jan, 2010. "How to succeed? Get more sleep", TEDTalks, Dec, 2010.

Sleep

POSSIBLE MORAL

Still reading this? If it's in the middle of the night, put the book down and go get some rest. Sleep your way to success!

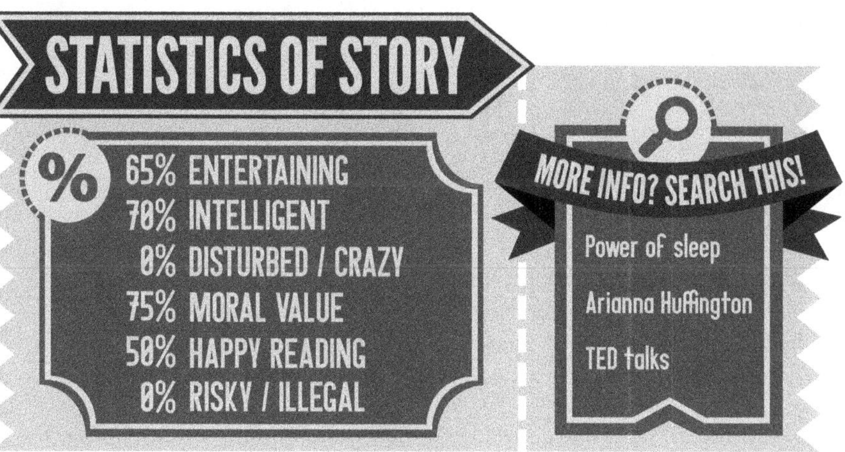

SIMPLE SOLUTIONS

TOOTHPASTE TUBE

INNOVATION SIMPLIFY IMAGINATION
SELL IDEA INCREASE SALES

Back in the 1950s a man approached one of the large toothpaste manufacturers and said that he had an innovation which would cost them almost nothing to implement, but would yield an immediate 40 percent increase in their business. He offered to sell them the exclusive rights to the idea for $100,000. This was a huge sum at the time, but given the high volume of toothpaste sales, it would be recouped rapidly. However, the executives of the company were greedy and would not spend such money if it could be avoided. They thanked the man and said they would get back to him.

Clearly interested in the man's innovation, the toothpaste manufacturer held a big meeting with the company's marketing and technical staff. They were tasked with proposing ideas for increasing business by 40 percent for little cost. Two weeks later, no useful ideas had emerged. So, they called back the man and said he had got a deal. After the legal niceties were completed and the money handed over, he gave them a brown envelope containing a small slip of paper. On this slip were the words: "Make the hole bigger".

By increasing the diameter of the hole from 5 mm to 6 mm, the volume of paste squeezed out for any given length of toothpaste along the brush is increased by 40 percent. So, most users will consume the tube that much faster and need to buy more.

POSSIBLE MORAL

This story serves to illustrate that simple ideas can come from simple imaginative thinking. Never question simple ideas for being "too simple". It's indeed easy to overlook these. Yet sometimes the best solution is to simplify the issue you're struggling with instead of looking for groundbreaking solutions.

Source: "Blue collar innovation", Wave, Katarina Ždraljevi, 17 Sep, 2011.

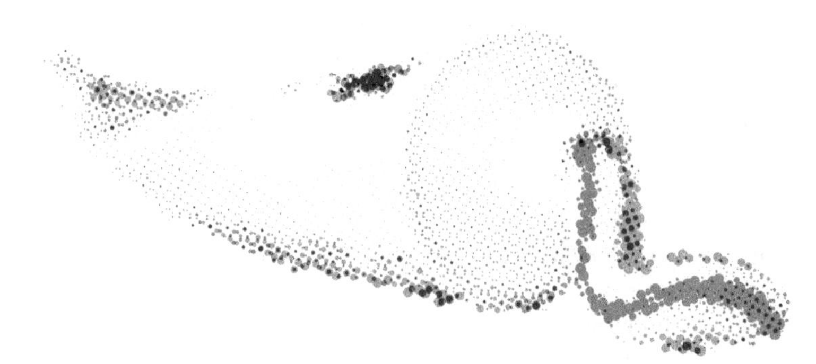

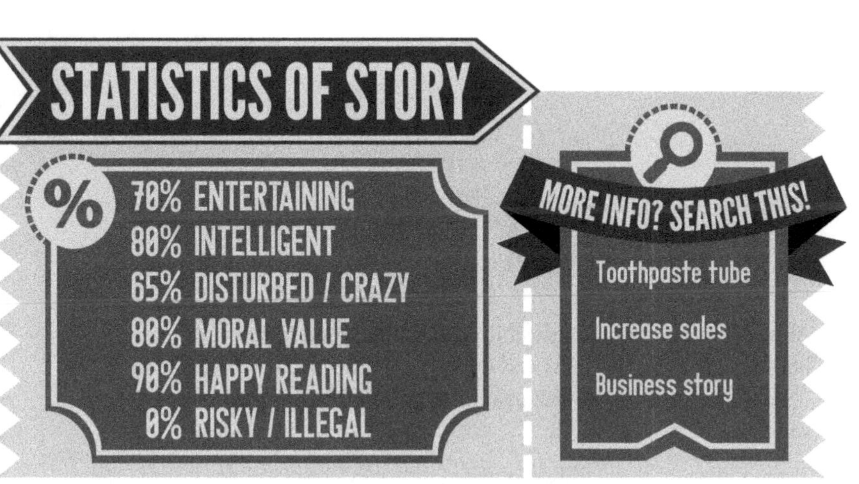
STATISTICS OF STORY
70% ENTERTAINING
80% INTELLIGENT
65% DISTURBED / CRAZY
80% MORAL VALUE
90% HAPPY READING
0% RISKY / ILLEGAL
MORE INFO? SEARCH THIS!
Toothpaste tube
Increase sales
Business story

SMART BUT DOUCHEY

LEON NORDIN SAYS NO

GOOD POINTS HARSH EGOISM
NEGATIVE AUTHORITY

Swedish copywriter and creative legend Leon Nordin is said to have been a man with both backbone and authority during his time in the advertising industry. He supposedly spoke his mind – to both clients and employees. In the 70's, Nordin is said to have created a list of ten "NO"-rules, somewhere along the following:

1. No, it will not be easy.
2. No, it will not be done quickly.
3. No, it's not going to be cheap.
4. No, you're not off the hook.
5. No, no committees.
6. No, we don't do pitch-missions.
7. No, we don't show any alternative solutions.
8. No, we don't do follow-up tests on communication.
9. No, you cannot take the sketch with you.
10. No, I don't care what your wife or husband thinks.

Although it may seem harsh, this list has some good points – which both people in the business and outside, can learn from. The different "NO"-rules probably works great in quite a number of customer situations. Use them wisely.

Source: "Leon Nordin säger nej. Tio gånger om", Please Copy Me – blog, Håkan Aludd and Mattias Åkerberg, 12 Aug, 2010.

NO

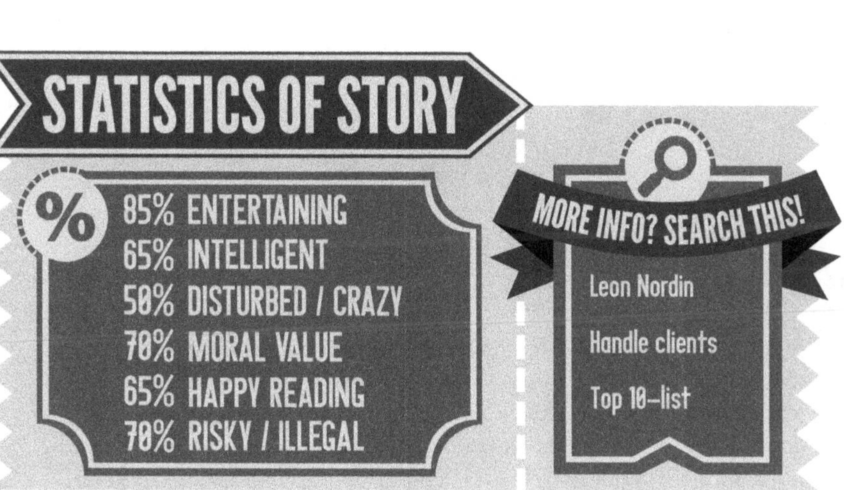
STATISTICS OF STORY
85% ENTERTAINING
65% INTELLIGENT
50% DISTURBED / CRAZY
70% MORAL VALUE
65% HAPPY READING
70% RISKY / ILLEGAL
MORE INFO? SEARCH THIS!
Leon Nordin
Handle clients
Top 10-list

SMART BUT DOUCHEY

NAIL STORY

RECRUITMENT HANDS POLICEMAN
ELIMINATION JOB INTERVIEWS

Tim Foster is a teacher at *Luleå University of Technology* in Sweden and holds classes in branding and marketing. As a guest lecturer for me and my graphic design class, Foster shared quite an interesting story about his father. His father worked as a policeman in the United States and later became responsible for recruitment of new personnel at his station. When holding these job interviews, his father had a trick that he used for years in order to tell what kind of person he was dealing with. At the end of each interview, he asked the applicant to show him their hands so that he could see their nails. If the nails were dirty, he assumed the person was lazy and would most likely do his job half-heartedly. If he or she couldn't even clean their nails for this interview, he sensed they wouldn't be fit for the job. If the person's nails were bitten, he saw it as a sign of the person being the nervous kind, a sign of low stress tolerance, not a suitable characteristic when being a police officer either. However, if the applicant had well kept nails he or she stood a better chance of being employed.

As a complement to the job interview, for Foster's father, this was a smart way of making sure he had the people he wanted on the force. Judging people by the look of their nails in an everyday situation would've been douchey, but in this specific situation I believe it was of good use.

Source: Anecdote from lecture with Tim Foster, "Karriärdagen", Luleå University of Technology, 19 Maj, 2011.

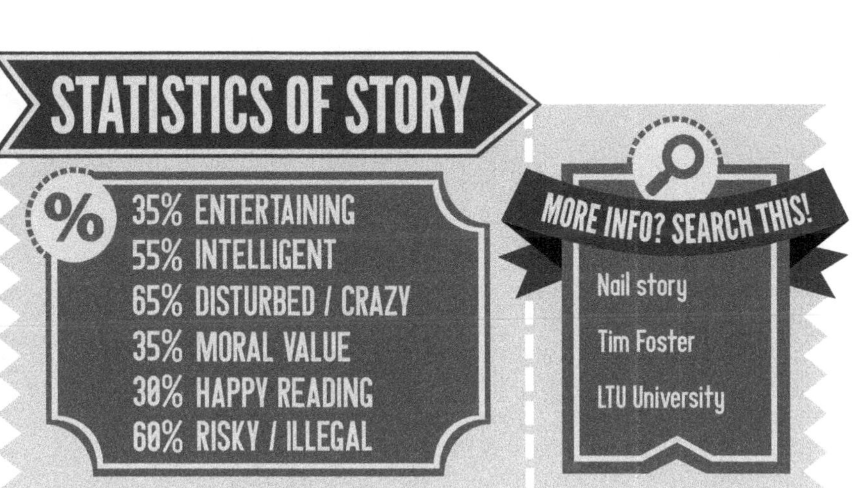
STATISTICS OF STORY
35% ENTERTAINING
55% INTELLIGENT
65% DISTURBED / CRAZY
35% MORAL VALUE
30% HAPPY READING
60% RISKY / ILLEGAL
MORE INFO? SEARCH THIS!
Nail story
Tim Foster
LTU University

SMART SAVERS

SQUARE MELONS

WATERMELON JAPAN SMALL SHOPS
LESS SPACE FARMERS

Japanese grocery stores have a problem. They are much smaller than the stores in the United States and therefore don't have a lot of space to waste. Watermelons, being big and round, wasted a lot of space. While most people would simply claim that watermelons grow round and there is nothing that can be done about it, some Japanese farmers took a different approach to the problem. If the grocery stores wanted more space, they asked themselves: "How can we provide it?".

It wasn't long before farmers in the southern Japanese town of Zentsuji found the solution: Making the watermelons square shaped. They found out that if you put a watermelon in a square box while it's growing, it will take on the shape of the box and grow into a square fruit. The result made the owners of the grocery stores happy since they could now stack the melons on top of each other like boxes. Another benefit was that it was much easier and cost effective to ship the watermelons. Consumers loved them because they took less space in their refrigerators, which are also much smaller than American ones. This also meant that the growers could charge a premium price for them.

POSSIBLE MORAL

Always look for a better solution. Creating square watermelons was simply a better and more convenient solution. The stores brought attention to a problem they were having and asked if a solution was possible. Remember, however, that it's impossible to find a better way if you are never asking the question in the first place. Get into the habit of asking yourself: "Is there a better way I could be doing this?" and you will find that there often is.

Source: "Square fruit stuns Japanese shoppers", BBC, 15 Jun, 2011.

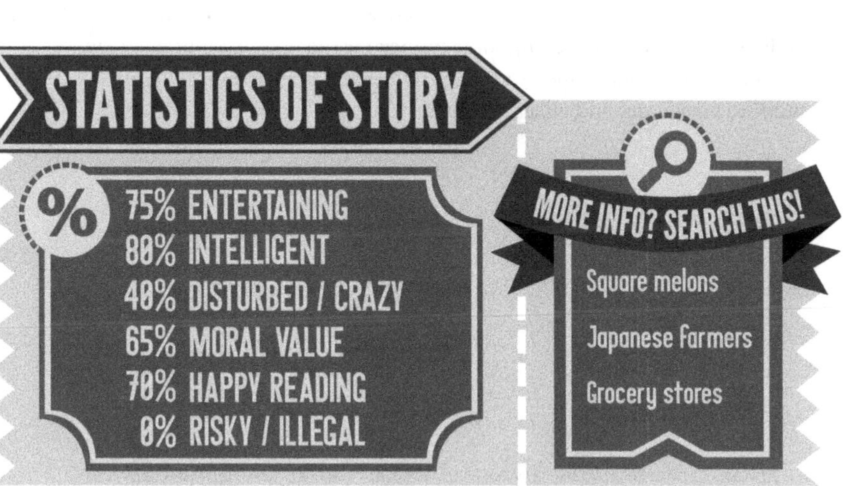
STATISTICS OF STORY
75% ENTERTAINING
80% INTELLIGENT
40% DISTURBED / CRAZY
65% MORAL VALUE
70% HAPPY READING
0% RISKY / ILLEGAL
MORE INFO? SEARCH THIS!
Square melons
Japanese farmers
Grocery stores

SPREAD OF JOY

A WALK AROUND BRITAIN

HOSPITALITY JOURNEY SINGING
FOLK SONGS BRITISH ISLANDS

During the years 2003 to 2011, two young men (Ed and Will) travelled by foot across Britain. They made journeys around the British Islands for as long as they could; some of these lasted for about nine months, while others were much shorter. They had no money, but managed simply by living in the wild and relying on the hospitality of strangers. Ed and Will have been nicknamed everything from "the hobbits" to "the smelly ones", and have been greatly appreciated by the people they've met. They claim that their faith in English hospitality has been restored after being treated so well.

Their adventures was documented and put on a website, where their project termed *A Walk Around Britain* is presented. On the website they share skills they've learned and experiences they've had along the way. During their walks they've also gathered local stories which they also share on their site.

Ed and Will's tips for other people eager to make journeys like theirs is to always carry something with you to give away, and to give away things as often as possible. For Ed and Will, that something was songs. This was a practical gift in the sense that songs don't weigh anything and there is an endless supply. When needing some money for the occasional beer, a new pair of socks or toilet paper, they sang traditional English folk songs in pubs, town squares and village gardens.

Sources: "The modern troubadours who sing for their supper", The Telegraph, 16 Apr, 2009. "About", awalkaroundbritain.com, 2011.
Quotes: From awalkaroundbritain.com, "Who We Are", 2011.

POSSIBLE MORAL

Quotes from awalkaroundbritain.com, "Who We Are" (2011):
"Walking defines us. We are the upright strollers of the great ape family. The perspectives opened by walking are the keys to our kind. For the mind, soul and body, walking is an expansive act – it opens gates into the landscape, turning quick blurry images into smells, aches and wonders. It shows the hedgerows daily bubble toward glory, then fade to cold sleep. It lets you hear the birds, screaming the seasons. It welcomes you direct into the great event of life on these islands. No other qualifications are needed; just go out, and be on foot".

"For today's people, living in 21st century England, coming-of-age ceremonies are plastic and terrible. With our elders locked in overheated boxes, our children protected from everything, how then shall we grow? With whose help shall we learn our abilities and strengths, to know our land, and our place amongst everything?".

"The journey gives encounters that can shake everything previously learned, meetings whose significance seems to echo through earliest memories. Walking allows fate to get closer".

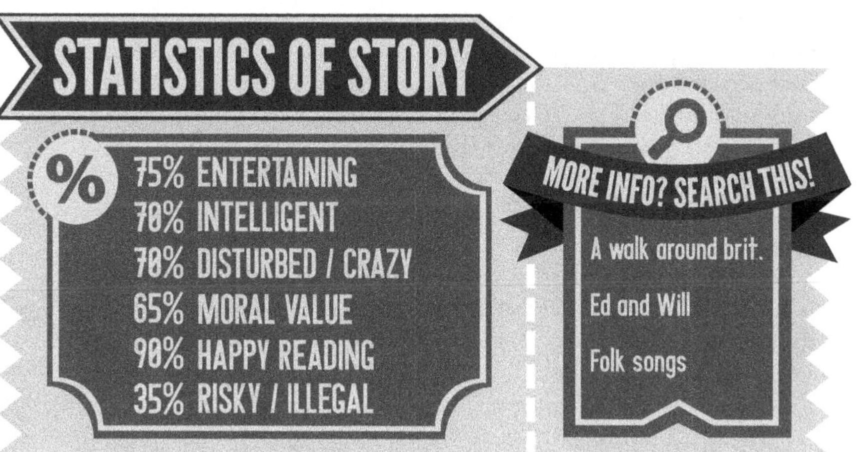

STATISTICS OF STORY
%
75% ENTERTAINING
70% INTELLIGENT
70% DISTURBED / CRAZY
65% MORAL VALUE
90% HAPPY READING
35% RISKY / ILLEGAL
MORE INFO? SEARCH THIS!
A walk around brit.
Ed and Will
Folk songs

SPREAD OF JOY

ALICE'S BUCKET LIST

BRAVERY CANCER BONE MARROW DONATION
GOALS #ALICESBUCKETLIST

Alice Pyne, aged 16, has been battling a deadly form of cancer for the last five years, and unfortunately the cancer is spreading throughout her body. Alice started a blog as a way to keep her friends and family updated on her progress, and thought it would be "fun" to write a so-called "bucket list". Inspired by the movie *The Bucket List*, she writes about 17 things she wants to do before she dies.

On the blog Alice writes: "Mum always tells me that life is what we make of it and so I'm going to make the best of what I have, and because there were so many things I still wanted to do, mum suggested that I turn my ideas into a bucket list. I'm 16 and I have terminal cancer. I've created a bucket list because there are so many things I still want to do in my life... some are possible, some will remain a dream. My blog is to document this precious time with my family and friends, doing the things I want to do. You only have one life... live it!".

Alice's Bucket List has since become one of the most popular topics online with people from all around the world, including pop star Katy Perry, using *Twitter* to spread the *hashtag* (a form of metadata tag) *alicesbucketlist*. Alice's first post on the blog has received more than 900 comments. Her second post, where she expressed her surprise at the number of people who read her first post, had nearly 300 posts after just a few hours of being online. Alice says she's excited about crossing items off her bucket list, and hopes to take pictures and blog about her experiences, but most of all, she's glad people are joining bone marrow donation registers because of her.

Thousands of people have left messages of support on Alice's blog and many have even offered to help her tick off some of the items on her list. Swimming with sharks, having her hair done "if they can do anything with it", and entering her dog, Mabel, in a regional Labrador show are among the things she still wants to do. One of her biggest wishes is that "everyone sign up to be a bone marrow donor", something that has now even been discussed in the British parliament. Prime Minister David Cameron

Sources: "Alice's Bucket List: dying girl's blog...", The Guardian, 9 Jun, 2011. "About Me", alicepyne.blogspot.com, 2012.
Quotes: From Alice Pyne's offical blog, alicepyne.blogspot.com.

promised to work with the Leader of the Opposition to try and achieve Alice's wish, addressing the problem that too few people are currently on this life-saving register.

POSSIBLE MORAL

We can't control what happens to us, but we can control how we react to challenges. Our responses to those obstacles are an important part of who we are. With her blog, Alice spreads joy and hope to the world, and at the same time put a lot of effort in encouraging her readers to become donors. Alice has an amazing goal and is doing a very brave and admirable act. She is savoring every moment she can, and challenging the rest of us to consider something we often try to avoid thinking about: "If today was your last day on earth, how would you spend it?".

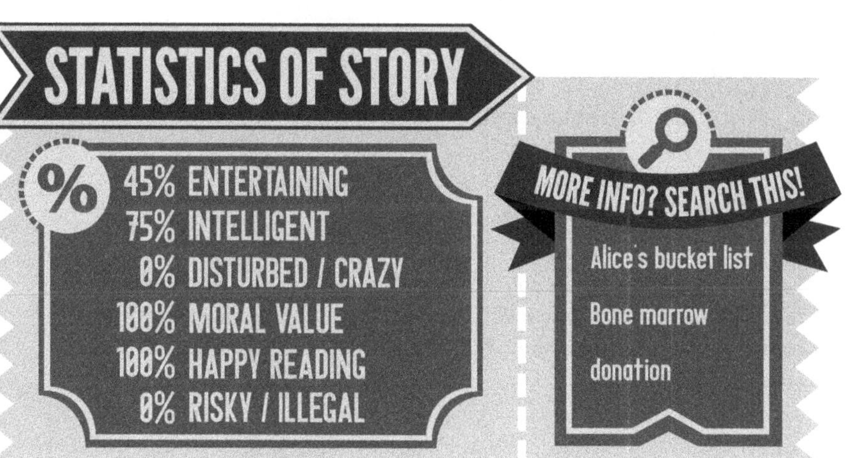

SPREAD OF JOY

FAKE IT TILL YOU MAKE IT

PERFORMANCE YOUTUBE RONALD JENKEES
INSPIRATIONAL MUSIC PRODIGY

Ronald Jenkees is an American *YouTube*-fenomena best known for his entertaining keyboard performances. Jenkees is an odd fellow that loves what he's doing. He doesn't read music, he plays by ear, and he's self-taught. He plays music just because it's pure fun for him, and he wants to share his joy with everyone else. Jenkees is promoting the exact right thing: It shouldn't be about the money, it should be about the music.

His *YouTube* videos has been viewed over 60 million times, and he's released two independent albums. Needless to say, people fell in love with this happy Kentucky nerd and his music. However, a recent rumor has it that Ronald Jenkees is a made up persona, an entertainment act. This has created a internet fuss, with fans showing anger and disappointment towards him because they feel betrayed.

In my own opinion, real or fake, the man is a musical prodigy. If he's using a fake persona, it's a brilliant marketing move. I'm certain this act of his is what made him grow so popular. Had he just been playing his music, far less people would have noticed him. What's so bad about having a fake persona? Here's a little story for you haters out there. There was a kid named David Jones who wanted to be a rock star. He took on a fake name, created a fake persona, complete with makeup and outlandish outfits and ended up doing pretty well for himself. His "fake" name? *David Bowie.*

Sources: "About me", ronaldjenkees.com, 2012. "ronaldjenkees" at YouTube.

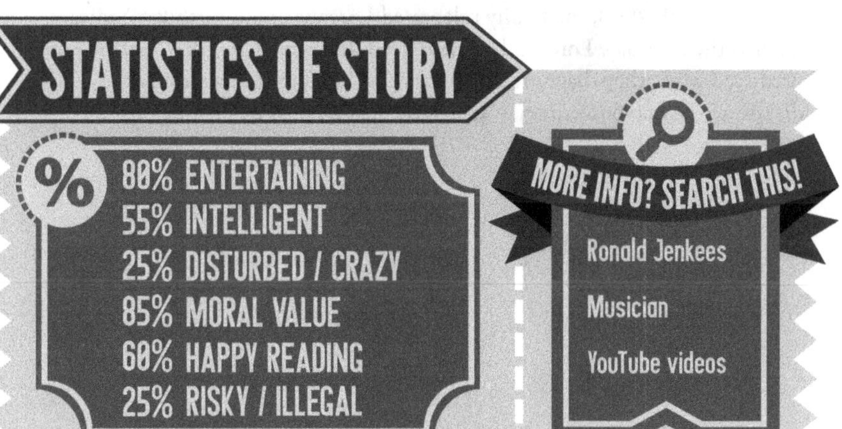
STATISTICS OF STORY
80% ENTERTAINING
55% INTELLIGENT
25% DISTURBED / CRAZY
85% MORAL VALUE
60% HAPPY READING
25% RISKY / ILLEGAL
MORE INFO? SEARCH THIS!
Ronald Jenkees
Musician
YouTube videos

LORENZO'S OIL

TREATMENT LOVE DID THE IMPOSSIBLE
RESEARCH INCURABLE DISEASE

In 1984, Lorenzo Odone, only 6-years-old, was diagnosed with a disease so rare that nobody was working on a cure, so his father, Augusto Odone, decided to learn all about it and tackle the problem himself. Lorenzo's father asked the doctor if he could read the available medical papers. He said: "Don't bother, you won't understand them". Undeterred, Augusto spent night after night in the library scouring every single paper about his son's illness. He discovered that the brain damage seemed to be linked to a buildup of dangerous, long chain fatty acids in the blood. Augusto invited all the worlds experts to a conference to discuss the research, and it was at the conference that he first found a glimpse of hope. An oil, oleic acid, was able to destroy the fatty acids.

Less than a year later Augusto and his wife Michaela had created a treatment for their son: A combination of oils that effectively reduced the long chain fatty acids in his blood. It was astonishing. Where the entire medical profession had failed, two ordinary parents had succeeded. *Lorenzo's Oil*, as the treatment oil has been named, is showing a significant preventive effect. According to Dr. Hugo Moser, taking the oil reduces the chance of getting the disease by 50 percent.

On May 29, 2008, the family celebrated Lorenzo's 30th birthday. Sadly, he died the next day. Lorenzo had then lived 22 years longer than doctors predicted when they diagnosed him with this incurable, degenerative disease of the nervous system at the age of six.

Sources: "Lorenzo's oil: The full story", BBC, 21 Jul, 2004. "The boy who inspired Lorenzo's...", The Daily Mail, 31 May, 2008.

POSSIBLE MORAL

There's nothing like a parent's love for their child, and due to their love Augusto and Michaela Odone created their own miracle. They chose not to give up and struggled to overcome the obstacles. Despite the negative circumstances they went to look for ways to develop a cure and eventually they triumphed over the disease that was slowly taking their son away from them. In the end, they didn't only save their son but a lot of other people as well through their creation.

SPREAD OF JOY

RELATIONSHIP MARKETING

HELIKOPTER CLIENTS FUN
STAND OUT COMPETITION

Gunnar Forslund is a Swede who has worked with advertising and marketing for over 25 years, primarily as an entrepreneur. In the last 20 years, he's founded a number of companies such as *Reklamcity*, *Piteå Dansar och Ler*, *North Bend Sweden* and *Helikopter Advertising Agency*. During an interview I had with Forslund, he shared stories from his time working at *Helikopter*. At the time, there was a ongoing war between advertising agencies on who could think of the best ways of making themselves seen and heard. This wasn't happening in public, but on the *relationship marketing* battlefield, i.e. only targeting the agencies current or future clients. For *Helikopter* it was a way of saying "we like you", or "please come back". In this non-public marketing platform, they could also show off their level of creativity in a much more relaxed and fun way than in the everyday situations with clients. Giving the client the feel that this agency is up to date, a trendsetter and what not. These are three of Forslund's favorite memories from his *relationship marketing* with *Helikopter*:

Sweets with invoice/bill

Helikopter ordered hundreds of lollipops with their logo printed on them. They then posted them together with the invoices sent to the clients. A simple act that made them stand out from the crowd. They included something appreciated together with something that's not as appreciated. One day they'd almost run out of lollipops. When Forslund was asked by a colleague if they should order new ones he said: "Nah, I don't think anyone will miss them". However, when the last lollipop had been sent, it didn't take long before costumers got in touch with them asking: "Have you stopped with the sweets?". The people at *Helikopter* was pretty chocked about how appreciated their lollipops had been.

Invisible Ink

At one time they printed a flyer-advertisement for their agency with invisible ink: Really expensive, and really fun. The ink reacted to heat.

Source: Anecdotes from interview with Gunnar Forslund (www.2tango.nu), Feb, 2012.

If one held the paper close to a lamp, a tea light or a radiator – the ink would get visible. It went back being invisible when you removed it from the heat. The flyer had some hints printed in regular ink, on what could be done with the paper. *Helikopter* created a possible interaction with a simple dull paper.

Millennium
In the end of year 1999, many companies fought over who could create the best New Year's greeting. It was a big thing, entering a new millennium. *Helikopter* got the great idea of focusing on a completely different date than the rest of the agencies. They chose to send out their greeting-cards on the 5th of February instead. Why? Simply because *Chinese New Year* is celebrated on that date. Year 2000 was the year of the Dragon, and according to the Chinese zodiac the Dragon is the mightiest of the signs. Dragons symbolize such character traits as dominance and ambition. After learning about this, the people at *Helikopter* bought semi-transparent paper bags, and filled them with tarragon spice (also known as *dragon's wort*). Including the message: "Now you might think we're a little behind. But we just want to greet you a Happy New Year – the Chinese way!". A cute message, looking like the paper inside a Chinese fortune cookie read: "If you're successful, so will we be".

POSSIBLE MORAL

The over-all moral of story is that competition is a good thing. It makes us perform more, and do better! Never underestimate the effect of a small action or gesture. Also, be sure to take good care of your clients.

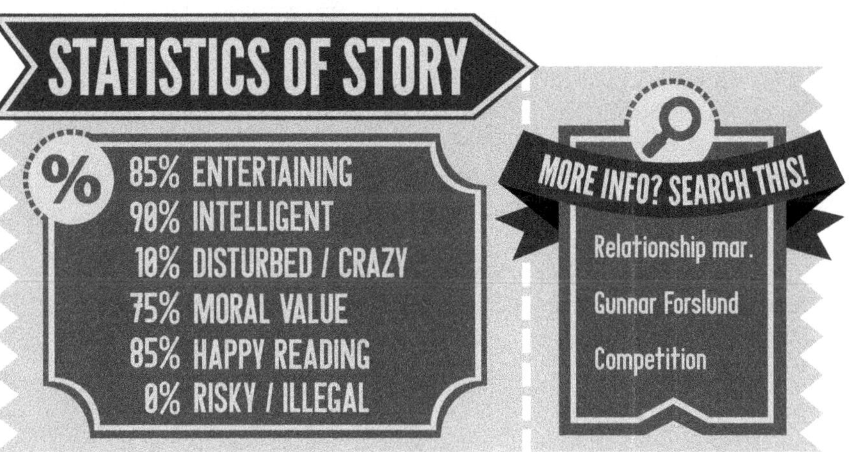

SPREAD OF JOY
SCIENTIST CUPCAKE BAKER

MOTIVATIONAL DREAMER HELLO SUGAR
HARD WORK COMPUTER SCIENTIST

The cupcake trend has swept both retail and in-store bakeries and has extended its reach to supermarket shelves. The popularity of cupcakes grew with help from the TV-show *Sex and the City*, where the lead characters ate cupcakes at Manhattan's upscale *Magnolia Bakery*. It didn't take long before the cakes took its place as the new favorite on-the-go snack, and suddenly cupcake towers begun to replace traditional wedding cakes.

Åsa Hellgren was living in the United States studying to become a system analyst (computer scientist), and later got work as an IT-manager in Texas. The company was doing a lot of events where they offered participants snacks and Åsa was the one who ended up taking care of the catering-part. She felt that she had an underlying passion for baking, and she wanted to get involved. In her spare time she had always loved baking. She soon discovered the art of American cupcakes, and fell in love with the impressive looking cakes with their colorful frosting. In Sweden, cupcakes were far from as popular as in the United States, and Åsa started thinking that there was a market for them there as well. So, after four years she decided to quit her job and move back home. After six months she had started her business *Hello Sugar* and was suddenly baking cupcakes from early morning to late at night, creating handmade cakes for weddings, birthday-parties and other festive events.

Åsa works alone, both baking and managing invoices and orders on her computer. She has run her one-person business in Stockholm since 2009. She's behind all of it – from concept to baking and cake design research. Having only herself to thank for the business's success is part of the charm of a solo enterprise, she says it feels really great when you feel you've managed to get through all the obstacles on your own.

Åsa Hellgren is one of those who contributed to introducing the American cupcake-wave to Sweden. *Hello Sugar* has become a successful business and has been praised in both newspapers, magazines and on TV.

Sources: "Smarriga cupcakes – vi guidar...", Expressen, 5 May, 2010. "Åsa vågade satsa på drömjobbet", Piteå Tidningen, 31 Dec, 2010.

POSSIBLE MORAL

It's unexpected that Åsa, a trained computer scientists, would become a full-time cupcake baker. Åsa Hellgren's story is about leaving your comfort zone, and going all in for something you truly love. A great and encouraging example of the "following your dream"-mindset.

What's your dream? What would you love to do with your life if you had the time and resources? Travel? Work as a volunteer? Devote yourself to a craft or hobby? By knowing your dream, you have a powerful motivator to make changes in your life.

SPREAD OF JOY

SPOT-ON JOB INTERVIEW

CARLSBERG GOALS FEEDBACK ATTITUDE JOB INTERVIEW

The Danish brewing company *Carlsberg* has a lovely attitude towards job applicants. Instead of, like many other companies, who either ignore applicants or call and say: "We're sorry, you didn't get the job", *Carlsberg* choose a much smarter approach. They simply don't want people to leave thinking *Carlsberg* is a lousy company. Therefore, those who don't get the job are answered: "Sorry, we can't give you the job, but if you want we can offer you feedback on your interview to tell you what was good and what you can improve". This is of course very much appreciated by the men and women who apply. Even if they don't get the job, they can still go home with some feedback on how to improve, rather than having to wonder what they did wrong.

What a great thing to do. Without feedback it's hard to understand what you may be doing wrong. Receiving feedback after an interview provides important pointers to improve and prepare you for the next one. This is also a smart marketing move by *Carlsberg*. I'm just waiting for the "probably the best job interview in the world" campaign.

Source: Anecdote from lecture with Tomas Hellgren (www.kreatek.se), Piteå Företagarcentrum, 27 Feb, 2012.

INTERVIEW
IN PROGRESS

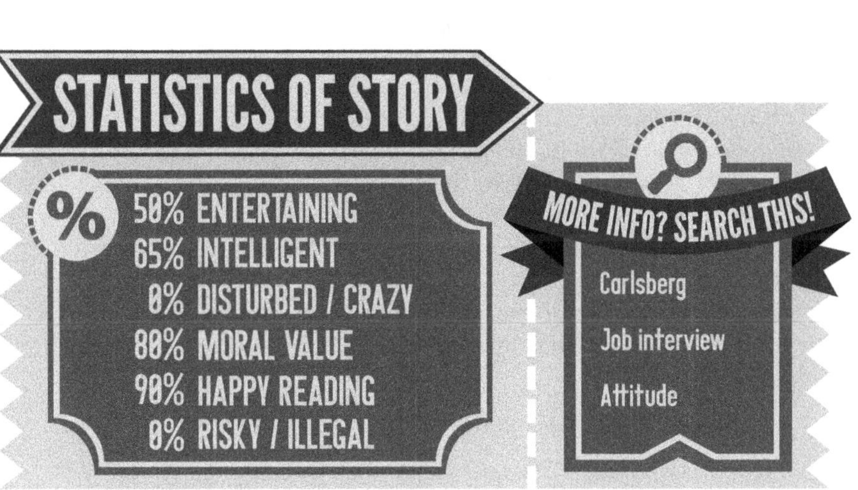
STATISTICS OF STORY
%
50% ENTERTAINING
65% INTELLIGENT
0% DISTURBED / CRAZY
80% MORAL VALUE
90% HAPPY READING
0% RISKY / ILLEGAL
MORE INFO? SEARCH THIS!
Carlsberg
Job interview
Attitude

SPREAD OF JOY

THE FUN THEORY

BEHAVIOR GUERRILLA EXPERIMENT
PIANO STAIRS VOLKSWAGEN

The Fun Theory is an advertising campaign created by *Volkswagen* in 2009. It was launched to generate interest in *Volkswagen*'s *BlueMotion technologies* that deliver the same great car performance with reduced environmental impact, and to do this, they found an insight around how "fun" could change human behavior for the better. They installed different experiments, used hidden cameras and recorded the reactions of the people in true guerrilla marketing fashion. Volkswagen created a competition called *The Fun Theory Award*, where they encouraged people to create their own fun theories (concepts and sketches) and compete with them. The prize? €2,500 and turning your idea into reality.

The result of the campaign became a huge success with a tremendous amount of views for the uploaded videos. One part of the project that has been greatly appreciated is *Piano stairs*, which was installed by the worldwide marketing communications network *DDB* in Stockholm, Sweden. "Take the stairs instead of the escalator or elevator and feel better" is something we often hear or read in the papers. Few people follow that advice. *Volkswagen* wanted to see if they could get more pedestrians to take the stairs than the escalator, by making it fun to do so. *DDB* turned the regular metro-stairs into a full working piano. The steps were made into keys that played notes when walking on them. The result was that people chose the stairs 66 percent more often. In October of 2009, the video *piano stairs* ranked at the top of *The Viral Video Chart*, a list of the world's most widely circulated viral videos. The film is the most commented and referenced movie there of all time.

Another experiment that was part of *The Fun Theory* was successful in testing whether making a trash can sound like a 50ft-deep well would make people stop littering. An additional experiment turned a bottle-recycling center into an arcade game.

Sources: "Viral marknadsföring växer", Svenska Dagbladet, 2 Nov, 2009. "Volkswagen's Viral Video Serie...", Viralblog, Oct, 2009.

POSSIBLE MORAL

This campaign is dedicated to the concept that something as simple as having fun is the easiest way to change people's behavior for the better; be it for yourself, for the environment, or for something entirely different. The only thing that matters is that it's change for the better. This is social marketing: Remember that it's not always about the monetary profits, but about the social profits too.

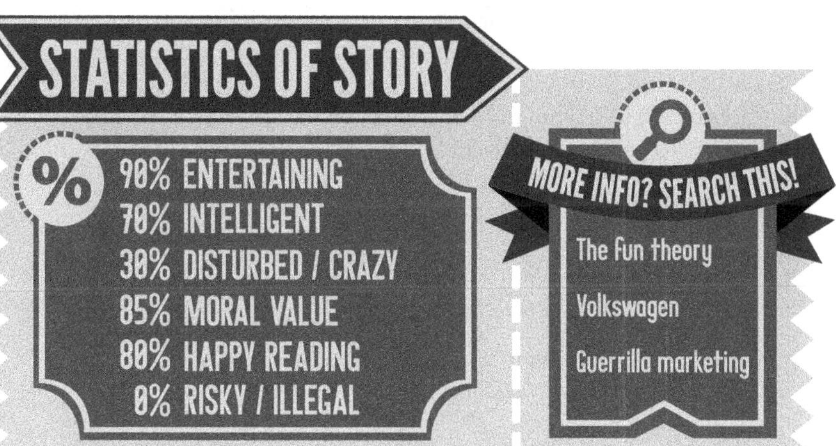

STORIES OF TIMING

ARTIST STOCK PAYMENT

PAYMENT GAMBLE PAINTING
FACEBOOK STREET ARTIST

In 2005 the 35-year old artist David Choe did some gambling and made himself into a millionaire. He was hired by former *Facebook* president Sean Parker to paint a mural at *Facebook*'s first office in Palo Alto, California. When the mural was finished, Parker gave Choe the option of being paid in cash or in stock options. At the time, *Facebook* was only a year old and only open to college and high school students. There was no "like" button, no revenue from advertising and no hype of a $5 billion dollar initial public offering (IPO). Even so, he chose to go with the stocks as payment.

Choe was added on as an "adviser" and received 0.1 to 0.25 percent of the company earnings. Today, after the huge success of *Facebook* – you do the math! Choe's share of the company is now worth somewhere around $200 million. That's a mind-blowing figure, especially if you consider that he was homeless after having painted that fateful mural. In 2003 he led a difficult life, doing jail time for cashing forged checks, stealing, and assaulting a security guard. Choe, who now lives in Los Angeles, said he thought that the idea of *Facebook*, famously founded in 2004 by Mark Zuckerberg in his *Harvard University* dorm room, was "ridiculous and pointless" at the time.

Today, his work can be seen in galleries all over the world. The artist, who began spray-painting in his teens, created the cover art for Jay-Z and Linkin Park's multi-platinum album *Collision Course* in 2004. In 2008, he also painted a portrait of the then Senator Barack Obama – a painting that now hangs in *the White House.*

Source: "Facebook IPO Turns Graffiti Artist David Choe Into Multi-Millionaire", ABC News, 2 Feb, 2012.

POSSIBLE MORAL

The decision seven years ago by a Korean-American muralist and graffiti artist to turn down thousands of dollars in cash for his work made him a very, very, rich man. The story points out why one should think twice before choosing the instant reward, in this case getting paid in money. Do more jobs for free. Take a chance to be repaid in other ways, but remember that gambling on a dot com can either make you miserable or make millionaires out of receptionists.

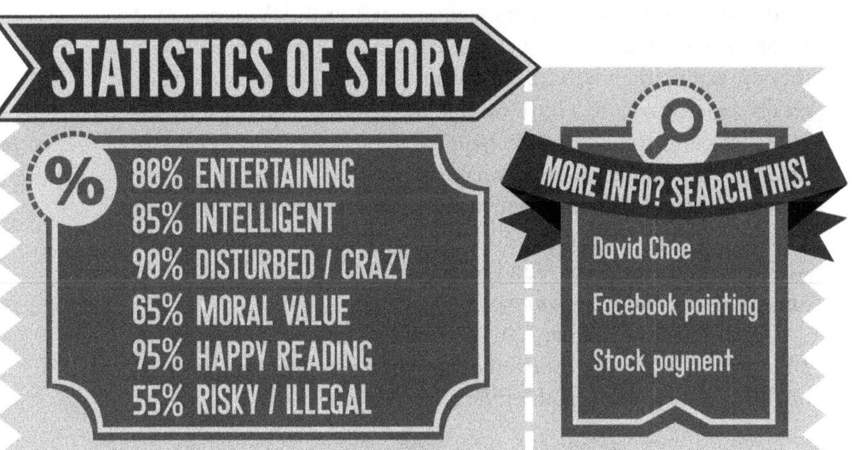

STATISTICS OF STORY
%
80% ENTERTAINING
85% INTELLIGENT
90% DISTURBED / CRAZY
65% MORAL VALUE
95% HAPPY READING
55% RISKY / ILLEGAL
MORE INFO? SEARCH THIS!
David Choe
Facebook painting
Stock payment

STORIES OF TIMING

SERENDIPITY

COINCIDENCE SUCCESS ACCIDENT
GREAT VALUE STUMBLING UPON

Serendipity refers to looking for one thing and stumbling over something else that proves to be of greater value. *Serendipity* means a "happy accident" or "pleasant surprise"; specifically, the accident of finding something good or useful without looking for it.

The music group Roxette got their breakthrough in the United States in 1989. How? Because a college DJ played their song *The Look* continuously for weeks. The song topped the singles chart later that year, all thanks to this young DJ's choice of music.

Harry Potter books have made J. K. Rowling one of Britain's wealthiest people and a whole generation are now familiar with the concept of *Muggles*, *Hogwarts* and *Platform 9 3/4* at *Kings Cross Station* in London. When she wrote the first *Harry Potter* book, Rowling worked hard to get the book published. Twelve different publishing houses rejected her. Finally, Barry Cunningham from *Bloomsbury*, a small publishing house in London gave the green light. The decision to publish Rowling's book apparently owes much to Alice Newton, the eight-year-old daughter of *Bloomsbury*'s chairman, who was given the first chapter to review by her father and immediately demanded the next.

The Swedish humor duo Filip Hammar and Fredrik Wikingsson shares a story over their podcast. When they visited the *Apple store* in New York, they opened up their website on various computers in the store. Filip recalls standing next to a little kid thinking: "What if he was to like one of our video clips, and his dad just happens to be Leslie Moonves and head of CBS? Then you never know what happens".

Whisky distillery *Ardbeg* happened to mix the contents of their own whiskey barrel of single malt whiskey with another distilleries single malt whiskey. The mixture was found to be successful and bottled and sold under the very name *Serendipity*.

On the night of February 24, 1987, while working in Chile for the *University of Toronto*, Ian Shelton discovered a previously undetected bright light on a photograph of the *Large Magellanic Cloud*. Initially

Sources: "Lägesrapport!", Filip & Fredrik blog, 20 Feb, 2012. "Revealed: The eight-year-old girl who saved Harry...", New Zealand Herald, 3 Jul, 2005. "Serendi(pity)", The Ardbeg Project, 1 Apri, 2005. '"Whole new science...", Edmonton Journal, 25 Feb, 2007.

sceptical, Shelton went outside to look with a naked eye, and saw that the bright light was indeed present. His discovery turned out to be a supernova, the first visible to the naked eye since Johannes Kepler's observation in year 1604. One of the greatest astronomical discoveries of the twentieth century unfolded. At a lecture at *Telus World of Science* in Edmonton year 2007, Sheldon jokingly said that discovering a supernova tends to look good on an astronomer's resume. It helped him get into graduate school and still makes good conversation at cocktail-parties. Sheldon's discovery is a great example of *serendipity*. Someone else would have seen it first if he hadn't. As it later turned out, an amateur astronomer in New Zealand saw it the same night.

POSSIBLE MORAL

The triumph of coincidence. *Serendipity* or "fortunate discovery" stories teach us that things can change in an instant. Things aren't always what they seem. Struggling and depressed one minute, and rich and happy beyond our wildest dreams the next. Sometimes we people fantasize about these scenarios, and sometimes they actually happen.

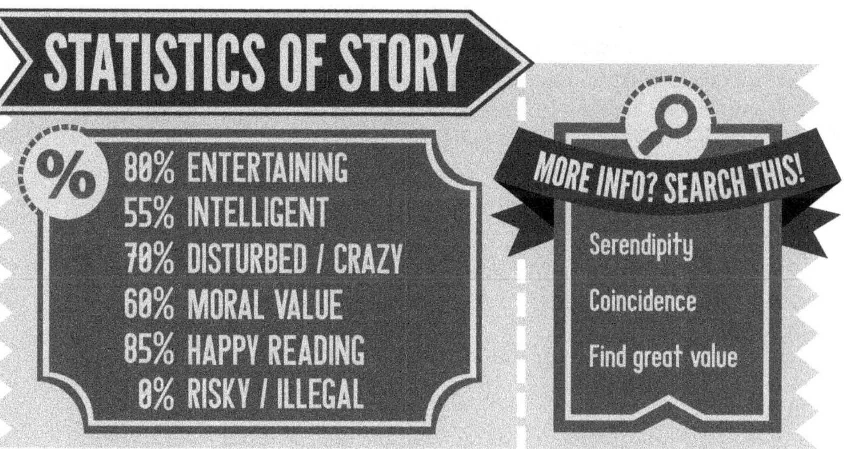

WHERE THE ACTION IS

LUCKY BREAKS CONTROL GET INVOLVED
STAY ACTIVE MEET LIKE-MINDED

As we all know it's not always the ones that get educated and work hard that become successful. Being at the right place at the right time is a great way to reach success. You most likely know of someone that has the mysterious ability to always be where the action is. But what does it really mean to be in the right place at the right time? And can we control it? I do believe we can.

My first tip to get more "lucky breaks" in your life is to make it a habit to meet regularly with like-minded people that have the same or similar goals you want to achieve. The more you gather with these people the more opportunities you'll discover to learn, advance and network. To stay active gives you the best chance of being at the right place at the right time. So, tip number two is to create this habit for yourself. You can do so by being active in various organizations, clubs and groups. Stay active on social network websites, blogs and online forums that focus on your profession or topics of interest. The third tip involves the importance of getting involved and contributing to organizations in your neighborhood, for example where you live or work. This is one of the best ways to establish connections and relationships. Share suggestions and ideas, help out, ask questions, answer questions and help others get answers. In an age where everyone wants to be a spectator, entertained or helped, do the opposite by helping others. Listening instead of talking is also of great importance. Most people don't realize the power to simply sit down, listen and pay attention to what someone has to tell you (look up *The power of listening* on page 96).

Sources: Thoughts by Simon Zingerman and "How To Be In The Right Place At The Right Time More Often", Lifehack, 1 Apr, 2010.

POSSIBLE MORAL

Being in the right place doesn't mean standing in a physical location, it means having your life in the right place. It means creating opportunities and setting yourself up to take advantage of them. It also means being responsible, live cheap, reserve some free time and have some savings, so that when an amazing opportunity comes around you can take it. What most see as luck I see as an opportunity. By trying out these different methods you will soon find yourself ending up where the action is more frequently than before.

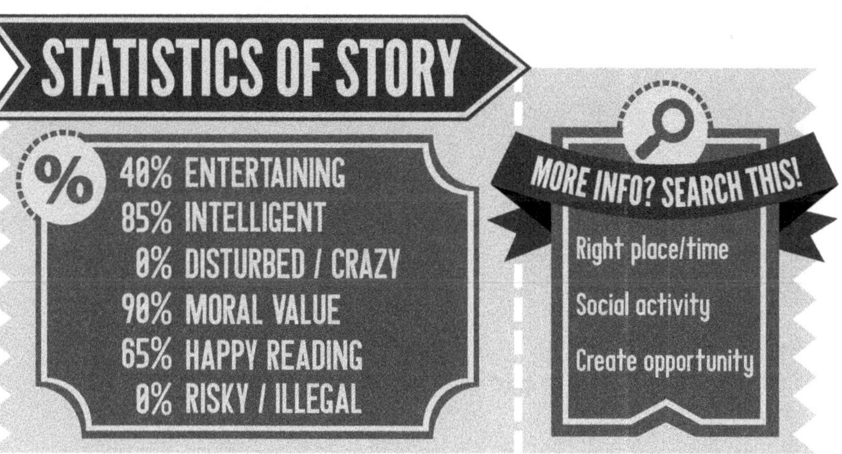

STUPID STUFF, STUPID AUDIENCE

AFTERLIFE TELEGRAMS

GREETINGS DEATH TERMINALLY ILL
VOLUNTEERS MEMORIZE

Afterlife Telegrams offers to send greetings from the living to the dead. For a donation of $5 per word (five word minimum), one can have telegrams delivered to those who have passed away. This is done with the help of terminally ill volunteers who memorize the telegrams and then deliver them after they die. Since the company can't guarantee delivery nor prove that a message has been delivered successfully, the customers do not pay for "deliveries". They pay for "delivery attempts". The paid fee, depending on the wishes of the messenger, is either given to a relative, donated to a charity or used to pay for medical bills.

No matter how stupid this idea might seem, one needs to remember that the market, just like humanity, takes twists and turns and is also determined by demand. What we at first deem useless might end up being the next best-seller. It can be the product's novelty, fun factor or sheer stupidity. Whatever the case, just remember there's always room on the market for an original business idea, which might just earn you success.

Source: "Afterlife Telegrams", Something Awful, 7 Feb, 2003.

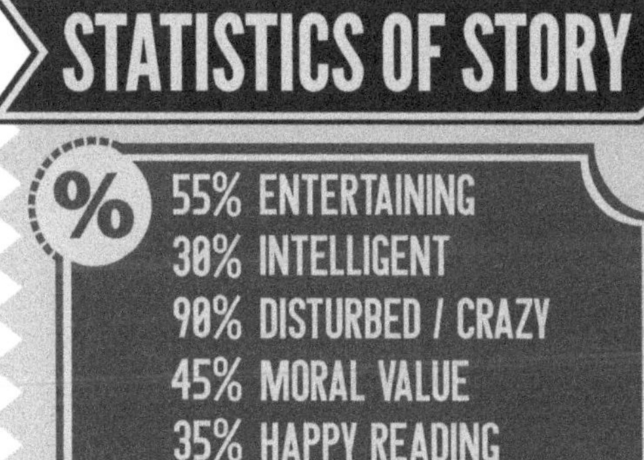
STATISTICS OF STORY
%
55% ENTERTAINING
30% INTELLIGENT
90% DISTURBED / CRAZY
45% MORAL VALUE
35% HAPPY READING
50% RISKY / ILLEGAL

MORE INFO? SEARCH THIS!
Afterlife telegrams
Send greetings
Volunteers

STUPID STUFF, STUPID AUDIENCE

AULD SOD GIFTS

UNIQUE GIFT IRELAND ANCESTRY
IRISH SOIL FINDING A MARKET

Can you sell anything under the correct headline? Well, *Auld Sod Gifts*, based in Ireland showed that it's possible to sell potting soil to Irish patriots in the United States, using the right approach. *Auld Sod Gifts* sell genuine 100 percent Irish soil and shamrock for online ordering. Their slogan is: "We have made it possible for you to own a little piece of Ireland no matter how far from the Emerald Isle you are!". So, whether you or your family emigrated from Ireland long ago, you have a deep love of Irish turf or you're simply looking for an original and unique gift – this is the product for you. Imported directly from Ireland and sold to anywhere in the United States or Canada.

POSSIBLE MORAL

Some might ask whether this really is a recipe to becoming a millionaire or not. To those who doubt I would say, think again. An 87-year-old lawyer in Manhattan, originally from Galway, recently bought $100,000 worth of the dirt to fill in his American grave, yet undug. A native of County Cork spent $148,000 on seven tons of dirt to spread under the house he was having built in Massachusetts. With some 40 million Americans claiming Irish ancestry, you can definitely say that there's a market out there.

Sources: "Filthy Rich", Mirror.co.uk, 28 Oct, 2006. "Our story", auldsodgifts.com, 2012.

IRISH
DIRT

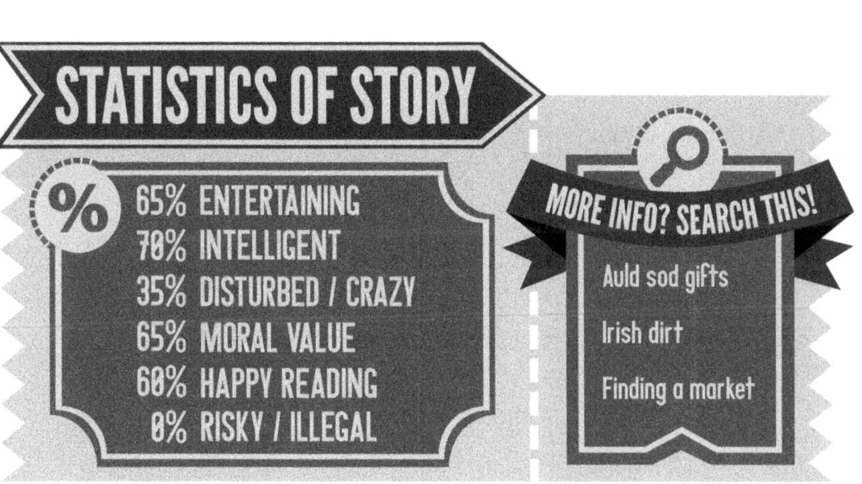
STATISTICS OF STORY
%
65% ENTERTAINING
70% INTELLIGENT
35% DISTURBED / CRAZY
65% MORAL VALUE
60% HAPPY READING
0% RISKY / ILLEGAL
MORE INFO? SEARCH THIS!
Auld sod gifts
Irish dirt
Finding a market

STUPID STUFF, STUPID AUDIENCE

IFART

JOEL COMM IPHONE POPULAR APPLICATION SOUND EFFECTS

iFart is a *iPhone* application released by *Infomedia* in 2008. As the name suggests, it's an application that plays a wide variety of fart noises. It's best described as a digital *Whoopie Cushion.* Open up *iFart* and you're presented with a list of 20 sound-effects to choose from. Of course, they're all just variations on the same "theme" – but some are better than others. There's "Jack the Ripper", "The Wipe Out" and "Squeezer" – just to name a few.

So, what's so special about this *iFart*? Well, it quickly became one of the most popular *iPhone* applications of all time. The developer, Joel Comm, noted that over Christmas Eve and Christmas day of 2008, more than 58,000 people purchased a copy of *iFart*, netting him over $40,000 dollars in just two days. *iFart* went on to reach the number one spot on the application charts before Christmas 2008, remaining there for three weeks and staying in the top ten until mid-January 2009, by which time it had sold more than 350,000 copies.

POSSIBLE MORAL

As an observer of human nature, let's just face the facts: stupid stuff sells, and often the more stupid and silly it is, the better it sells. I see *iFart* as being the modern smartphone equivalent of the *Pet Rock* craze of the 70's (read more on page 200), perhaps lasting about as long. The humor of teenage boys probably hasn't changed for millennia, so I'd say Joel Comm was just young enough at heart to see this market opportunity. In short: Be the first to think stupid.

Sources: "iFart developer makes $40,000 in 2 days", Edible Apple, 28 Dec, 2008."iFart Mobile to Pull...", CNET News, 13 Feb, 2009.

STUPID STUFF, STUPID AUDIENCE

PET ROCK

HOUSE PET 70'S FAD TRAINING MANUAL
IMMORTAL SIX MONTHS

Pet Rock is the business idea of Gary Dahl from California. In the 70's he sold this new kind of pet that doesn't die, never needs to be fed, walked, bathed or groomed. Dahl began by creating the company *Rock Bottom Productions*. He imported rocks from Rosarito Beach in Baja, California, Mexico. The package for the rock included a pet training manual and a cardboard box, designed like a pet carrier. The manual contained instructions on how to properly care for one's pet, including how to house train a *Pet Rock* by placing it on a piece of newspaper and teaching it other commands including sit, stay, roll over, play dead, and come.

Dahl started selling *Pet Rock*'s in 1975, and believe it or not they sold like crazy. He got a million dollar profit from his sales during Christmas of that same year. He sold over five million of his rocks in a six month period. Shortly after that, the demand of his product declined, but by then Dahl had already collected a million dollar bonus from his silly idea.

Unlike most fads, the *Pet Rock* continues to live on and has seen resurgence on the internet. There are memorial pages, spin-offs, and one can still purchase such a pet, though new manufacturers have given their rocks new features and looks. There is also a *Pet Rock USB* available, plug it in and it… does absolutely nothing – as could be expected.

Source: "Pet Rock That Made Man A Multi-Millionaire In 6 Months Lives On", PetsDo, 25 Aug, 2007.

POSSIBLE MORAL

For parents who don't want to deal with the mess, noise, feeding, medical and pet insurance costs this must have been great. I can really imagine the face and reaction of a kid opening his presents for Christmas, hoping to get the kitten he so badly wished for – to face a box containing a cold grey piece of rock. Heart warming.

Though what's really impressive with this story is that it only took Dahl six months to achieve his multi-millionaire status, which was mainly possible due to the extremely low production costs. His idea was simple, effective and highly successful. The *Pet Rock* idea gives me inspiration to create the next multi-million dollar hit. As indicated by Dahl, what's needed is a good idea, a thorough plan, hard work, and good marketing.

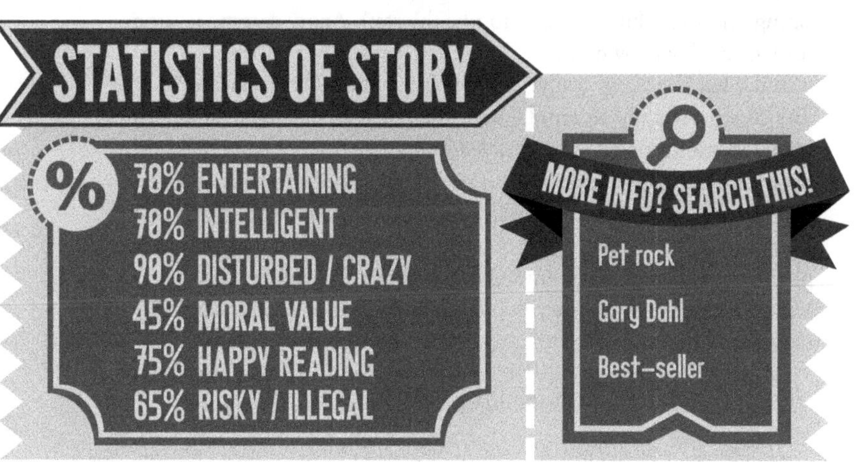

VASKNING

CHAMPAGNE SINKING REACTION
BUSINESS IDEA PEOPLE'S IDIOCY

Vaskning (*sinking*) champagne is the act of pouring out champagne in the sink. *Sinking* started in Sweden as a reaction to the ban on spraying champagne in many bars and is usually done by a person who orders two bottles of champagne and asks the bartender to pour out (sink) one of them. In 2007 and 2010 respectively, bars in the Swedish cities of Båstad and Visby, popular party destinations for the wealthy youth, banned the spraying of champagne. The ban was enforced with reference to champagne spraying possibly violating the requirement for servers of alcohol to maintain good order. The ban caused some people to pour out the champagne instead, and thus *sinking* was born. It soon turned into an idea virus of enormous potential and suddenly people where talking about *sinking* all over the place. Those who sink are either actually wealthy people, or people wanting others to think they are wealthy. It's all about getting as many as possible to see that you can waste $500 without blinking twice.

The disapproval of *sinking* is very strong with the Swedish people. The newspaper *Aftonbladet* published an article about the latest *sinking* trend – *burger dumping* (ordering 50 burgers at a fast food restaurant, eating one and asking the staff to toss the rest). Angry comments from readers quickly grew online.

But what is *sinking*, really? Is it art? Is it politics? Is it retarded? The concept has spread rapidly over the past year and accelerated in the media in connection to the so called *brat weeks* (the invasion of wealthy people during a few weeks of summer) in the Swedish towns of Visby and Båstad. However, it's unclear how much *sinking* that actually occurs. Everyone seems to have heard of it, but few have actually witnessed the phenomenon. In a survey among barkeepers in Båstad, Stockholm and Visby, one of them said they get "approximately one serious sinking request per night", while others claimed *sinking* was a myth.

During the summer of 2010, an extension of the *sinking* phenomena was introduced online. In addition to all the *YouTube* footage of

Sources: "Vaskning är bratsens provokation", Dagens Nyheter, 2 Aug, 2010. "Blås iväg deg på löpande band", Feber.se, 2 Aug, 2010.

at-home-do-it-yourself-sinkers a mysterious man in his thirties started the site *smsvaska.se*. The site promotes a phone number to which you send super expensive text-messages to simply "sink" $30. Three messages will get you the *Social Democrat champagne*, 15 a *Champagne Party*. In one month, people had been text-*sinking* for $3,700. Today it's over $10,000. When sending the text message, absolutely nothing happens. It's just like pouring money into the sink and down the drain. Brilliant, right?

Suddenly all kinds of different applications on the topic started to appear. With the *vaskningsapp* anyone could now sink using their *iPhone* or *Android*. You could also follow the leaderboard to see who sinks the most. "Show that YOU belong to upper class! This application doesn't do anything at all! It's just expensive as hell". Another one, called *Most Expensive Android Application*, costs $220 and its only purpose seems to be the ability to brag about it to like-minded friends. Well spent money.

POSSIBLE MORAL

This is a simple lesson on how easy it can be to create a business using other people's idiocy. The basic idea behind *sinking* is that the spent money and purchased product isn't used for something, it's there to go to waste. If sinkers felt they spent money on something worthwhile, the magic of it would disappear. It's like giving street graffiti artists a legal wall to paint on, it kills the excitement. If the man running *smsvaska.se* would have donated his earned money to charity, no one would have used his service to sink. Sad but true.

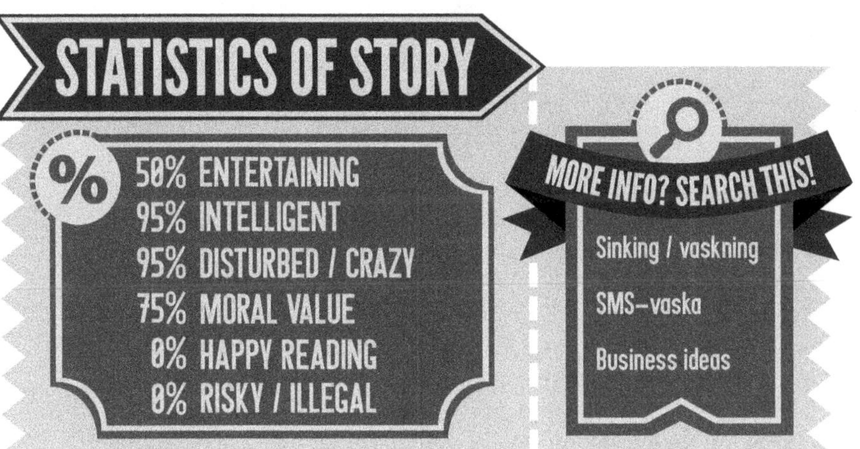

GREAT MISTAKES

UNEXPECTED RESULT DISCOVERY
SERENDIPITY SOLUTION

The Post-it note

The *Post-it note* were not a planned product. It was in fact the result of a failure. A man named Spencer Silver was working in the *3M* research laboratories in 1970 trying to find a strong super glue (adhesive). Silver managed to developed the new adhesive, but it was even weaker than what *3M* had already manufactured. It stuck to objects, but could easily be lifted off. It was super weak instead of super strong, and never really seemed to dry. Fascinated rather than embarrassed, Silver shared his results with co-workers, among them Arthur Fry. No one knew what to do with the stuff, but Silver didn't discard it.

One Sunday four years later Fry was singing in the church's choir. He used markers to keep his place in the hymnal, but they kept falling out of the book. Remembering Silver's adhesive, Fry used some to coat his markers. Success! With the weak adhesive, the markers stayed in place, yet lifted off without damaging the pages. The idea of the *Post-it note* was born. In 1980 *3M* began distributing *Post-it notes* nationwide and today they are one of the most popular office products available.

The Microwave

During the year 1945, Percy Spencer carried out some experiments with a new vacuum tube called a magnetron. He had a candy bar in his pocket, which suddenly began to melt. And that's how one melted chocolate bar led to the discovery of the *microwave oven.*

The Penicillin

In 1928, Alexander Fleming went on vacation without cleaning his workstation. On his return he saw that strange fungus had formed on the cultures on his desk and found that bacteria couldn't thrive on such cultures and thus he had by mistake invented the most widely used antibiotic in the world – *Penicillin.* Ironically, Fleming was searching for a "wonder drug" that could cure diseases at the time of the discovery, however, it wasn't until he threw away his experiments that he found what he was looking for.

Sources: "The Power Of Serendipity", CBS News, 11 Feb, 2009. "Inspirational Stories II: The 3M Post It Notes Invention", GoalSettingCollege, Ellesse. "The Origin of Twitter's "Fail Whale"", 2 Aug 2010.

The Fail Whale

Regular *Twitter* users are familiar with the image of a smiling whale being lifted out of the ocean by a flock of birds. It appears when the hugely popular social media service crashes due to overloading. This now iconic image (it even has its own fan club) dubbed the *Fail Whale* has changed the life of its young designer. Yiying Lu, a university graduate from Sydney, says in an interview from *Sydney Morning Herald*, *'How Fail Whale became a hit'* from 2009, that it's "kind of a kismet (fate) thing" that her career is now associated with a failure page. It could have been disastrous for the young artist to have her most recognized work associated with failure but it turned out to be welcomed attention. Rather than having a page saying: "The page cannot be found" or "Server overloaded", Lu's illustration actually made it more interesting and gave an alternative way of taking failure.

POSSIBLE MORAL

These are four great examples of how failure can be turned into success. Failure is nothing more than not getting the desired outcome the first time around. No one who is living their dreams started out perfectly. They just didn't quit when failure was the results of their efforts. Learn to open up your mind and to see things from different perspectives.

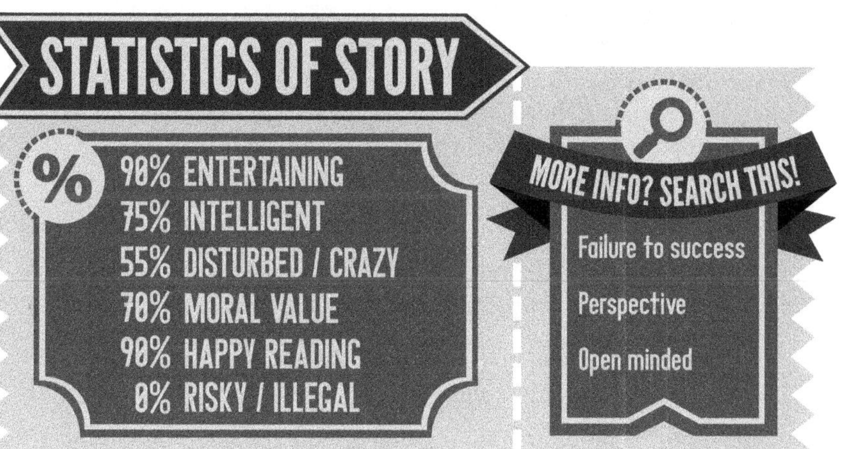

ICON OF FAILURE

ARCHITECTS ACCIDENT STATUS
FAKING IT IMPORTANT SYMBOL

Buschetos Cathedral in Pisa, Italy, is one of its era's most beautiful buildings. When the church was consecrated by Pope Gelasius II in year 1118 it was greater than both the contemporary *St. Peter's Basilica* in Rome and *Hagia Sophia* in Constantinople. The church was Pisa's pride, and admired by the world. It would probably still be the pride of Pisa, if not due to the act of an unknown architect, who long after Buschetos death built a jerry-building in 1173 and accidentally created an icon that today overshadows the Cathedral – The *Leaning Tower of Pisa*. It was designed to be perfectly vertical, but due to a lack of architectural skills and poor knowledge of the marsh it was being built on, the clock tower started to lean during construction. While contemporary architects would be sure to carve their name into the wall of their buildings, even today, no one knows who designed the tower. Perhaps the leaders in the city were embarrassed and wiped out all the records of this person.

It wasn't until the Romantic period in the early 1800's that the tower was given its status as an important symbol of the city. A couple of visiting architects started spreading the theory that the tower's dangerous slope was a deliberate move. The unknown architect had been able to balance the tower on a knife edge, they said. This rumor made many people travel to Pisa to view this "masterpiece" and poets such as Shelley and Byron soon turned Pisa into a famous city. The myth that the leaning tower was designed by a genius architect only lived on for about 20 years, but by then the structure had already been given its status as one of the world's most famous buildings.

Many suggestions have been given on how to straighten the *Leaning Tower of Pisa*, including taking it apart stone by stone and rebuilding it at a different location. In the 1920s the foundations of the tower were injected with cement grouting that has stabilized the tower to some extent. Until recent years tourists were not allowed to climb the staircase inside the tower, due to consolidation work, but the *Leaning Tower of Pisa* was reopened and is today one of the most popular tourist attractions in Italy.

Sources: "Leaning Tower of Pisa, A Magnificent...", Symon Sez, 9 Aug, 2010. "Leaning Tower of Pisa", en.wikipedia.org, 2012.

POSSIBLE MORAL

The *Leaning Tower of Pisa* was from the beginning an embarrassing failure, but now millions of people from around the world make pilgrimages to the city every year to view the tower. This brings up the "fake it till you make it" way of thinking. Sometimes this of course backfires, but for the most part, especially in business, pretending to know what you're doing can take you a long way. It's okay to admit when there's things you don't understand, but mastering that overall vibe of "I know what's going on" will open doors. The truth is that no one knows everything, but we're all experts in our own way. Own what you know; fake the rest. The Italian poets faked the story about the tower being a genius architectural piece, and when people found out that the story was a hoax – they pretty much just went along with it.

SUCCESS FROM FAILURES

NOSTALGIA OF MUD

AHEAD OF TIME MISTAKE FASHION
SHORT-LIVED CLOTHING STORE

Vivienne Westwood and Malcolm McLaren opened a clothing store called *Nostalgia of Mud* in the early 80s. The facade was covered by a world map. The interior was styled like an archaeological excavation. Visitors descended on recycled scaffolding to an earth floor and a heaving "mud" pond surrounded by voodoo-like artefacts. The clothes sold in the store were 20 years ahead of their time, impossible to wear and impossible to sell. In this way it made the clothes outdated right away. *Nostalgia of Mud* was an odd store that was shut down after just two years.

Perhaps it was lucky that it went as badly as it did? Westwood is now an acclaimed world famous fashion designer and McLaren was the manager for, among others, the bands Sex Pistols and New York Dolls.

The failure led to a crossroad in life for both Vivienne and Malcolm. Being ahead of their time turned their careers into something else, which might otherwise never have happened. A profitable mistake for both.

Sources: "Vivienne Westwood: An Unfashionable Life", Jane Mulvagh, 22 Jul 2011. "Nostalgia Of Mud", Ellie Thea, 19 Jan, 2011.

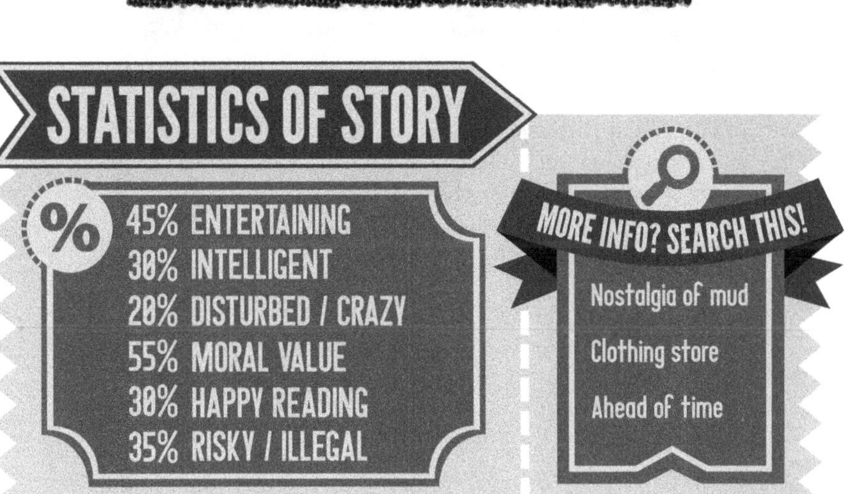
STATISTICS OF STORY
%
45% ENTERTAINING
30% INTELLIGENT
20% DISTURBED / CRAZY
55% MORAL VALUE
30% HAPPY READING
35% RISKY / ILLEGAL
MORE INFO? SEARCH THIS!
Nostalgia of mud
Clothing store
Ahead of time

SILLY TOY, GREAT VALUE

WORLD WAR II GENIUS MARKETING
SUCCESS TOY TO HANDLE FAILURE

The story of a failure that turned into a successful toy that's been used in everything from children's play to space voyages. A combination of engineering, accident and entrepreneurship produced one of the most successful toys of the twentieth century.

Early in World War II, James Wright was working in *General Electric*'s Connecticut labs under a government contract to create an inexpensive substitute for synthetic rubber. One day in 1943, Wright happened to drop boric acid into silicone oil, and was astonished to find that the resulting "goo" would stretch and bounce further than rubber, even at extreme temperatures. Wright had tried to make synthetic rubber, but failed. Nobody could figure out what to do with the result until a marketing genius named Peter Hodgson gave it a name (*Silly Putty*), put it in a little plastic egg and sold it as a novelty toy.

Ironically, it was only after its success as a toy that practical uses were found for *Silly Putty*. It picks up dirt, lint and pet hair, can stabilize wobbly furniture, and it copies any newspaper or comic-book print that it touches. It has also been used in stress-reduction and physical therapy, and in medical and scientific simulations. The crew of *Apollo 8* even used it to secure tools in zero-gravity.

Peter Hodgson's product left him an estate of $140 million at his death in 1976. More than 300 million little eggs have been sold. *Silly Putty*, still a recognized name in over 95 percent of American households, remains one of the classic novelty products of modern times.

Sources: "The Silly Putty Story", The New York Times, 19 Jan, 1992. "The Amazing Origin of Silly Putty", GE Reports, 3 May, 2011.

POSSIBLE MORAL

You won't reach success without failure. A history of human failure would make for a long and interesting book, yet we prefer books about success stories – like the one you're holding in your hand. Going through life, we'll experience both successes and failures, but it's how we handle success or failure that makes the difference in the long run. A greater value was found in *Silly Putty* due to Peter Hodgson's way of seeing things. When Wright and the rest of *General Electric* saw failure, Hodgson saw an opportunity.

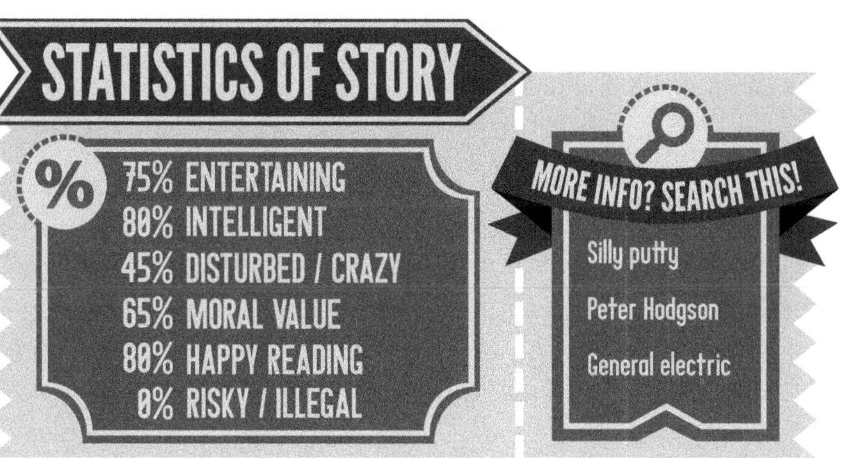

SUCCESS FROM FAILURES

THE CABIN OF BON IVER

MEDITATION PURPOSE MUSIC
DISCOVERY FINDING HAPPINESS

In the fall of 2007, after dual breakups (a girl and his band, DeYarmond Edison) a depressed Justin Vernon make his way to a remote hunting cabin in Wisconsin that belongs to his father. He lived there alone for three months, filling his days with wood chopping and other chores around the property. Vernon wanted to heal himself after the series of breakups. He didn't intend to write or record any music during the time, he wanted to recover from the events of the previous year. Even so, living in the cabin slowly began feeding a bold, uninhibited new musical focus for him. That cabin became the birthplace of *For Emma*, a lonesome recording in which Vernon discovered a gift he never knew he had until the song *Flume* came tumbling out of him: A very special falsetto he had only used before while singing along in cars to female singer-songwriters.

After a modest self-production of just a few hundred copies, the album was snapped up by Indiana indie label *Jagjaguwar* for wide release in February 2008. It became the indie label's biggest album release ever, with over 320,000 copies sold. During Vernon's time in the cabin, he had alone created a collection of nine ethereal, folk-music based tracks. He also formed what would later become Bon Iver. Vernon have later said in interviews that he will continue to make albums without engineers and producers because he's capable of doing it all himself. In 2012, Bon Iver was nominated for four *Grammy Awards*. They won for *Best new artist.*

Sources: "For Emma, Forever Ago", Jagjaguwar, 19 Feb, 2008 "Who, What and Where is Bon Iver?", The New York Times, 3 Jun, 2011.

POSSIBLE MORAL

Not looking for the solution was the key for Justin Vernon when finding happiness again. On top of that he wrote some pretty great music as well. When no one knows what they want, they look for things they think they need but really don't – satisfied for a brief second, only to go back searching. But some things in life don't need searching for, they're already there. The thing you do need to find, is purpose and finding purpose is finding happiness.

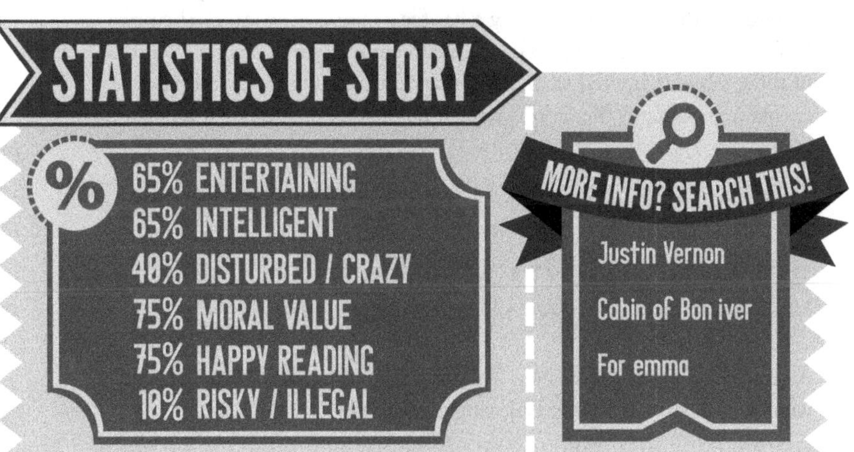

A TABLE FOR GOOD

CITY HARVEST CONCEPT FIGHT POVERTY
SKIP THE LINE DONATIONS

Over one point five million New Yorkers live in poverty, struggling to afford basic necessities such as rent and medical care while trying to put food on their tables. As more people are affected by the recession and high unemployment in New York City the need for emergency food has increased dramatically. For over 30 years, the food rescue organization *City Harvest* have been working to address the demand for food.

A Table for Good is a concept thought of by students from *Miami Ad School New York* and *Berghs School of Communication* for *City Harvest*. It won the *Interactive silver pencil* in the *One Show* of 2011. The concept is to give New Yorkers a way to skip the restaurant queue and at the same time feel good about it. *A Table for Good* is simply a way to donate by buying a dinner reservation. In collaboration with a number of restaurants, the idea is to offer a table for special reservations, that people can buy every day. The money goes directly to *City Harvest*. A new table is available every night on a first paid, first served basis. People can make reservations like they've always done, on the phone, online and via the *A Table for Good*-application. They're also making it possible to find the *A Table for Good* reservation box on all the restaurants websites as well. Guests can choose whether they want to pay a flat fee or bid on the table. The price is based on demand and popularity. Each company that sits down at one of these tables is invited to digitally market the table – and become a permanent name in the fight against hunger.

POSSIBLE MORAL

A great concept that gives New Yorkers a way to donate simply by doing what they're already doing: Enjoying great food.

Source: "A Table for Good", vimeo.com, Jacob Sempler, 2011.

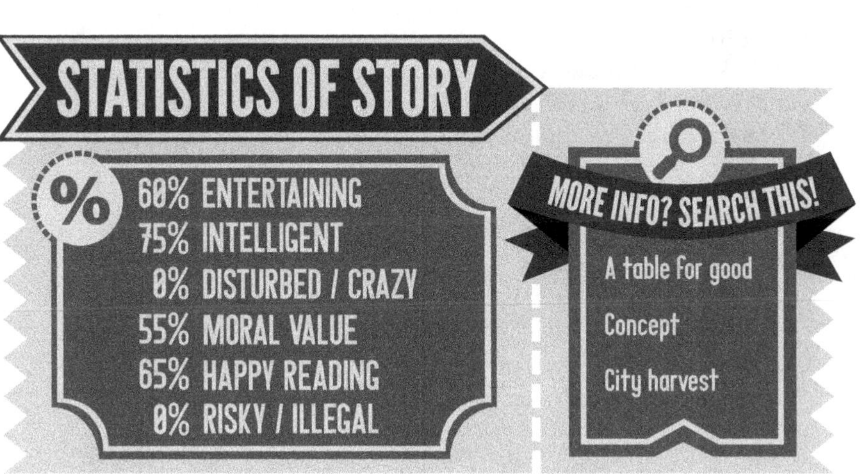
STATISTICS OF STORY
60% ENTERTAINING
75% INTELLIGENT
0% DISTURBED / CRAZY
55% MORAL VALUE
65% HAPPY READING
0% RISKY / ILLEGAL
MORE INFO? SEARCH THIS!
A table for good
Concept
City harvest

SUSTAINABLE TREATS

BOBBLE

ENVIRONMENT PLASTIC POLLUTION FILTRATION DRINKING TAP WATER

Over seven billion pounds of *PVC*-plastic (the most environmentally damaging plastic) is thrown away in the United States each year. Only 18 million pounds of that, about one quarter of a percent, is recycled. Two million plastic beverage bottles are used every hour. Much of this plastic ends up in the oceans. One great thief is the plastic water bottle. Why do Americans buy bottled water, instead of drinking from the tap? Because of the taste. The tap water isn't in any way dangerous, as in some countries, but the majority of people simply think it taste worse.

Bobble is a reusable bottle that filters water as you drink, using an ingenious replaceable carbon filter. It's intended for making municipal tap water taste better. When water passes through the filter, the carbon removes chlorine and organic contaminants. *Bobble* is a good-looking, sleek alternative to single-serve plastic water bottles, which harm the environment (and your wallet). The bottle is free of *BPA*, *Phthalates* and *PVC*. Both *BPA* and *Phthalates* mimic the body's hormones and have, in laboratory animal tests, been shown to cause reproductive and neurological damage as well as increasing childhood asthma and allergy. The *PVC* lifecycle (its production, use and disposal) results in the release of toxic, chlorine based chemicals.

Bobble's water filter can be used on pretty much any bottle. Every filter equates to 300 single-serve bottles. After a year, you've removed thousands of bottles from the environment, simply by filtering the water from your own tap.

POSSIBLE MORAL

A smart way of getting people to stop consuming bottled water since it's a major environmental problem. Save money, save the environment and at the same time get water that tastes good – brilliant!

Sources: "Could this be the Perfect Water Bobble?", Treehugger, 24 Feb, 2010. "Our story", waterbobble.com, 2012.

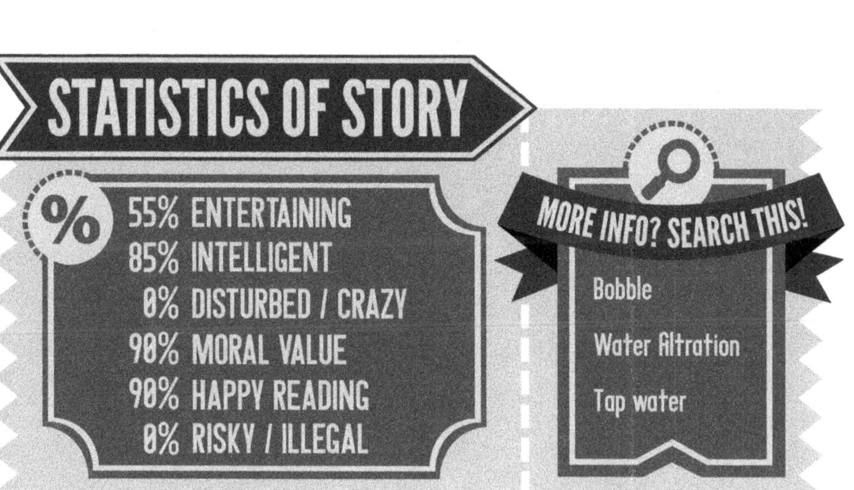
STATISTICS OF STORY
55% ENTERTAINING
85% INTELLIGENT
0% DISTURBED / CRAZY
90% MORAL VALUE
90% HAPPY READING
0% RISKY / ILLEGAL
MORE INFO? SEARCH THIS!
Bobble
Water filtration
Tap water

SUSTAINABLE TREATS

DIRTY WATER

REACTIONS DISGUST AWARENESS
DONATIONS VENDING MACHINE

One day in 2009 *UNICEF* asked themselves: What if we bottled the dirty water that millions of people in developing countries drink every day and offer it to people on the streets of New York? Together with advertising agency *Casanova Pendrill* they took a very ordinary object, a water vending machine, and filled it with bottles of disease-laden H_2O. This was done in order to enlighten New Yorkers about how something we in the West take for granted, is considered luxury to millions of people in the developing world. They placed the machine in the Union Square Park area, with the goal of raising awareness of this alarming issue. New Yorkers were startled to find the choice of malaria, yellow fever and hepatitis-flavored *Dirty Water*. They looked at the vending machine in disgust. Though no one drank *Dirty Water*, many did donate to the cause – paying in the same way you normally would when paying for a bottle in your average vending machine. If you didn't have any change, you could also donate with your phone.

The real dirty water currently has 900 million consumers in the world. Over 4,200 children die of water-related diseases every day and millions of people around the world lack access to clean water resources. The idea of "selling" dirty water was inspired by *UNICEF*'s promise that every dollar donated would provide clean drinking water to 40 children for a day.

This is a clever way to convey a big and important message which is unfortunately rarely in the spotlight of the media. *UNICEF* confronted those that live a life of luxury with the harsh realities from other parts of the world, they created awareness, raised funds and changed perceptions.

Sources: "Dirty water kills 5,000 children a day", The Guardian, 10 Nov, 2006. "UNICEF's Dirty Water...", TriplePundit, 19 Jul, 2010.

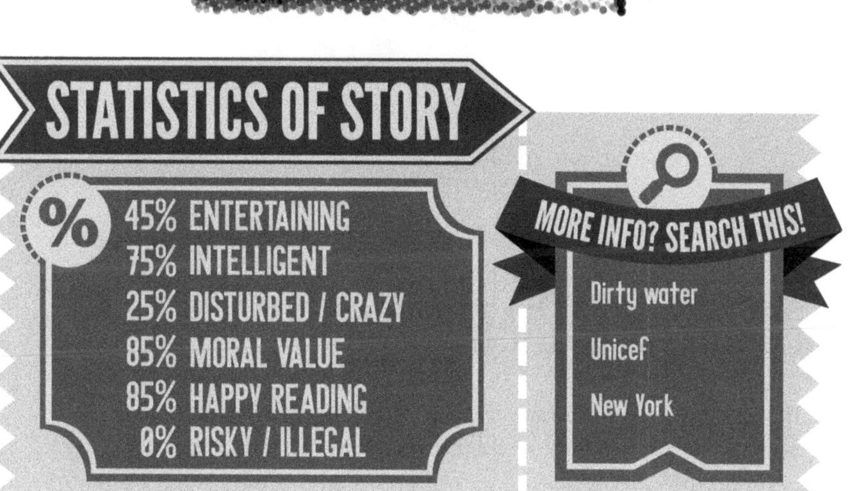
STATISTICS OF STORY
45% ENTERTAINING
75% INTELLIGENT
25% DISTURBED / CRAZY
85% MORAL VALUE
85% HAPPY READING
0% RISKY / ILLEGAL
MORE INFO? SEARCH THIS!
Dirty water
Unicef
New York

MORE THAN A SLOGAN

CULTURAL ICON SLOGAN LITTERING
POPULAR CAMPAIGN

The phrase *Don't Mess with Texas* is a trademark of the *Texas Department of Transportation*, which began in 1986 as part of a statewide advertising campaign. The intention behind the campaign was to reduce littering on Texas roadways and it received statewide attention. *Don't Mess with Texas* was prominently shown on road signs on major highways, television, radio and in printed advertising. The campaign is credited with reducing litter on Texas highways with roughly 72 percent between 1986 and 1990. The campaign's target market was 18 to 35 year old males, who are statistically shown to be the most likely to litter.

Beyond its immediate role in reducing litter, the slogan became a cultural phenomenon and it's been popularly appropriated by Texans. Though the origin of the slogan isn't well known outside of Texas, it appears on countless tourist souvenirs. The phrase is actually a federally registered trademark. The transportation department has tried at times to enforce its trademark rights with cease and desist letters, but has had very limited success. The phrase *Don't Mess with Texas* is a frequently cited example of pride in Texas culture.

The state famous for *American football, Texas Rangers, BBQ* and *Chuck Norris* shows the rest of the world that it's cool not to litter. Respect.

Source: "Why there's no messing with Texas", CNN, 8 Jul, 2011.

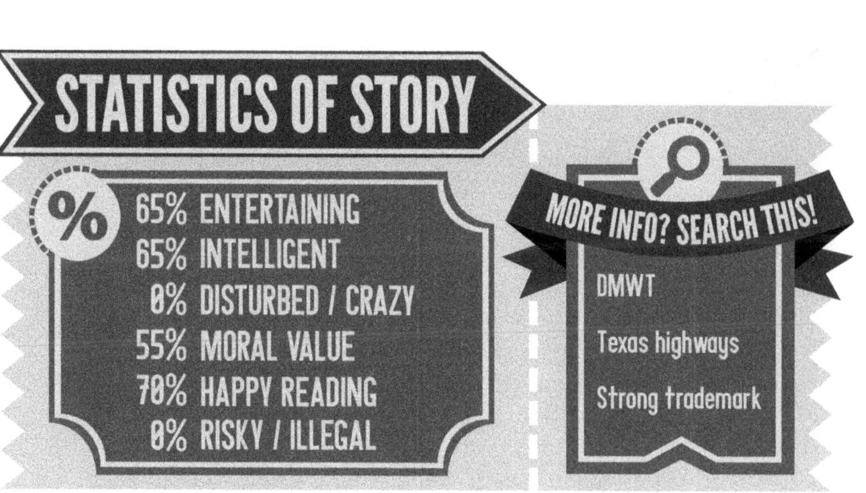
STATISTICS OF STORY
65% ENTERTAINING
65% INTELLIGENT
0% DISTURBED / CRAZY
55% MORAL VALUE
70% HAPPY READING
0% RISKY / ILLEGAL
MORE INFO? SEARCH THIS!
DMWT
Texas highways
Strong trademark

PRINTED WIKIPEDIA

EXPERIMENT STUDENT SAVING TREES
5000 PAGES 400+ ARTICLES

Student Rob Matthews from the United Kingdom has printed 0.01 percent of the English part of the Internet encyclopedia *Wikipedia* into a book that has about 5000 pages and 400+ featured articles. The book is huge, about 1' 7" (48.3 cm) tall. The English edition of *Wikipedia* contained around 3 million articles in 2011. If someone were to print the entire *Wikipedia* encyclopedia into a book the size of it would roughly be equivalent to 952 volumes of the *Encyclopedia Britannica*, contain 2.25 million pages and take you over 123 years to read. The sheer volume of information stored on *Wikipedia* is simply massive. A text based archive of the English version takes up 2.5GB of digital storage space and if you include images, that number jumps to over 78GB.

POSSIBLE MORAL

In the majority of human history, physical encyclopedias were at least this big (but divided into several books) and printed many thousands of times. *Wikipedia* has, in many instances, rendered the printed encyclopedia obsolete in most households, thereby saving a lot of natural resources. Of course many, including myself, will still be using printers from time to time, but then you will only print the sections you need instead of thousands of articles that you've got no use for. Sometimes, a project like this can be needed to remind us about some of the really great things that the digital world has given us (read more about *Wikipedia* on page 138).

Sources: "Wikipedia as a Printed Book—Seriously!", Digital inspiration, 1 Jan 2012. "Wikipedia", rob-matthews.com, 2010.

SUSTAINABLE TREATS

STATISTICS OF STORY
25% ENTERTAINING
75% INTELLIGENT
35% DISTURBED / CRAZY
85% MORAL VALUE
80% HAPPY READING
0% RISKY / ILLEGAL
MORE INFO? SEARCH THIS!
Printed wikipedia
Rob Matthews
Digital vs analog

SUSTAINABLE TREATS

SELF-POWERED GYMS

GENERATE ENERGY HUMAN-POWERED EXERCISE REVOLUTIONARY

In 2007 French inventor Lucien Gambarota and entrepreneur Doug Woodring, originally from United States but now living in Hong Kong, started producing clean and sustainable energy to gyms using good old-fashioned human-power Using generators connected to exercise bikes and treadmills, the gyms are able to power themselves by harnessing energy from their members' workouts. Gambarota and Woodring have joined forces with *Hong Kong's California Fitness*, a subsidiary of *24 Hour Fitness Worldwide*, and launched a revolutionary concept in which energy burned off by exercisers is diverted and converted to power lighting fixtures, while excess energy is stored in a battery. One person has the ability of producing 50 watts of electricity per hour when exercising at a moderate pace. If a person spends one hour per day running on the machine, he or she could generate 18.2 kilowatts of electricity and prevent 4,380 liters of CO_2 from being released per year.

Any movement on the gym's stationary bikes contributes to power a set of batteries which are used to generate electricity for anything from lights to TVs and stereos. Though the energy output is still relatively small, the goal is to someday provide 100 percent of the electricity used in the gym through working out.

POSSIBLE MORAL

I love the idea of burning calories by not burning fossil fuels. Lucien Gambarota and Doug Woodring are true pioneers in this field. Today there are other great spin-offs of the idea: *The Green Microgym*, *Ecogym* and *Fortum Active* are some examples. Hopefully we'll see even more human-powered gyms in the near future.

Sources: "Human-Powered Gyms in Hong Kong", Inhabitat, 3 Aug, 2007. "More Gyms Are Tapping...", Treehugger, 29 Dec, 2008.

STATISTICS OF STORY

55% ENTERTAINING
75% INTELLIGENT
0% DISTURBED / CRAZY
55% MORAL VALUE
70% HAPPY READING
0% RISKY / ILLEGAL

MORE INFO? SEARCH THIS!
Manpowered gyms
Lucien Gambarota
Doug Woodring

THE BITTER TRUTH

BAD-MOUTHING

CAR REPAIR POSITIVE TAKING FOR GRANTED WRONG FOCUS NEGATIVE NATURE

In a situation where something bad happens to us, it's natural to talk about it with friends and family. If something good happens, we enjoy and treasure it, but are not as likely to speak of it. It's as if we take it for granted. So, when experiencing a scenario where both something good and something bad happens, our human negative nature makes us bound to highlight and talk more about the bad stuff. That's simply the way most of us work. Here's a story for you, told by a guest lecture of mine:

A woman went to a car repair service to get her car fixed. She received poor service. They told her they found several problems she hadn't ask about in the first place and told her she needed to leave the car overnight. She had an important deadline early the next day, so leaving the car wasn't an option. Being stressed about it, she got upset and left. The woman went to another car service nearby. They managed to help her with her car in just a few hours. She was really happy and grateful for the help and superb service she had gotten with such short notice. When she came back home she talked with her family and friends about her day. What do you think was the favorite topic? Not so unexpected the focus was set on bad-mouthing the first car repairing service she visited. The woman went on and on about the bad service she was given and spent very little time explaining about the great help she received from the second car service.

POSSIBLE MORAL

When I first heard this story it made me think, why is it so difficult to put focus on the good stuff? Amongst many things, I wanted to change this behavior of mine as I felt like that woman in the story could just as well have been me. If you're the positive kind by nature, kudos to you, but if you're like me – maybe it's time for a change?

Source: Anecdote from lecture with Tomas Hellgren (www.kreatek.se), Piteå Företagarcentrum, 13 Feb, 2012.

CRAP-O-METER

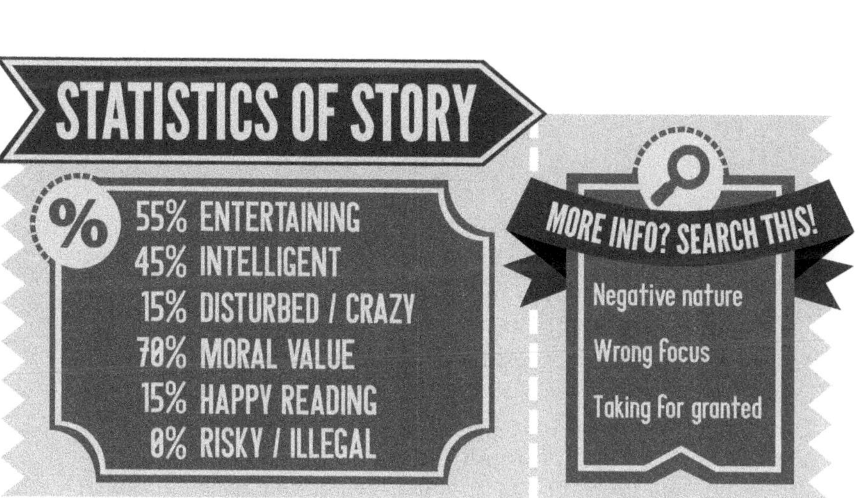
STATISTICS OF STORY
55% ENTERTAINING
45% INTELLIGENT
15% DISTURBED / CRAZY
70% MORAL VALUE
15% HAPPY READING
0% RISKY / ILLEGAL
MORE INFO? SEARCH THIS!
Negative nature
Wrong focus
Taking for granted

THE BITTER TRUTH

DON'T WIN AWARDS

TIMELESS LIMITS TRENDS
ORIGINALITY COMMITTEE

The creative director, author and genius Paul Arden was a true maverick and perfectionist who cared passionately about the standard of ideas and often went to the edge to make them happen. An original character who with his books and lectures taught people to listen to their guts and to always try and do the unexpected.

At the *D&AD*'s (British educational charity, promoting excellence in design and advertising) *President's Lectures* in 1994, Arden amongst many other things gave his thoughts on the subject *awards*. He said that nearly everybody likes to win awards. Because awards create glamour and glamour creates income, but people should be aware that awards are judged in committees by consensus of what is known. In other words, what is in fashion. Arden believes originality can't be fashionable, because it hasn't as yet received the approval of the committee.

POSSIBLE MORAL

A story of advice that can be applied anywhere, except in sports perhaps. Don't try to follow trends. Create them. Be true to your subject and you will be far more likely to create something that is timeless. Simply, listen to Arden's advice – don't win awards.

Sources: "Paul Arden's Lecture at the D&AD", Adland.tv, 31 Jul, 2007. "It's not how good you are...", Paul Arden, 2003.

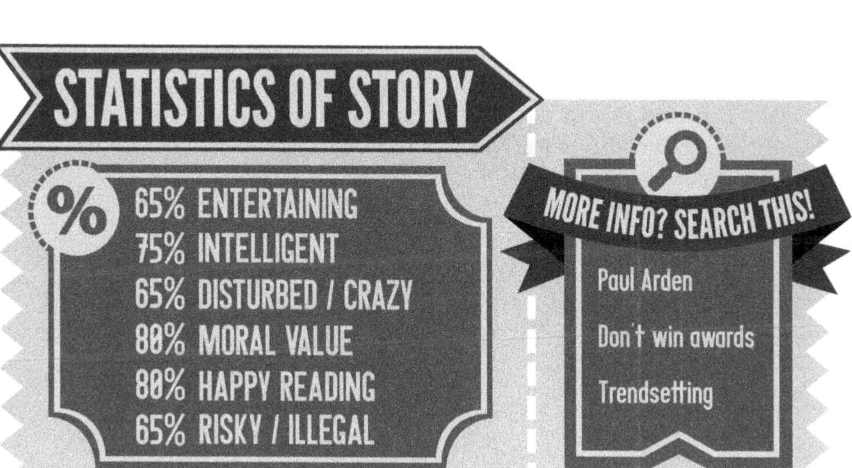
STATISTICS OF STORY
65% ENTERTAINING
75% INTELLIGENT
65% DISTURBED / CRAZY
80% MORAL VALUE
80% HAPPY READING
65% RISKY / ILLEGAL
MORE INFO? SEARCH THIS!
Paul Arden
Don't win awards
Trendsetting

THIRD WORLD BRILLIANCE

A LITER OF LIGHT

PHILIPPINES BULB PLASTIC BOTTLE
DARKNESS SOLAR POWER

Did you know that millions of families still live in the dark? *MyShelter Foundation*'s project *Isang Litrong Liwanag* (*A Liter of Light*), is a sustainable lighting project which aims to bring the eco-friendly *Solar Bottle Bulb* to disprivileged communities. It's a simply brilliant idea that uses recycled plastic bottles to provide home lighting. A single bottle can provide light equivalent to a 60 watt bulb, free, for up to five years! How does it work then? Recyclable PET bottles are installed in the roof, with half of the bottle outside the house and half inside. They're then filled with filtered water and bleach (two caps full). The sun hitting the bottle reflects in the water and creates a bright light. The communities who benefit from this idea live in areas where the houses hardly have windows and therefore live in darkness, even during daytime. Up until this innovation their only alternative has been to turn on the light bulb and use electricity.

The concept behind *A Liter of Light* was designed and developed by students from the *Massachusetts Institute of Technology*. The *Solar Bottle Bulb* is based on the principles of *Appropriate technology* – a concept that provides simple and easily replicable technologies that address basic needs in developing countries.

MyShelter Foundation aims to brighten up one million homes in the Philippines by the end of 2012. According to statistics from the *National Electrification Commission* in 2009, three million households still remain powerless outside the centre of Manila and even in the city centre, families still continue to live in darkness.

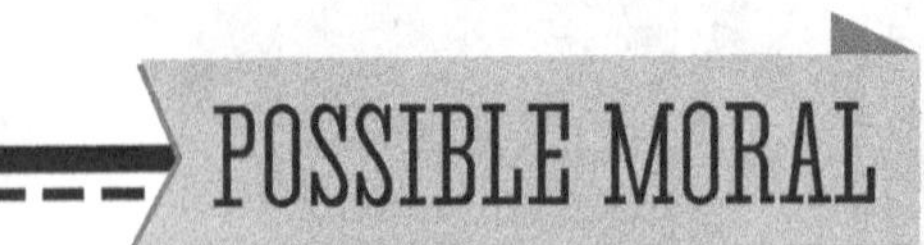

A genius idea! Bringing free eco-friendly light to people that need it. It's this sort of intelligence and ingenuity that the world needs a lot more of.

Sources: "How water bottles create cheap lighting in Philippines", BBC News, 19 Sep, 2011. "About", aliteroflight.org, 2012.

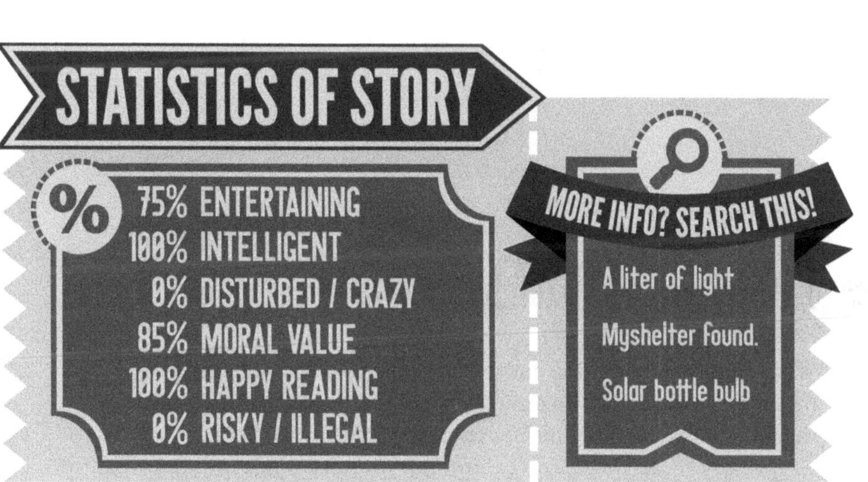
STATISTICS OF STORY
%
75% ENTERTAINING
100% INTELLIGENT
0% DISTURBED / CRAZY
85% MORAL VALUE
100% HAPPY READING
0% RISKY / ILLEGAL
MORE INFO? SEARCH THIS!
A liter of light
Myshelter found.
Solar bottle bulb

THIRD WORLD BRILLIANCE

LUNCH BOX BATTERY

ELECTRICITY STUDY LIGHTING
RECHARGEABLE AFRICA

A child in a developing country goes to school with a lunch box for his or her meals. Upon arrival the child connects and charges the box in the school's charging station. When school's over and the child is back home the lunch box will provide the family with light for less than half its earlier cost. More than two billion people worldwide lack access to electric lighting. For example, only two percent of western Kenya has access to grid electricity and 97 percent of the homes use kerosene wick lamps, which at $37 per year, offer mediocre lighting and consumes a significant portion of the villagers' yearly income.

Professor Vijay Modi at *Columbia University* in New York designed this rechargeable lunch box that serves as a light. The lunch box light will provide a better study or work environment for villagers, while lowering recurring costs and soot levels in the home. It can provide the 20 lux of light at two meters that is required for reading.

What a neat way of getting power to these people. Since the children travel to school anyway, no extra effort needs to be made. A true win-win situation. Hopefully the lunch boxes aren't too heavy to carry!

Source: "Portable Power-Pack", The Earth Institute at Columbia University, 31 Mar, 2006.

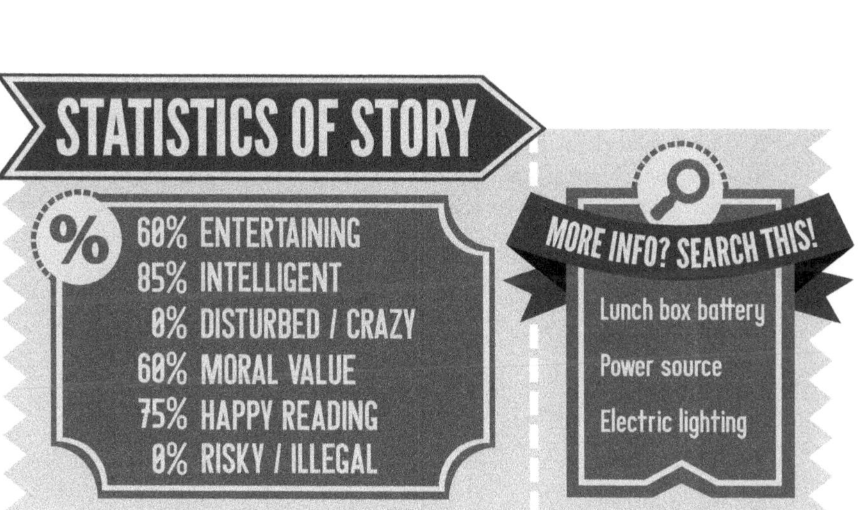
STATISTICS OF STORY
%
60% ENTERTAINING
85% INTELLIGENT
0% DISTURBED / CRAZY
60% MORAL VALUE
75% HAPPY READING
0% RISKY / ILLEGAL
MORE INFO? SEARCH THIS!
Lunch box battery
Power source
Electric lighting

COUCHSURFING

HOSTING GLOBAL COMMUNITY
SLEEPING FACE TO FACE

Couchsurfing is a neologism referring to the practice of moving from one friend's house to another, sleeping in whatever spare space is available, floor or couch, generally staying a few days before moving on to the next house. *CouchSurfing International Inc.* is a corporation based in San Francisco that offers its users hospitality exchange and social networking services. It has more than three million profiles in 246 countries and territories. The *couchsurfing* project was conceived by Casey Fenton in 1999. According to Fenton's account, the idea arose after finding an inexpensive flight from Boston to Iceland. Fenton randomly e-mailed 1,500 students from the *University of Iceland* asking if he could stay in someone's home. He ultimately received more than 50 offers of accommodation. On the return flight to Boston, he began to develop the idea that would establish his *couchsurfing* project.

Registering is free and members have the option of providing information and pictures of themselves and of the sleeping accommodation they offer (if any). More information provided by a member, and other members, improves the chances that someone will find the member trustworthy enough to be his host or guest. Security is often measured in the references accumulated by networking. Volunteers may verify names and mailing addresses. Members looking for accommodation can search for hosts using several parameters such as age, location, gender and activity level.

At *CouchSurfing International*'s website they explain their mission: "We envision a world where everyone can explore and create meaningful connections with the people and places they encounter. Building meaningful connections across cultures enables us to respond to diversity with curiosity, appreciation and respect. The appreciation of diversity spreads tolerance and creates a global community".

Sources: "196 – How to couchsurf", 23 May, 2011. "How it works", couchsurfing.org, 2012.
Quote: From CouchSurfing International's offical website, couchsurfing.org, "Our Mission", 2012.

POSSIBLE MORAL

In today's social climate, virtual encounters are more trusted and popular via increasingly well-managed websites designed for easy navigation. This creates more legitimate opportunities to meet other individuals that earlier would only have happened by pure chance. *Couchsurfing* promotes meeting face to face, having experiences together, or helping one another. This is not an online environment where people stay on for endless hours to chat or kill time, but one which members use to transform their online connections into flesh and blood friends or acquaintances.

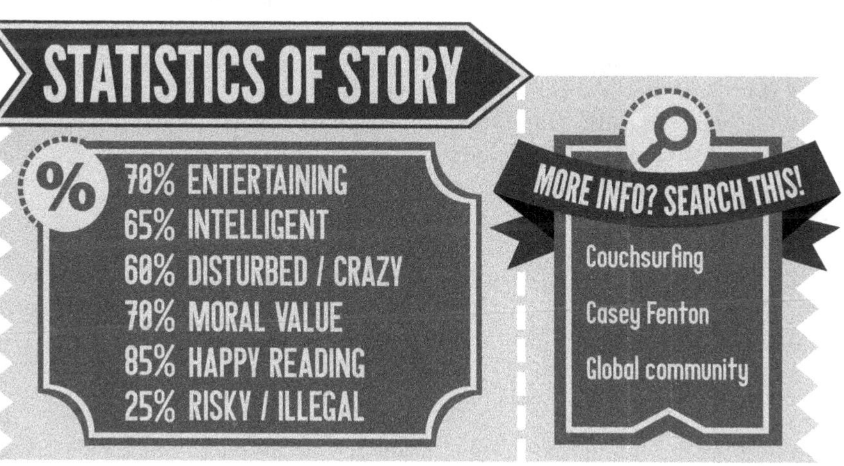

WHEN PEOPLE CONNECT

CROWDFUNDING

POSSIBILITIES FINANCIAL CULTURE
KICKSTARTER TRUST

For many people, the thought of taking significant financial risks holds them back from jumping head first into launching the idea that has been stuck in the creases of their brain. *Crowdfunding* is designed to take the risk out of that creativity and innovation, allowing even the little guy to do something amazing. Inspired by *crowd sourcing*, *crowdfunding* describes the collective cooperation, attention and trust by people who network and pool their money together. *Crowdfunding* occurs for a variety of purposes: Disaster relief, citizen journalism, artists seeking support from fans, political campaigns etc. If you've been holding back because of lack of funds, you might just find there's help out there. Fueled by the community, and managed by some fantastic sites, crowdfunding can help you fund your idea, business startup or music project.

Crowdfunding website *Kickstarter* is the largest funding site there is. Fund anything, from life sized mousetrap games to one man's cultural journey across Mexico – *Kickstarter* has clearly captured the imagination of its audience. The key lesson to the most successful projects being funded, is that they make people feel like they're contributing to support something neat, but also that they're paying for inside access to a product they've committed to.

What really got the world to notice *Kickstarter* and the true power of crowdfunding was the success of video game producer *Double Fine*'s campaign in early 2012. They were aiming high. They hoped to raise $400,000 to fund an upcoming adventure game. The campaign ended up raising almost $3.4 million (!), shattering records and publisher's hearts worldwide. This success was to change game financing forever.

Sources: "What is crowdfunding?", Startups, 2012. "Double Fine Adventure Kickstarter concludes...", Gamespot, 14 Mar, 2012.

POSSIBLE MORAL

Could this be the best thing that ever happened to modern culture? A new and exciting universe where possibilities seem endless for both creative professionals and amateurs. The power is in the hand (and wallets) of the people! Now go fund something awesome.

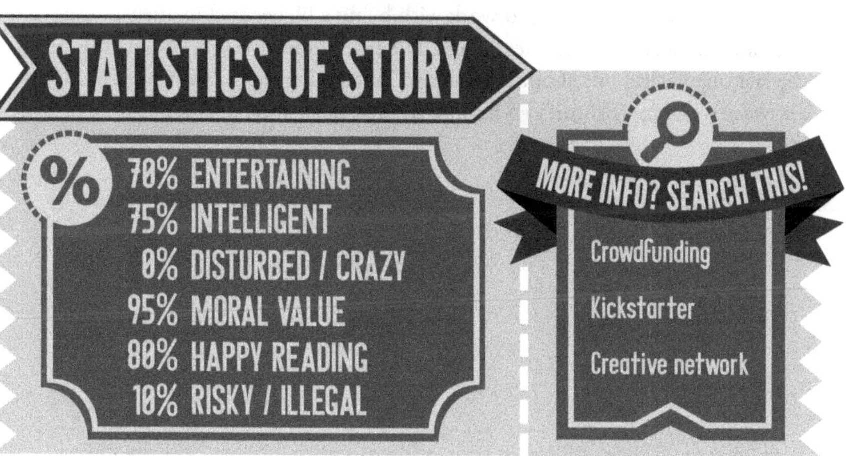

DON'T TELL ASHTON

SOCIAL MEDIA TWITTER ASHTON KUTCHER
ARTWORK INTERNET HISTORY

In 2010, the interactive communication class at *Berghs School of Communication* in Stockholm, Sweden, introduced an impressive social experiment through *Twitter* they called *Don't Tell Ashton*. The idea was to create a piece of art consisting only of *Twitter* users' profile images (avatars). When the users *tweeted* about the project, their avatar was added to the artwork. The size of the avatar depended upon the persons *Twitter* influence – the more followers the person had the bigger the image was.

The project was created and kept a secret from none other than the American actor, producer and former fashion model – Ashton Kutcher. In 2009, Ashton became the first user of *Twitter* to have more than one million followers. For the students, this "Twitter god" was the perfect choice for the experiment. On the 17th of May, the website *donttellashton.com* went live. It spread quickly, and after only three days the artwork was finished.

Don't Tell Ashton reached over 4 million people from 151 countries. It got picked up by all major industry press, and was written about all over the world. On *Google* the phrase "Don't tell Ashton" generated 130,000 results the first week, but still, no one had told Ashton. The students actually ended up traveling to Los Angeles to hand him the artwork personally as a gesture of "big up & keep up the good work with being a bigger frickin' megaphone than any news channel on the planet". Finally Ashton *tweeted*: "Why am I the last one to find out about everything?" and wrote about the project on *Facebook*, reaching Ashton's +5 million followers.

Sources: "Don't Tell Ashton – Eurobest 2010 Gold", YouTube, tobiasfant, 17 Sep 2010. "Don't tell Ashton...", Binero, 21 May, 2010.

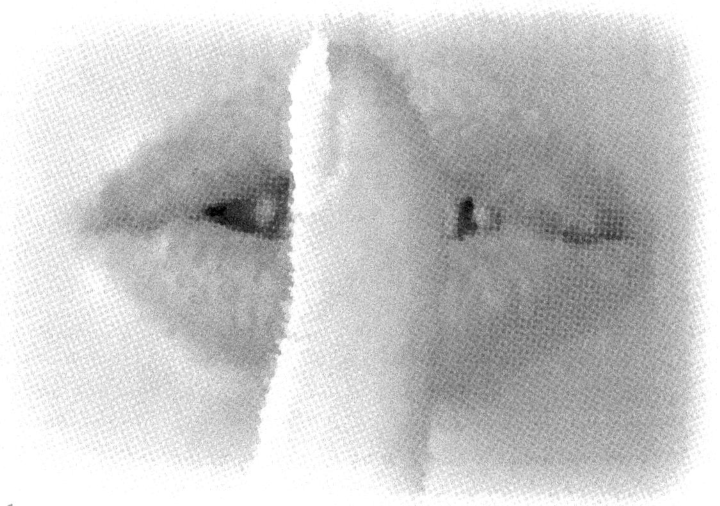

POSSIBLE MORAL

With this experiment, the students created the world's first artwork made by *Twitter* users. It's a story that shows the great influence and power of social media. These students took a pretty new and unexplored medium at the time, played around with it and created a piece of internet history. Choosing Ashton Kutcher was a genius move, and they really reached an impressively big audience, but what's maybe even more impressive was how they were able to keep it all a secret from Ashton.

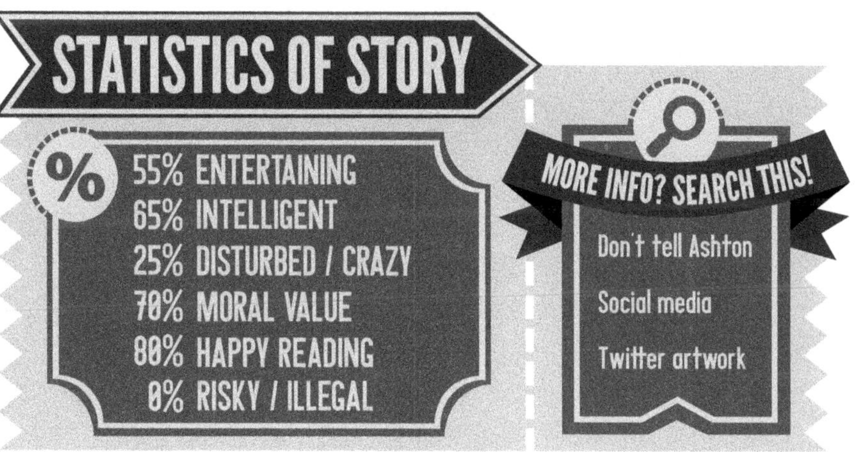

STATISTICS OF STORY
%
55% ENTERTAINING
65% INTELLIGENT
25% DISTURBED / CRAZY
70% MORAL VALUE
80% HAPPY READING
0% RISKY / ILLEGAL
MORE INFO? SEARCH THIS!
Don't tell Ashton
Social media
Twitter artwork

FOUND SONGS

CONNECTING FANS INCREASING VALUE
INTERACTION STORYTELLING

In 2009, little-known Icelandic multi-instrumentalist Ólafur Arnalds felt the need to come up with a good story to go with his music, that would help attract both new and old fans and better connect them to him while also giving them a reason to support him monetarily. So, with that idea (having a story behind the music) as his base, he came up with a project called *Found Songs*, where he would write, record and release a new song every single day for seven straight days. He did it all out of his bedroom. His fans then stepped up and created artwork for each song, and in some cases, amazing videos that within days had thousands upon thousands of views.

Arnalds made the tracks available via the online social networking service *Twitter*. At the project's website you can watch the videos, look at the artwork people created for the songs and even download all the songs for free. There's also a store where you can buy the beautifully packaged vinyl or CD-versions of the album, and some higher quality digital downloads.

Arnalds fan base increased massively after this project. He has since been involved with various other projects and his music has appeared in many films, television shows and advertisements. His song *Brotsjór* was featured on the eighth season of *So You Think You Can Dance*. He also spoke at length on the subject of fan-submitted art in the 2011 documentary film, *PressPausePlay*.

Sources: "PressPausePlay"-documentary, House of Radon, 2011. "Found Songs", foundsongs.erasedtapes.com, 2012.

POSSIBLE MORAL

A perfect example of connecting and interacting with fans. By letting anyone join his project Arnalds gained new fans that had never before heard his music. Participation increased the value of Arnalds work and made *Found Songs* into a big success. Remember that your fans are your life-blood. See that you know who they are, and give them a reason to follow you. Be sure to thank them, often, for caring enough to support you. They're responsible for your success just as much as you are.

WHEN PEOPLE CONNECT

MIND IF WE JOIN YOU?

ENCOUNTERS RANDOM TRAVEL
SOCIALIZE FEEL-GOOD

Swedish humor-duo Filip Hammar and Fredrik Wikingsson recorded a show in the summer of 2011 called *Får vi följa med?* translated *Mind if we join you?*. The idea was to let chance/coincidence decide their fate on a journey through Sweden in which the goal was to meet interesting people that they were to join up with. Filip and Fredrik simply asked people "Mind if we join you?", and if they were given permission they followed the person for a while until that same person in some way led them to meet the next interesting person. This created a long journey through the whole country which made them experience both small and large events, life stories and happenings of everyday people in Sweden.

The first episode begins with Filip and Fredrik getting help by some people at the Central Station of Stockholm to randomly select a train, trolley and seat number. On the train they meet a man who is about to travel to Sundsvall to dance and to honor his deceased girlfriend. The man agrees for them to join him. They end up dancing at a Casino, meeting a woman they follow – and thus the adventure continues.

POSSIBLE MORAL

A story of unexpected encounters with strangers without a script, which is unusual to witness on TV. This is a show with a feel-good vibe to it. An original idea implemented in a "On the road" type of concept. A fun and interesting way to get a feel for Swedish society. Just how friendly are people? How hospitable are they? Hopefully this show can encourage the viewers to socialize more with their fellow citizens, without having to actually know them first.

Sources: "Får vi följa med?", Kanal5, 2012. "Får vi följa med?", sv.wikipedia.org, 2012.

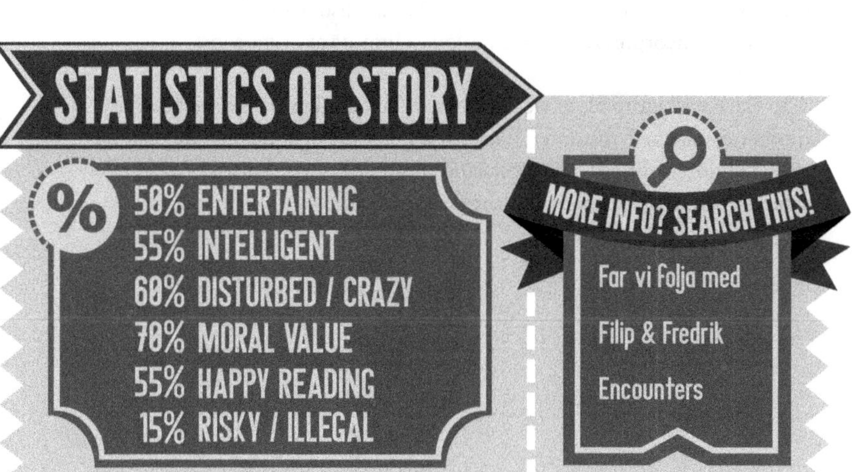
STATISTICS OF STORY
%
50% ENTERTAINING
55% INTELLIGENT
60% DISTURBED / CRAZY
70% MORAL VALUE
55% HAPPY READING
15% RISKY / ILLEGAL
MORE INFO? SEARCH THIS!
Far vi folja med
Filip & Fredrik
Encounters

WORD OF MOUTH

DELL HELL

CONSUMERS BLOG PUBLICITY CRITICISM WORD OF MOUTH

In June 2005, *Dell Inc.* received some major complaints concerning its customer support services. Blogger Jeff Jarvis posted a series of rants, coined *Dell Hell*, about the *Dell* laptop he'd recently purchased. Jarvis' posts caught the attention of others who also began to share their own negative experiences with *Dell*'s customer service. It wasn't long before Jarvis's blog posts began to catch the attention of the mainstream media. The initial blog post received approximately 253 comments, all of which were written by other consumers who'd been on the receiving end of *Dell*'s poor customer service. As a result of the bad press and *Dell Inc.*'s continued silence regarding the issue, the computer industry giant's sales and reputation began to plummet.

A year after the *Dell Hell* incident, *Dell* created two new corporate communication initiatives which incorporated social media technology. In June 2006, they launched their own blog, *Direct2Dell*. The blog changed how the company viewed online customer service. *Dell* now understands the importance of participating and reacting to online conversation. They have been taught how powerful social media can be and how it cannot be simply ignored. *Dell* has also learned of new ways in which to incorporate new technologies into its existing communications platform.

In the days before blogs were invented, Jarvis might just have been another dissatisfied customer, but today, his widely circulated criticism has triggered dozens of other bloggers and hundreds of commenters to publicly complain about the bad service they've received.

Sources: "My Dell hell", The Guardian, 29 Aug, 2005. "You Can Learn From "Dell Hell." Dell Did", Customer Think, 11 Mar, 2008.

POSSIBLE MORAL

There really is power in numbers. In today's society one has to understand the true power of word of mouth. It's true that the new tastemakers are us. Don't simply ignore what people are saying about you and your business and make sure to leave a good impression because thanks to the web, there's a risk that if a customer has a bad experience with you or your salespeople, it'll end up as a post on a blog or a social network site.

MY STORIES

POSSIBLE MORAL

MY STORIES

POSSIBLE MORAL

MY STORIES

POSSIBLE MORAL

MY STORIES

POSSIBLE MORAL

MY STORIES

POSSIBLE MORAL

MY STORIES

POSSIBLE MORAL

MY STORIES

POSSIBLE MORAL

MY STORIES

POSSIBLE MORAL

PERSON/PRODUCT/COMPANY INDEX

PERSON/PRODUCT/COMPANY INDEX

PERSON/PRODUCT/COMPANY INDEX

ILLUSTRATION INDEX

The majority of the illustrations in this book are based on original photographs. Photos that I have either purchased, photographed myself or been given permission to use by the copyright holders. In the last creative process, these photos have been turned into vector graphics (vectorized) using *Adobe Illustrator*. In this index these are listed with the license, filename and/or the name of the copyright holder. The illustrations that are not based on original photographs is a mixture of sketched/painted art in both analog and digital format, created by me from scratch – and also vectorized (with halftone effect) in the very end. These illustrations are listed in this chapter with my name as the copyright holder.

The halftone effect that's been applied on all of the illustrations is inspired by the printing technique from the early 1850s, and used to give them a timeless feeling where old meets new.

The purchased photographs/illustrations are all from *iStockphoto*, using the standard license. Below you can read parts of the license agreement which is of interest for the use of these products in this book (quoted from *iStockphoto*'s website):

*"**Legal Guarantee***
Every royalty-free file licensed on iStockphoto includes a free Legal Guarantee. This is our promise that content, used within the terms of the license agreement, will not infringe any copyright, moral right, trademark or other intellectual property right or violate any right of privacy or publicity.

Standard License
- Books and book covers, CD & DVD covers. Up to 499,999 impressions.
- Online or electronic publications or uses, including web pages to a maximum image size of 1200 x 800 pixels; video image size limitation is 640 x 480. Any size reproduction is acceptable with substantial changes to the content".

ILLUSTRATION INDEX

The illustrations

Page 6 – "Pointing hand" – Based on image from iStockphoto, Standard license. (File #17789992).

Page 7 – "QR-reader" – Illustration © Simon Zingerman.

Page 11 – "Martin" – Nominative use, Illustration © Simon Zingerman.

Page 13 – "Black cab" – Based on image from iStockphoto, Standard license. (File #20049013).

Page 15 – "Paper clip" – Based on image from iStockphoto, Standard license. (File #5390779).

Page 17 – "Prospector" – Illustration © Simon Zingerman.

Page 19 – "The Winner" – Based on image from iStockphoto, Standard license. (File #4688622).

Page 21 – "Green Island" – Original photograph © Tourism Queensland.

Page 23 – "David's gear" – Illustration © Simon Zingerman.

Page 25 – "Happiness machine" – Original video © Definition 6 agency and The Coca-Cola Company.

Page 27 – "Street musician" – Original photograph © Malyshka Malyshka.

Page 29 – "Take Me Out" – Original video © Benjamin Espiritu, Atomic Tom and Reid Carrescia.

Page 33 – "Great Beer Delivery" – Original advertisement © Publicis Mojo Auckland, Lorenz Perry and Lachlan McPherson.

Page 35 – "Sopranos guerrilla marketing" – Original photograph © New York Post.

Page 37 – "Info concept" – Based on image from iStockphoto, Standard license. (File #5195112).

Page 39 – "Anchor" – Based on image from iStockphoto, Standard license. (File #21166563).

Page 43 – "Icebar" – Private photography © Simon Zingerman.

Page 45 – "The fashion center" – Private photography © Simon Zingerman.

Page 47 – "Coca Cola production" – Original photograph © Sven Kaestner, The Guardian.

Page 49 – "Waiting" – Illustration © Simon Zingerman.

Page 51 – "Stock Market Chart" – Based on image from iStockphoto, Standard license. (File #15176922).

Page 53 – "Salami pizza" – Based on image from iStockphoto, Standard license. (File #20548303).

Page 55 – "Small shop owner woman" – Based on image from iStockphoto, Standard license. (File #17986908).

Page 57 – "Funny pose" – Illustration © Simon Zingerman.

Page 59 – "Google Stress Bricks" – Original photograph © Google, Inc.

Page 61 – "Chevy apprentice" – Original video © General Motors Company.

Page 63 – "Million Dollar Homepage" – Original website graphic © Alex Tew.

Page 65 – "Santa - Daily Delivery" – Based on image from iStockphoto, Standard license. (File #1050524).

Page 67 – "Sorry, We're Closed" – Based on image from iStockphoto, Standard license. (File #5816357).

Page 69 – "Cleaning Crew" – Original photograph © Betsy Malloy Photography.

Page 71 – "Chess: King Down" – Based on image from iStockphoto, Standard license. (File #5670435).

Page 73 – "Monkey business" – Illustration © Simon Zingerman.

Page 75 – "Good News" – Based on image from iStockphoto, Standard license. (File #17913369).

Page 77 – "Joshua Bell" – Original video © Gene Weingarten, Joshua Bell and The Washington Post Company.

Page 79 – "Adam Sacrifice" – Original graphic/photo © Burger King, Crispin Porter & Bogusky, Pelun Chen and Hook Studios.

Page 81 – "Yakuza" – Illustration © Simon Zingerman.

Page 83 – "Eternal Reefs" – Original photograph © Eternal Reefs Inc, George Frankel, Don Brawley and Chuck Kizina.

Page 85 – "Bag Of Groceries" – Based on image from iStockphoto, Standard license. (File #15450579).

Page 87 – "Cross" – Illustration © Simon Zingerman.

ILLUSTRATION INDEX

Page 89 – "Vigilante Phoenix Jones" – Original photograph © Peter Yang, The Magazine GQ (Condé Nast).
Page 91 – "Cup of Tea" – Based on image from iStockphoto, Standard license. (File #8405151).
Page 93 – "The Bubble Project" – Original photograph © Ji Lee.
Page 95 – "Free Speech Movement UC Berkeley 1964" – Original photograph © Paul Richards.
Page 99 – "Wifi" – Original photograph © Roo Reynolds.
Page 103 – "Smashed" – Illustration © Simon Zingerman.
Page 105 – "VOIP Phone" – Based on image from iStockphoto, Standard license. (File #18137332).
Page 107 – "Romantic envelope" – Based on image from Jupiterimages. Old Visuals Collection. (Item: bca57061).
Page 111 – "Do not give up" – Based on image from iStockphoto, Standard license. (File #18180137).
Page 115 – "Boxing Gloves #2" – Based on image from iStockphoto, Standard license. (File #497781).
Page 117 – "Mirror Cube" – Illustration © Simon Zingerman.
Page 119 – "Sagres Preta Chocolate" – Original video © Grand Union Portugal, Manuel Garcia.
Page 121 – "Comparing apples to oranges" – Based on image from iStockphoto, Standard license. (File #5455107).
Page 123 – "Bus Stop for Humans Only" – Original photograph © Daniel Lubetzky.
Page 125 – "LBP BillBoard" – Original photograph © VinylMadness.
Page 127 – "Daniel Kish" – Original video © PopTech.
Page 129 – "FCUK" – Illustration © Simon Zingerman.
Page 131 – "Lejon" – Based on private photograph © Simon Zingerman. Original design © Lisa Larson.
Page 133 – "Swedish national costumes" – Original image from Nordisk familjebok (The copyrights for the book have expired and this image is in the public domain).
Page 135 – "Salman Khan" – Original photograph © Robyn Twomey.
Page 137 – "Child Head with symbol" – Based on vector image from iStockphoto, Extended license. (File #20385819).
Page 139 – "Internet education. Books and computer mouse" – Based on image from iStockphoto, Standard license. (File #21696539).
Page 141 – "Angry Birds in Space" – Original advertisement © Rovio Entertainment ltd.
Page 143 – "Litago" – Original video © Dist Creative and Tine.
Page 145 – "Wordfued" – Based on Wordfeud logotype © Håkon Bertheussen.
Page 147 – "Ammo chef" – Part of original logotype © Season Shot Inc, Brett Holm, David Feig and Tom Smith.
Page 149 – "Donut Cop" – Nominative use © Simon Zingerman.
Page 151 – "Empty box" – Illustration © Simon Zingerman.
Page 153 – "Red Toddler Piano" – Original photograph © Hardwood and Hardboard.
Page 155 – "Cosmonaut" – Nominative use © Simon Zingerman.
Page 157 – "Spoonachos" – Original photograph © Denis Bostandzic.
Page 159 – "Swan Vestas Extra Long Matches" – Original photograph © House of Swan.
Page 161 – "George Eastman" – Original photograph © Corbis.
Page 163 – "Push Sleep" – Illustration © Simon Zingerman.
Page 165 – "Comparing apples to oranges" – Festland via Stock Xchng (Royalty free).
Page 167 – "Say No" – Nominative use © Simon Zingerman.
Page 169 – "Nail bite" – Nominative use © Simon Zingerman.

ILLUSTRATION INDEX

Page 171 – "Square watermelons" – Original photograph © CNN.
Page 173 – "A Walk Around Britain" – Original photograph © Ed and Will (A Walk Around Britain).
Page 175 – "Green bucket" – Based on image from iStockphoto, Standard license. (File #14900549).
Page 177 – "Jenkins" – Original photograph © Ben Feltes.
Page 179 – "Lorenzo's Oil" – Original photograph © Augusto Odone and Michaela Odone.
Page 183 – "Cupcakes" – Illustration © Simon Zingerman.
Page 185 – "Interview In Progress" – Based on image from iStockphoto, Standard license. (File #2144669).
Page 187 – "The Fun Theory" – Original photograph © Volkswagen Personbilar Sverige AB and DDB Stockholm.
Page 189 – "Splashes of paint" – Based on image from iStockphoto, Standard license. (File #19637419).
Page 193 – "Clock" – Original icon © Aleksandra Wolska.
Page 195 – "Mailman holding blank form outdoors" – Based on image from iStockphoto, Standard license. (File #1331397).
Page 197 – "Irish dirt" – Original photograph © Irish Gifts, Sod of Irish dirt and Belleek and Shamrock Gifts from Ireland.
Page 199 – "Gas Mask" – Based on vector image from iStockphoto, Extended license. (File #1528738).
Page 201 – "Pet Rock" – Original photograph © Gary Dahl.
Page 207 – "Tower of Pisa" – Illustration © Simon Zingerman.
Page 209 – "Nostalgia of Mud" – Original logotype and invitation © Vivienne Westwood and Malcolm McLaren.
Page 211 – "Silly Putty" – Original photograph © Crayola LLC.
Page 213 – "Alpine Hut" – Based on image from iStockphoto, Standard license. (File #2813553).
Page 215 – "Set" – Based on image from iStockphoto, Standard license. (File #18875214).
Page 217 – "Bobble" – Original photograph © Move Collective, LLC.
Page 219 – "Dirty Water" – Original photograph © Casanova Pendrill, NY. Dámaso Crespo and Gustavo Villanueva.
Page 221 – "Recycle can" – Based on image from iStockphoto, Standard license. (File #19772849).
Page 223 – "Wikipedia" – Original photograph © Rob Matthews.
Page 225 – "Energy bike" – Original photograph © PlugOut Fitness.
Page 227 – "Crap-o-Meter" – Nominative use © Simon Zingerman.
Page 229 – "Poo Award" – Illustration © Simon Zingerman.
Page 231 – "A Liter of Light" – Original photograph © MyShelter Foundation.
Page 233 – "Vintage Lunch Box" – Original photograph © Teresa Yates.
Page 235 – "Couchsurfing" – Original design © Joseph Matthew Brauer.
Page 237 – "Savings rush" – Based on image from iStockphoto, Standard license. (File #14173519).
Page 239 – "Shhhhh" – Based on image from iStockphoto, Standard license. (File #2252632).
Page 233 – "Found Songs" – Original photograph © Stuart Bailes and Ólafur Arnalds. Graphics © Jónas Valtýsson and Ólafur Arnalds.
Page 243 – "Travel Suitcase" – Based on image from iStockphoto, Standard license. (File #19623926).
Page 245 – "Hell" – Original logotype © DellHell.net.

LITERATURE

Did You Know That...?: *Surprising-But-True Facts about History, Science, Art, Inventions, Origins and More* - Marko Perko, 2001. Backinprint.com.

Farliga idéer - Alf Rehn, 2010. BookHouse Editions.

Freakonomics - Steven D. Levitt, Stephen J. Dubner, 2009. Harper Collins USA.

Fuck Logic 2 - Per Robert Öhlin, 2009. Lucky Man.

In the bubble - John Thackara, 2006. MIT Press.

It's not how good you are, It's how good you want to be - Paul Arden, 2003. Phaidon.

Making Ideas Happen: *Overcoming the Obstacles Between Vision and Reality* - Scott Belsky, 2010. Portfolio Penguin.

One Red Paperclip: *Or How an Ordinary Man Achieved His Dream with the Help of a Simple Office Supply* - Kyle MacDonald, 2007. Three Rivers Press.

Paradise Lost - John Milton, John A. Himes, 2005. Dover Publications Inc.

The Long Tail: *Why the Future of Business Is Selling Less of More* - Chris Anderson, 2008. Hyperion Books.

The Tipping Point - Malcom Gladwell, 2000. Little Brown.

Whatever You Think Think the Opposite - Paul Arden, 2006. Penguin Books.

LECTURES/INTERVIEWS

Carina Wedin - Lecture - 2012. Agera. Piteå Företagarcentrum (START).

Caroline Törnberg - Lecture - 2011. Vocal Devotion. Karriärdagen at Luleå University of Technology.

Gunnar Dagnå - Lecture - 2010. Creative methods. Luleå University of Technology.

Gunnar Forslund - Lecture & interview - 2012. Tango. Piteå Företagarcentrum (START).

Hjärta Smärta - Lecture - 2009. Design history and Hall of Femmes, Samira Bouabana and Angela Tillman Sperandio. Luleå University of Technology.

Marcus Gärde - Lecture - 2009. Typography and Grid systems. Luleå University of Technology.

Mari Ramnek - Lecture & Interview - 2012. Zebra workshops & coaching. Piteå Företagarcentrum (START).

Maria Juhlin - Lecturer - 2009-2012. Bachelor of Arts Programme in Media Design. Luleå University of Technology.

Mikael Wiberg - Guest supervisor & Lecturer - 2009, 2011-2012. Luleå University of Technology.

Niklas Berg - Interview - 2012. Creative at In The Cold.

Stefan Hattenbach - Lecture - 2009. Typography. Luleå University of Technology.

Tomas Hellgren - Lecture - 2012. Scenario Sweden. Piteå Företagarcentrum (START).

Tim Foster - Lecture - 2011. Karriärdagen at Luleå University of Technology.

DOCUMENTARY/FILM/TV

Art & Copy - 2009. Doug Pray, Jimmy Greenway & Michael Nadeau.

Big River Man - 2009. John Maringouin, Molly Lynch.

Dragons' Den - Series 1-9, 2005-2011. Sam Lewens, Zoe Thorman. BBC Manchester. Sony Pictures.

Exit Through the Gift Shop - 2010. Banksy, Revolver Entertainment.

Life in a Day - 2011. Liza Marshall, Ridley Scott. Scott Free Productions, YouTube, Inc., LG Corp.

PressPausePlay - 2011. David Dworsky, Victor Köhler.

Shark Tank - Series 1-2, 2009-2011. Mark Burnett Productions, Sony Pictures Television.

TED Talks - Richard Saul Wurman, Sapling Foundation. 2004, Stefan Sagmeister: Happiness by design. 2006, Ken Robinson says schools kill creativity. 2009, Stefan Sagmeister: The power of time off. 2010, Arianna Huffington: How to succeed? Get more sleep. 2011, Steve Jobs: How to live before you die. 2012, Andrew Stanton: The clues to a great story.

The Greatest Movie Ever Sold - 2011. Morgan Spurlock, Sony Pictures Classics, Stage 6 Films, POM Wonderful.

AUDIO

Filip & Fredrik - Podcast - Season 1-3, 2010-2012. Filip Hammar and Fredrik Wikingsson (Season 1-3), Aftonbladet (Season 1 and 2).

Uppfinnaren - Audiobook - 1998. Alf Mork, Virgin.

WE ALL NEED HEROES

The search for stories continues at
www.weallneedheroes.com

www.ingramcontent.com/pod-product-compliance
Lightning Source LLC
Chambersburg PA
CBHW060230050426
42448CB00009B/1373

* 9 7 8 9 1 6 3 7 1 7 2 0 8 *